A GUIDE TO THE

Identification and Control of Exotic Invasive Species

IN ONTARIO'S HARDWOOD FORESTS

Lisa M. Derickx and Pedro M. Antunes

Invasive Species Research Institute
1520 Queen Street East, BT300
Sault Ste. Marie, Ontario, Canada
P6A 2G4

Algoma University
ISBN 978-0-929100-21-0

ISRI has been granted permission to reproduce the photographs and range maps in this book by their rightful copyright holders and through the Bugwood Network Image Archive. A full list of photography credits appears in section 8.0.

Disclaimer: This publication contains recommendations for chemical control that are intended to serve only as a guide. It is the responsibility of the pesticide applicator to follow the directions on the pesticide label. Pesticide labels and registrations change periodically. If any information in these recommendations disagrees with the label, the recommendation must be disregarded. No endorsement is intended relating to pesticide use or a particular product. The authors and the Invasive Species Research Institute assume no liability resulting from the use of these recommendations.

Design: Carmen Misasi Design
Cover photo credits: English ivy leaves: James H. Miller, USDA Forest Service, Bugwood.org (left) & Chris Evans, Illinois Wildlife Action Plan, Bugwood.org (right); Japanese barberry, garlic mustard & Himalayan balsam: Lisa Derickx, Invasive Species Research Institute; Norway maple keys: Leslie J. Mehrhoff, University of Connecticut, Bugwood.org; tree-of-heaven samaras: Chuck Bargeron, University of Georgia, Bugwood.org; emerald ash borer adult & tunneling damage: David Cappaert, Michigan State University, Bugwood.org; emerald ash borer feeding galleries: Joseph O'Brien, USDA Forest Service, Bugwood.org; Asian long-horned beetle: Melody Keena, USDA Forest Service, Bugwood.org; beech bark disease: Linda Haugen, USDA Forest Service, Bugwood.org; gypsy moth larva: Jeffrey Fengler, Connecticut Agricultural Experiment Station Archive, Connecticut Agricultural Experiment Station, Bugwood.org; Dutch elm disease: Fabio Stergulc, Università di Udine, Bugwood.org; crown dieback and epicormic shoots: Daniel Herms, The Ohio State University, Bugwood.org
Back cover photo credits: Emerald ash borer feeding on leaf: Jared Spokowsky, New York State Department of Agriculture and Markets, Bugwood.org; Asian long-horned beetle exit hole: Steven Katovich, USDA Forest Service, Bugwood.org; Asian long-horned beetle feeding damage: Dean Morewood, Health Canada, Bugwood.org; elm bark beetle larval galleries: James Solomon, USDA Forest Service, Bugwood.org; butternut canker: Joseph O'Brien, USDA Forest Service, Bugwood.org; dog-strangling vine seedpod: Leslie J. Mehrhoff, University of Connecticut, Bugwood.org; common buckthorn, Japanese knotweed, periwinkle, dog-strangling vine flowers and exotic bush honeysuckle: Lisa Derickx, Invasive Species Research Institute.

This book is dedicated to Errol Caldwell for everything he does for Northern Ontario's social and economic development. The creation of an Invasive Species Research Institute at Algoma University in Sault Ste. Marie and this guidebook were only possible due to his foresight.

Acknowledgments

Funding for this book was provided by the Invasive Species Centre (ISC) to the Invasive Species Research Institute (ISRI) at Algoma University. As a not-for-profit organization, part of ISRI's mission is to ensure that our research findings reach as many people as possible. In the case of this publication, the external funding received was essential to produce this guidebook and to print and distribute it at the lowest possible cost (i.e., only that of printing).

We are thankful to Dr. Michael Irvine, Vegetation Management Specialist from the Ontario Ministry of Natural Resources (OMNR), for providing constructive criticism throughout the development of this guide. His consultation in the early stages of writing and his thorough review of the manuscript have lent to the significance and value of this publication. Thanks to Professor John Klironomos from the University of British Columbia for writing the foreword; to Dr. Richard Wilson, Forest Program Pathologist (OMNR), for his expert advice and helpful suggestions regarding forest pathogens; to Dr. W.D. McIlveen, Terrestrial Biologist, and Susan Meades, Director of the Northern Ontario Plants Database, for their advice and review of plant species taxonomy; to the ISRI staff, Laura Sanderson and Kim Mihell, for proof reading the text and assistance with editing.

We are grateful to Jeff and JoAnn St. Pierre from North Country Photography and James Smedley from James Smedley Outdoors for assistance in photographing all aspects relating to maple syrup production. A special thanks is extended to the many other people who provided permission to use the high quality photographs found in this guide. A full list of photo credits follows to acknowledge these contributions. We are also thankful to our designer, Carmen Misasi of Carmen Misasi Design, for all of the time and effort he put into working with us to create this publication.

We are thankful to Calvin Gilbertson (Gilbertson's Maple Products) and David Thompson (Thompson's Maple Products) for permission to photograph their maple syrup operations on St. Joseph Island and for sharing their expert knowledge of maple syrup production in Ontario. Also, thanks to the Ontario Maple Syrup Producers Association (OMSPA) and all of their members for a wonderful and educational experience at the summer tour and meeting in Belleville, 2011.

Thanks to Lindsay Burtenshaw at the Royal Botanical Gardens and Bruce Cullen from the Toronto Zoo for their information on managing invasive plants, for tours of the gardens and zoo, and for permission to take photographs for use in the guide. Thanks to Freyja Forsyth of Credit Valley Conservation (CVC), Hayley Anderson of the Ontario Invasive Plant Council (OIPC) and Fraser Smith of the Ontario Federation of Anglers and Hunters (OFAH) Invading Species Awareness Program, for providing us with hands-on experience in invasive plant management at their various volunteer events.

Finally, thanks to our family and friends for their patience and encouragement over the course of producing this guide.

About the Authors

Lisa M. Derickx, B.Sc., is a Research Associate at the Invasive Species Research Institute (ISRI) in Sault Ste. Marie, Ontario. She has a B.Sc. Honours Degree in Environmental Science from Carleton University and a diploma in Fish and Wildlife Conservation from Sault College of Applied Arts and Technology. Lisa has obtained funding from the Ontario Trillium Foundation to develop a citizen scientist approach to identify and map terrestrial invasive plants. Her interests lie in plant and wildlife identification and environmental conservation.

Pedro M. Antunes, B.Sc. & Ph.D, is a Research Chair in Invasive Species Biology (funded by the Ontario Ministry of Natural Resources) and Associate Professor (Department of Biology, Algoma University) since 2010. Currently, he is also the Research Director of the Invasive Species Research Institute at Algoma University and Chair of the North American Invasive Species Network. He began his academic studies in Biology at the University of Évora, Portugal (1999). He then undertook his doctoral research in Soil Science at the University of Guelph (2005) followed by post-doctoral research in Soil Microbial and Plant Ecology (2005-07). In 2008, he moved to Berlin, Germany, to assume a Research Assistant Professor position in Ecology at the Freie Universität. He is broadly interested in science and environmental conservation. His research in ecology focuses on the roles that soil microorganisms play in controlling plant productivity and community structure.

Foreword

As humans, we love to place things into groups. It is how we organize the various objects that we come into contact with, it is the filing system that we have for our thoughts. It is how we make sense of the world. When taking a walk in nature, we may not know how to identify every organisms that we see, but we can typically divide them into broad groups: Plant, animal, fungus - and from there (and often with the help of a field guide) we can get more specific, a particular Phylum, and then all the way down to a species.

The species binomial (or latin name) is the gateway to all information that is known for that organism - its life history, its morphological and behavioural characteristics, its geographic range, and whether it is native or exotic. Interestingly, a large proportion of the species that we encounter in most habitats are exotic. They originated elsewhere and immigrated to our local ecosystems. Where did these species come from? Well, the vast majority of exotic organisms that are found in Ontario have origins in Eurasia, from locations with comparable climate. If we want to learn more about these species, then a visit to their home of origin may provide significant insight into their biology and ecology.

Why worry about exotic organisms? Is this a form of xenophobia? One major reason for concern is that they lead to the homogenization of our natural ecosystems. Everywhere we go, we see the same species, diminishing the uniqueness of local ecosystems. As humans, this has a strong psychological effect on us. It is unnerving, similar to when we travel to a distant location overseas and find the same fast food restaurants that we just left behind. We don't yet understand the ecological consequences of such homogenization. However we do know that many exotic organisms, those that are invasive, can have great ecological and economic consequences.

Being exotic is one thing. Being invasive is another. It is important not to confuse the two. All invasive organisms are exotic but not all exotics are invasive. How do we define an invasive species? There are two main categories. The first are those species that grow, reproduce, and spread at unusually high rates. Such species can be found at very high densities in local habitats, often in widespread monoculture. The second are those species that have significant local impact. They can negatively affect the growth and reproduction of local native species, or may alter the functioning (productivity, stability) of local ecosystems. Some of the most problematic and worrisome invasive species can do both, spread rapidly and harm native systems.

Scientists are currently placing a lot of effort in the study of invasive species. There are many unanswered questions, such as: what factors cause certain species to become invasive? Why are certain ecosystems more invasible than others? What are effective ways to control invasive species? Such questions are not just academic. We need to know the answers to these questions, so that we can properly manage our landscapes. In this context, any new information on invasive species, particularly the most serious of them, needs to be communicated to other scientists and to the public. So it should be clear just how important this book is. A guide that focuses on invasive species in Ontario - one that is comprehensive and science-based, yet accessible to any audience.

Dr. John Klironomos
University of British Columbia

Table of Contents

SECTION ONE

5.0 Invasive Species Accounts

SECTION ONE

1.0
INTRODUCTION

1.1
An Introduction to Exotic Invasive Species of Hardwood Forests

Exotic invasive species are those not native to the habitat in which they are causing harm to either the environment, economy or society (Environment Canada, 2004). Invasive species are increasingly prevalent in Ontario's hardwood forests. Forestry represents an important part of Ontario's economy, at an estimated $14 billion in 2008 (MNDM, 2011). Ontario's hardwood forests also provide high value non-timber forest products such as the iconic maple syrup (Mohammed, 1999) (Fig. 1). They provide us with ecological goods and

Figure 1: A non-timber forest product (sap for 'maple syrup')[2.]

services, such as clean air and wildlife habitat, provide areas for recreational enjoyment, contribute to the natural aesthetics of Ontario and sustain a resource-based tourism industry. For all these reasons, proper management of invasive species is a vital step to sustaining our existing hardwood forests (Daily et al. 1997).

Invasive species can alter forest integrity through rapid population expansion. This may affect biodiversity by causing shifts in species abundances and in some cases can lead to local extinctions (Wyckoff & Webb, 1996). Studies have shown that exotic plant invasions can alter soil physicochemical properties and affect nutrient cycling (Leicht-Young et al. 2009; Kourtev et al. 1998). Moreover, exotic insects and pathogens (i.e., microorganisms that cause disease in their hosts) can severely damage and cause large-scale mortality of indigenous trees and shrubs (Allen & Humble, 2002). Consequently, invasive species can result in reductions to timber value and the quality and quantity of other forest-derived products such as maple syrup (Kota et al. 2007).

The majority of exotic plants were introduced to North America intentionally for agriculture and horticultural purposes and were thus prized for their fast-growing, sun-loving habits. Since forest understories are generally subject to low light levels, they tend to be inhospitable to many of these introduced horticultural varieties. However, some shade-tolerant exotic species have been introduced and, not surprisingly, many are spreading in forest environments (Martin et al. 2008).

In general, invasive forest plants have relatively long lag-times (i.e., the time it takes before a species' population grows exponentially and becomes invasive in the new introduced environment), which may give a false sense of security when assessing the risk of invasion (Crooks, 2005). Some of the invasive plants described in this book are still available for sale in garden centres across Ontario. Only recently has evidence arisen concerning the detrimental effects of invasive vines such as periwinkle (*Vinca minor*; Darcy & Burkart, 2002) and English ivy (*Hedera helix*; Dlugosch, 2005). Other species, such as common barberry (*Berberis vulgaris*), have been banned for sale due to reported detrimental effects to agriculture; yet its close relative, Japanese barberry (*B. thunbergii*), is still sold and used as a common garden plant (Fig. 2) because it is not known to cause any ill effects to agricultural crops (CFIA, 2008). More research is required to determine the factors responsible for different lag-times in exotic plant species. However, the exotic status should be sufficient for the inclusion of these species in monitoring programs (Simberloff, 2011). For highly invasive species, research on their ecological effects as well as preventative measures need to be considered to minimize negative effects to hardwood stands in Ontario.

Figure 2: Two varieties of a common garden shrub, Japanese barberry[6].

1.2
How to Use this Book

Considering the increasing number of invasive species establishing in Ontario's forests, there is a clear need for management guidelines focusing on those species that have the largest potential to be detrimental to hardwood stands. In addition, challenging economic times are leading to increasing awareness that public involvement in environmental issues is crucial to overcome these challenges. This guide, based on evidence from the peer-reviewed scientific literature, focuses on invasive plants, insects and pathogens that exhibit ecological, economic and social impacts that are detrimental to Ontario's hardwood forests. It is intended to serve as an educational resource and a field guide to aid woodlot owners in invasive species management.

There are two sections in this guide. The first section describes the risks associated with invasive species in hardwood forests. These forests are valuable to woodlot owners in Ontario who rely on them for timber and high-valued products such as maple syrup. It introduces managers to the basic principles associated with different management strategies and outlines various methods of invasive species control.

Species invasions are dynamic and each case is unique. Management recommendations in this guide may not be the most appropriate for everyone. Forest managers and woodlot owners should gauge their level of expertise, commitment and finances when considering control options. It is also important to understand that these recommendations and management strategies may change as ongoing research provides new insights into invasive species management. We point out gaps in the literature throughout the guide and recommend that the reader keeps informed on highly invasive species and up-to-date with current management practices.

Individual invasive species descriptions make up the second section of this guide. These include invasive plants, insects and pathogens that have been identified as priorities for management in Ontario's hardwood stands (Tables 1 & 2). They have been selected as priorities for management based on the following risk categories:

Economic risks:
· Species that can directly affect commercial hardwoods by significantly reducing growth, causing widespread mortality and/or suppressing hardwood regeneration;
· Species that can alter the quality of timber or the quantity of maple syrup produced;
· Species whose environmental effects can result in the reduction of property value;
· Species that can cause losses resulting from movement restrictions related to timber products.

Environmental risks:
· Species that cause the loss of biodiversity;
· Species that reduce ecosystem goods and services;
· Species that can harm a species at risk.

Social impacts:
· Species that can interfere with traditional lifestyles;
· Species that can reduce aesthetic values of a hardwood stand;
· Species that affect the recreational enjoyment of a woodlot;
· Species that can impact human health.

Table 1: Invasive plants considered a high priority for management in hardwood stands and their associated risks (see Appendix 1 for referenced priority rating).

	Economic Risks			Environmental Risks			Social Risks			
	Cause reduced hardwood growth	Cause hardwood mortality	Suppress hardwood regeneration	Cause the loss of biodiversity	Affect ecosystem function	Harm species-at-risk	Interfere with a traditional lifestyle	Reduce aesthetic values of the forest	Affect recreational enjoyment	Impact human health
Norway maple (*Acer platanoides*)	✓		✓	✓	✓					
Tree-of-heaven (*Ailanthus altissima*)			✓	✓	✓					✓
Garlic mustard (*Alliaria petiolata*)	✓		✓	✓	✓	✓				
Barberry (*Berberis* spp.)				✓						✓
English ivy (*Hedera helix*)		✓	✓	✓					✓	✓
Himalayan balsam (*Impatiens glandulifera*)			✓	✓						
Japanese knotweed (*Fallopia japonica*)			✓	✓						
Common buckthorn (*Rhamnus cathartica*)			✓	✓	✓					
Periwinkle (*Vinca minor*)			✓	✓	✓					
Dog-strangling vine (*Vincetoxicum* spp.)			✓	✓	✓	✓				

The following information will be provided for invasive species considered a high priority in hardwood stands:

Identification - A tool to help managers accurately identify invasive species present in their woodlots. Signs and symptoms are provided to help identify invasive insects and pathogens.

Similar species - Visual aids and dichotomous keys are included to help distinguish similar species.

Biology - Understanding the biology and taxonomy of an invasive species provides important clues for its management. Taxonomic hierarchy, origin and distribution, habitat, type of reproduction, lifecycle and host species are included for applicable species.

Success mechanisms - Understanding traits likely to play an important role in enabling species invasibility can help managers

Table 2: Invasive insects and pathogens considered a high priority for management in hardwood stands and their associated risks (see Appendix 1 for referenced priority ratings).

	Economic Risks			Environmental Risks			Social Risks			
	Cause reduced hardwood growth	Cause hardwood mortality	Suppress hardwood regeneration	Cause the loss of biodiversity	Affect ecosystem function	Harm species-at-risk	Interfere with a traditional lifestyle	Reduce aesthetic values of the forest	Affect recreational enjoyment	Impact human health
Emerald ash borer (*Agrilus planipennis*)		✓		✓			✓	✓		
Asian long-horned beetle (*Anoplophora glabripennis*)	✓	✓		✓			✓	✓		
Chestnut blight (*Cryphonectria parasitica*)	✓	✓		✓		✓	✓	✓		
Gypsy moth (*Lymantria dispar*)	✓	✓						✓	✓	✓
Beech bark disease (*Neonectria faginata*)		✓	✓	✓	✓			✓	✓	
Dutch elm disease (*Ophiostoma* spp.)		✓		✓				✓		
Elm bark beetles (*Scolytus* spp.)		✓		✓						
Butternut canker (*Ophiognomonia clavigignenti-juglandacearum*)		✓		✓		✓		✓		

with the decision making process to select appropriate invasive species control strategies.

Ecological impacts – Understanding the ecological effects of invasive species is the basis for why they need to be managed.

Vectors and pathways – Understanding how and where an invasive species can reach and establish in a woodlot can greatly improve prevention and early detection techniques.

Management practices
· Prevention strategies – These strategies are the most efficient and cost effective methods of invasive species management. These strategies outline various ways whereby managers can limit invasive species introductions to woodlots.
· Early detection techniques – These techniques help maximize the capacity to detect invasive species before they spread in the woodlot.
· Control options – Outlines the most cost effective and environmentally sustainable management strategies for priority species.

2.0
INVASIVE SPECIES MANAGEMENT: AN OVERVIEW

2.1
Prevention Strategies

Prevention is the most efficient and effective approach to manage exotic invasive species. There are several things a manager can do to prevent the introduction of invasive species into a woodlot, regardless of whether they are plants, insects or pathogens. Creating a prevention plan that involves all those responsible for woodlot activities can go a long way to reducing the risk of invasion and the amount of time, effort and cost needed for invasive species management (Clark, 2003).

PREVENTION STRATEGIES FOR INVASIVE PLANTS

· Promote a healthy forest with diverse communities of native species. An undisturbed forest understory with diverse plant communities may be more resistant to exotic species introductions by imposing a high level of competition on newcomers (Clark, 2003). Remember to monitor both the canopy trees and the understory vegetation.

· Minimizing the agents of invasive species dispersal (i.e., vectors) will decrease the likelihood of introduction. Humans are a main vector of seed dispersal, so limiting access to the woodlot may be beneficial (Wilkins, 2000). However, this may not be possible in hardwood stands used for maple syrup production where access is required during the sugar season.

In this case, access should be restricted to existing trails and roads. Ensuring that shoes and tires are cleaned before entry could save a manager time and money (NCC, 2007).

· When planning for timber harvest, ensure that prevention measures are considered in the work plan. Survey the area to locate any existing invasions. Where possible, remove these species several years before harvesting. If eradication is not feasible, use an appropriate method of control. This will ensure that invasive plants are managed before activities that could contribute to further spread take place (Clark, 2003).

· Soil disturbance increases the forest's susceptibility to plant invasions. Try to minimize activities such as road or trail construction. As a mitigation strategy, plant native species where soil disturbance is unavoidable. This may help to deter establishment of invasive plants by promoting competition (Clark, 2003).

· Any equipment that must be brought into the woodlot such as tractors, skidders and all-terrain vehicles should be thoroughly cleaned. All mud and plant materials should be washed off in a designated area before entering the woodlot. These designated areas should be monitored frequently for invasive plants (USDA, 2001).

· Be careful when bringing any materials such as sand, gravel or soil into the woodlot. If possible, managers should take the initiative to visit the seller's warehouse beforehand to inspect materials for seedlings of invasive species. Ask companies whether they have implemented measures to prevent the transportation of invasive plants (USDA, 2001).

· Using the woodlot for recreational purposes such as hiking can also be a potential vector for seed dispersal. Shoes should be washed before entering and upon leaving the woodlot at a designated area. This area must also be frequently monitored for germinating seeds (NCC, 2007).

· Whenever possible keep pets on a leash because seeds can easily get caught in fur. This is especially important during the late summer and fall when seeds are ready to disperse (Clark, 2003).

· Avoid walking or driving through invaded areas. Traveling through these areas can spread seeds to un-invaded areas of the woodlot. Consider using signs such as flags to prevent others from walking through the invaded area (Clark, 2003).

· Continue to be conscientious outside the boundaries of the woodlot. Never plant an exotic invasive species in the garden as seeds can easily be carried into your woodlot (Miller et al.

2010). Ask local greenhouses about the possibility of buying native plants for the home garden (Havinga, 2000).

· Volunteer to help control invasive plants on neighbouring properties. It will help to decrease the likelihood of seed dispersal into your woodlot and will promote cooperation should a population establish on your own property (Peterson, 2007).

PREVENTION STRATEGIES FOR INVASIVE INSECTS AND PATHOGENS

· Increase species diversity in the woodlot. Many invasive insects and pathogens have a single host genus or species. Woodlots that are composed of one or two species are more likely to become infested and suffer greater negative effects when invasions do occur (OMNR, 2011).

· Don't move firewood. Many areas in Ontario have been put under various quarantines that restrict the movement of firewood and other wood products because they can harbour insects and pathogens. Check with the CFIA for quarantines in effect in your area (CFIA, 2012a).

· Maintain a healthy woodlot. Perform thinning activities when required to help decrease both interspecifc and intraspecific competition around high value trees, thereby promoting vigorous tree growth. Pruning high-value trees to remove dead or damaged branches may also decrease pathogen infections (Ostry et al. 1996).

· Avoid damaging trees during woodlot management activities. Wounds in the bark increase the chances of pathogen infection or insect establishment (Ostry et al. 1996).

· Inspect and clean any vehicles, camping equipment, boats or other objects that may harbour invasive insects, especially when moving through quarantine zones (CFIA, 2011a).

2.2
Early Detection and Rapid Response

Although a prevention plan is considered an effective management approach, these are not always foolproof and it is best to have a backup plan in place (Clout & Williams, 2009). Early detection is the identification of newly established invasive species at the initial stage of invasion. Invasive species may be eradicated and are clearly easier to control in these early stages. The larger a population is the greater the amount of labour and money required for its management (O'Neil et al. 2007). As such, management actions should occur promptly after detection to save money and minimize damage to the woodlot (NCC, 2007).

Monitoring is the key to early detection. A monitoring program is essential and can be carried out by managers, friends, family members or volunteers. It involves actively searching for invasive species in the woodlot. Be aware of invasive species present on adjoining properties because they can spread quickly (NCC, 2007). Once an invasive species is detected, implementing actions to immediately address the problem is highly recommended. Having a plan that outlines the management options for highly invasive and thus priority species will allow for quick and efficient control of new invasions (Grice, 2009).

EARLY DETECTION TECHNIQUES FOR INVASIVE PLANTS

· Early detection is important to prevent the establishment of an invasive plant species population and the consequent creation of a large seed bank. Remember that it is much easier to control a few individuals than a large population (Drayton & Primack, 1999).

· Learn how to properly identify priority invasive plant species. Become familiar with those species that are already present in your region (Strobl & Bland, 2000). Educate family, friends and employees on how to properly identify priority invasive species (Siegal & Donaldson, 2003).

· Create a species inventory of the woodlot. Many managers may already have tree species inventories as part of their woodlot management plan. These inventories should also include understory species. Create a basic map of the different species present in the woodlot. With that, if any new species appears, it can be more readily detected. These measures will decrease the likelihood of missing new invasions (Miller et al. 2010).

· Organize a monitoring program for invasive species. Monitoring activities should occur as frequently as possible and at least once during the spring, summer and fall (Miller et al. 2010). Pay particular attention to high risk areas such as forest edges, trails, roadways, flood water paths and disturbed areas. These are the pathways through which seeds can more easily disperse (Drayton & Primack, 1999).

EARLY DETECTION TECHNIQUES FOR INVASIVE INSECTS AND PATHOGENS

· Visual surveys and monitoring activities are important in the detection of invasive insects and pathogens in the early stages of invasion. Knowing what to look for is crucial. Invasive insects and pathogens usually leave visible signs of their presence in host trees (Cappaert et al. 2005).

· Check for signs of insect infestation or disease symptoms on host trees. Do not limit monitoring to the more valuable trees because many insects and pathogens will attack weakened or dying trees first (Seybold et al. 2008).

· Monitor host trees at various heights within the forest structure. Do not limit searches to what can be seen at eye level. Remember to pay attention to both the main stem and branches within the canopy (Turgeon et al. 2010).

· Look for multiple signs of invasion to help properly identify the causative agent. The signs and symptoms of harmful invasive species can easily be mistaken for those of less harmful native species and vice-versa. Symptoms caused by various environmental stresses may also be mistaken for invasions (Turgeon et al. 2010).

2.3
Management and Control Options

Management and control options for invasive species that affect hardwood stands should be based on maintaining a healthy forest. A healthy forest will provide the economic and aesthetic benefits desired by managers (Havinga, 2000). Effective management involves planning a strategy and having the ability to provide a certain level of commitment, effort and money (Clout & Williams, 2009; Holcombe & Stohlgren, 2009).

The following sections outline the three methods of invasive species control, including physical, chemical and biological control. Physical control consists of a person mechanically removing or destroying the invasive species with the use of hands or tools. Chemical control consists of using pesticides. Biological control consists of releasing living organisms that feed upon, parasitize or infect the unwanted species. When using chemical control an integrated approach to invasive species management should always be used. Integrated management requires thorough knowledge of the invasive species. All options including both mechanical and chemical control should be considered, taking into consideration all of the potential environmental and social risks, before a management strategy is implemented. Forest managers and woodlot owners should choose methods that are well aligned with their objectives and goals for the present and future use of the woodlot.

2.3.1
Physical Control

There are several ways of physically controlling invasive plants in a hardwood stand. They include hand-pulling, excavation, flower-head removal, cutting, mulching, solarization and using a directed flame. Hand-pulling consists of physically pulling whole plants, including the root system, out of the ground (Fig. 3). This is easiest when the soil is wet. Hand-pulling can be labour intensive and may not be appropriate for very large invasive species populations. The method is appropriate for herbaceous plants that do not easily break from the root and for small saplings of woody plants (Holt, 2009). Care should be taken while hand-pulling invasive vines to ensure that the extensive rooting system is completely removed from the soil. Minimize soil or other disturbance to native vegetation.

Figure 3: Removing invasive plants by hand[1] (left) and with a weed wrench[1] (right).

It is always important to protect yourself by wearing gloves, long-sleeved shirts, pants and appropriate footwear. For larger shrubs and small trees tools such as weed wrenches may be required to pry the roots from the soil (Miller et al. 2010).

Excavation involves using spades or shovels to remove the whole root system. It is only appropriate for very small populations because it is very labour intensive and causes a high degree of soil disturbance (Miller et al. 2010). Excavation can be an effective method of control for plants that break off easily from their roots such as dog-strangling vine (*Vincetoxicum* spp.; see section 5.1.10).

The purpose of flower-head removal is to prevent seed production. However, since it is very difficult to ensure that all flowers are removed throughout the season, this method should only be used to reduce seed production. Flower-head removal may be appropriate in sensitive areas where soil disturbance or chemical applications are restricted (Frey et al. 2005).

Cutting can be done using weed whackers, scythes and lawn mowers. The objective is to cut the stems as close to the ground as possible. Cutting may not kill a plant but it can reduce seed production. Cutting right after flowering is most efficient because the plant already spent a significant amount of energy in the production of flowers. This method generally needs to be applied several times throughout the season to prevent any late seedpod development. Cutting is appropriate for plants that rely on seeds for dispersal (Holt, 2009).

Mulching involves covering the area requiring control with materials such as straw, sawdust or mulched wood and bark. This effectively prevents light from reaching germinating seedlings. Solarization consists of covering the area with black plastic. This generates high temperatures that destroy the soil's seed bank (Holt, 2009)(Fig. 4).

Directed flame can be an effective treatment for some trees and shrubs. It involves applying a directed flame to the base of

Figure 4: Mulching[1] (left) and solarization[1] (right) management techniques.

the stem using a propane torch. The flame should be applied until the base is completely burnt. Several treatments may be necessary to kill the invasive plant. This method should only be used when the forest floor is wet or damp to decrease the risk of fire (Ward et al. 2009; Ward et al. 2010).

2.3.2
Chemical Control

The use of pesticides in Ontario is highly regulated. The Ontario Pesticides Act provides a legal framework for managing pesticides that is enforced by the MOE. Pesticides must be registered and classified in Ontario. Using an unregistered or homemade pesticide is illegal. It is also illegal to use a pesticide in any way other than that described by the pesticide product label (MOE, 2011). It should be noted that at the time of writing not all invasive species in this guidebook have labelled pesticides. Please consult with a licenced exterminator before attempting any chemical control methods. Refer to the PMRA, MOE and/or the OMNR for more information on pesticide use in Ontario.

There are currently 11 classes of pesticides in Ontario (Table 3). The regulations governing the Pesticides Act were recently rewritten to restrict the use of pesticides for cosmetic purposes. The purpose of the ban is to reduce public exposure to pesticides by preventing their use for aesthetic purposes on residential properties and in cemeteries, parks and school yards. Class 5 or 6 products containing class 11 ingredients are considered lower risk pesticides and biopesticides. These are the only pesticides that have not been banned for cosmetic uses. Some can be used for invasive species control in hardwood stands as long as they are being used according to the product label (MOE, 2011).

Table 3: Ontario pesticide classification (MOE © Queen's Printer for Ontario, 2011).

Class	Description	Details
1	Products intended for manufacturing purposes.	Manufacturing concentrates used in the manufacture of a pesticide product.
2	Restricted or commercial products.	Very hazardous commercial or restricted pesticides that continue to be used under an exception to the ban (i.e. agriculture, forestry, golf courses).
3	Restricted or commercial products.	Moderately hazardous commercial or restricted pesticides that continue to be used under an exception to the ban (i.e. agriculture, forestry, golf courses).
4	Restricted or commercial products.	Less or least hazardous commercial or restricted pesticides that continue to be used under an exception to the ban (i.e. agriculture, forestry, golf courses).
5	Domestic products intended for household use.	Less hazardous domestic pesticides that can be used by homeowners and include biopesticides and certain lower risk pesticides allowed for cosmetic purposes.
6	Domestic products intended for household use.	Least hazardous domestic pesticides that can be used by homeowners and include biopesticides and certain lower risk pesticides allowed for cosmetic purposes.
7	Controlled sale products (domestic or restricted).	Includes controlled sales domestic pesticides with cosmetic and non-cosmetic uses. Products are only allowed to be used for non-cosmetic purposes.
8	Domestic products that are banned for sale and use.	Banned domestic products.
9	Pesticides are ingredients in products for use only under exceptions to the ban.	Pesticide ingredients that are banned for cosmetic use. Products containing these ingredients may still be used for exceptions to the ban.
10	Pesticides are ingredients in products for the poisonous plant exception.	Ingredients contained in pesticide products allowed for use under the public health or safety exception. These are only ingredients that may be used to control plants that are poisonous to the touch under the public health or safety exception.
11	Pesticides are ingredients in products for cosmetic uses under the ban.	Ingredients contained in pesticide products that are biopesticides or contain lower risk pesticides.

In areas where an invasive species is widespread or causing a high degree of harm, a class 9 pesticide may be required. There are several exceptions to the ban that allow other classes of pesticides (e.g., class 9). Relevant exceptions pertaining to invasive species in hardwood stands include forestry, arboriculture, natural resources and agriculture (Table 4).

Table 4: Exceptions to the Ontario Pesticide Ban (MOE © Queen's Printer for Ontario, 2011).

Exception	Applicable circumstances	Reasons for exception
Forestry	Treed areas larger than 1 ha.	To protect trees from pests and to control competing vegetation.
Arboriculture	Upon written recommendation by a certified arborist or registered forester.	To protect tree health.
Natural resources	Upon MNR approval. Only relevant when no other exception applies.	To control an invasive species that can pose a threat to human health, the environment or the economy.
Agriculture	Uses related to agriculture by a farmer.	To protect agricultural operations.

Pesticides are often used to manage insect pests and pathogens affecting trees or to control competing vegetation. Class 9 pesticides can be applied if a hardwood stand is being used for forestry activities and if the stand is greater than 1 ha. Under the forestry exception, class 9 pesticides can only be applied by a person who holds a forestry exterminator licence. Landowners may apply for this licence or they may choose to hire a licenced exterminator (MOE, 2011).

If landowners are concerned about a particular tree in their woodlot, and if the woodlot is smaller than 1 ha or not being used for forestry, they may seek out the help of a tree care professional (i.e., a certified arborist or registered forester). If the tree care professional determines that the tree is at risk unless a pesticide is used he/she may write a letter stating their recommendation. The letter will allow the landowner to apply a class 5, 6, or 7 product containing a class 9 ingredient to the tree. A landscape licenced exterminator can be hired to either apply those pesticides or use a class 2, 3, or 4 product (MOE, 2011).

In natural areas where the forestry exception does not apply (e.g., hardwood stands greater than 1 ha that are not being used for forestry activities), a natural resources exception may apply. Products containing class 9 ingredients may be used for the purpose of protecting a native species or its habitat, protecting a rare ecosystem or parts thereof, or to control an invasive species. Woodlot owners must complete a written application at their local MNR office to receive approval before commencing chemical control (OMNR, 2010a).

Woodlot owners who also maintain an agricultural operation may use their agriculture class licence. However, these woodlots must be associated in some way with the agricultural operation in order for the licence to apply. Otherwise a forestry licence will be needed to use class 9 pesticides for management in the woodlot. Producing crops for use primarily by the owner's household is not considered an agricultural operation (MOE, 2011).

HERBICIDE APPLICATION TECHNIQUES FOR LICENCED FORESTRY EXTERMINATORS

FOLIAR SPRAY

The foliar spray technique is appropriate for use on herbaceous and woody invasive plants. Herbicides are applied directly to the foliage using a backpack sprayer or a spray bottle. Herbicides should completely cover any new growth on woody plants and all the foliage on herbaceous plants. Exterminators should completely cover the leaf surface with the herbicide while being careful to prevent any runoff. In areas where invasive plants intermingle with desirable vegetation a handheld wick or roller can be used to directly apply the herbicide to the foliage. This eliminates the chance of accidentally spraying the desirable vegetation (Miller et al. 2010). The foliar spray technique can only be used when leaves are present, thereby limiting management to a seasonal timeframe. On the other hand, foliar sprays may be used on a variety of both woody and herbaceous plants. Therefore, areas with multiple invasive species can be treated simultaneously (Swearingen & Pannill, 2009).

BASAL BARK

Basal bark application is appropriate for small diameter trees, shrubs and woody vines. Herbicides are applied to the lower portion of the stem using a spray bottle or backpack sprayer. Depending on the size of the invasive plant, a wide band is sprayed around the entire circumference of the stem. Herbicides should be applied abundantly so that the entire surface is coated. Any exposed roots should also receive treatment. Other techniques such as streamline and thin line application involve applying herbicides in a thin band around the circumference of the stem. Streamline application uses diluted herbicides whereas thin line uses non-diluted herbicides appropriate for small diameter stems (Miller et al. 2010). Basal bark application works best in the late winter or early spring when most native plants are still dormant. The stem needs to be completely dry and free of ice and snow for the herbicide to work effectively (Swearingen & Pannill, 2009).

STEM INJECTION

Trees, shrubs and large woody vines can be treated using the stem injection technique. Cuts are made in the stem diagonally towards the ground creating a small crevice through which the herbicide is poured. These cuts should be made around the entire stem and placed approximately 2.5cm apart (Miller et al. 2010). A spray bottle can be used to fill the crevice with just enough herbicide to prevent dripping. Herbicides must be applied to the cuts immediately, before the plant begins sealing off the wounded area. Herbicide applicators are available in various forms. Blades, drills and injection systems can be purchased. These applicators cause wounds in the bark through which herbicides are inserted simultaneously (Swearingen & Pannill, 2009). Caution should be taken when using stem injection techniques as some species may exude certain herbicides and translocation may affect neighbouring trees, thereby increasing the risk of non-target hardwood mortality (Lewis & McCarthy, 2008).

CUT-STUMP

Some managers may decide to first cut and remove invasive trees, shrubs or woody vines from the forest stand. Although this method may be labour intensive and time consuming it may be practical in areas where large infestations make access to the woodlot difficult. Investing time and energy in areas with dense invasions will ultimately make future management easier (Swearingen & Pannill, 2009). After the above-ground portion of the stem is removed, herbicides can be applied directly to the stump using spray bottles, brushes, handheld wicks or rollers. Most herbicides should be applied immediately after cutting, and with any sawdust removed, to allow for optimal absorption. Large invasions may need to be divided into smaller units so that cutting and herbicide application can be accomplished on the same day. For stumps larger than 7.5cm in diameter herbicides should be applied to wet the outer edge of the cut surface while the cut surface of smaller stumps should be completely covered (Miller et al. 2010).

3.0
A TRIBUTE TO HARDWOOD FORESTS OF ONTARIO

3.1
Timber Harvest

3.1.1
Ontario's Forests

Ontario has a total area of 107.6 million ha, of which 66% is forested. The majority of these forests, approximately 81%, is Crown land owned by the province (Fig. 5). A total of 27.1 million ha fall within the Area of Undertaking (AOU) where forest management activities actively take place. The majority of privately owned forests occur in southern Ontario and account for approximately 10% of the forested land in Ontario. A total of 9% are protected in parks and recreational areas (OMNR, 2012a).

There are four forest regions in Ontario, including the deciduous forest, the Great Lakes-St. Lawrence forest, the boreal forest and the Hudson Bay lowlands (Fig. 6). The occurrence of these forest regions is due to a combination of differences in bedrock, soil type and climate (Armson, 2001).

The deciduous forest region on the southern tip of Ontario is the most biologically diverse of the province's forest regions. It is unique to Ontario, not being found anywhere else in Canada (Armson, 2001). Most was converted to agricultural land during European settlement. Today this area is highly populated and the majority of forested land occurs in scattered woodlots, parks and conservation areas (OMNR, 2012a).

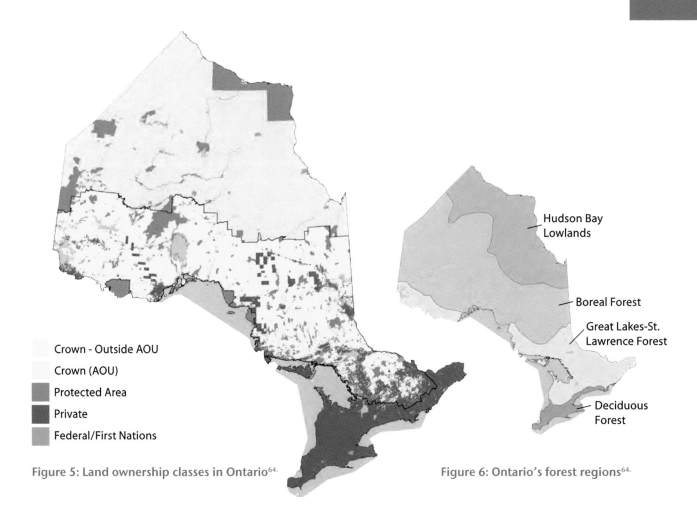

Figure 5: Land ownership classes in Ontario[64.]

Legend:
- Crown - Outside AOU
- Crown (AOU)
- Protected Area
- Private
- Federal/First Nations

Figure 6: Ontario's forest regions[64.]

Labels on Figure 6: Hudson Bay Lowlands, Boreal Forest, Great Lakes-St. Lawrence Forest, Deciduous Forest

The Great Lakes-St. Lawrence forest comprises a mixture of hardwood and softwood species. It is the second largest forest region in Ontario and occurs in both populated and rural areas (OMNR, 2012a). Both the deciduous forest and Great Lakes-St. Lawrence forest regions occur within the Great Lakes-St. Lawrence lowlands, which is characterized by sedimentary rock, level topography and relatively fertile soils (Wake et al. 1997).

The boreal forest and Hudson Bay lowlands lie within the northern latitudes of Ontario. The boreal forest region comprises mainly softwood species. It is the largest forest region in the province, containing 58% of Ontario's forested land (OMNR, 2012a). The boreal coincides with much of the Canadian Shield where thin soils and pre-Cambrian rock prevail (Wake et al. 1997). The Hudson Bay lowlands occur along the northern edge of Ontario. Spruce, tamarack, willow and birch dominate this forest region. Other prominent species are trembling aspen and balsam poplar (Armson, 2001). Areas of forested land are intermingled with large areas of open muskeg and the landscape is dotted with small ponds and lakes. This forest region occurs over sedimentary bedrock (OMNR, 2012a).

3.1.2
History, Economy and Culture of Timber Harvest

Historically, wood exports have played an important role in the Canadian economy. The wood trade in Ontario was a direct result of European demand. When the regular exports of wood from the Baltic region to Britain were compromised due to the Napoleonic wars, Britain was left in desperate need of wood for naval construction (Lower, 1933). As a result, demand for softwood timber more than doubled in the early 1800's (Armson, 2001).

The demand for wood products created a form of livelihood that allowed for the immigration of people to Upper Canada, now known as Ontario. British demand called for squared timber, which required logs to be cut on four sides. The method was wasteful, leaving behind 25 to 30% of the tree (Easterbrook & Aitken, 1988). However, square timber was in demand and accounted for over 50% of Canadian exports (Bothwell, 1986). As wood was slowly replaced by iron and steel in construction, the European demand for timber began to decrease. At this time, a new market was opening up with the United States where the demand for sawn logs was rising (Easterbrook & Aitken, 1988).

Historically, softwoods were the major commodity of the timber trade. White pine was the most solicited species followed by red pine and white spruce. Hardwood from maple and oak was also desirable, albeit to a smaller extent than softwood (Lower, 1933). Large, straight softwood trees were primarily targeted in forest stands since square timber greater than 20cm in width was in demand. As softwood species such as white pine became depleted, the industry shifted to hardwood exports; a result of a change in supply instead of demand (Armson, 2001).

Today, timber products continue to be an important part of Ontario's economy. Currently there are over 200 000 forestry-related jobs in the province, many in communities dependant on the industry. In 2008, forestry products made $14 billion in revenue for Ontario; the majority coming from pulp and paper products (MNDM, 2011).

3.2
Maple Syrup Production

3.2.1
History

THE ORIGINS OF MAPLE SYRUP

The exact origin of maple syrup is unknown. European settlers like to claim the discovery; however, there is evidence for sugar-making being long-established as part of the native traditions. The Algonquin word *Sinzibuckwud* (maple sugar) or the words *Sisibaskwatattik* (maple tree) and *Sisbaskwat* (sugar) of the Cree tribe have no similarities to the European settler's language. It stands to reason that there would be some similarities if the settlers had crafted those terms (Nearing & Nearing, 1950). The Cree did adopt a word for the white sugar that settlers brought with them. The word *Sukaw* has been said to be an attempt at pronouncing either the English word 'sugar' or the French word 'sucre' (Henshaw, 1890). There are also many early writings by settlers that mention the native people's previous knowledge of tapping maple trees and making maple syrup. The Nearings (1950) point out an example found in a letter written by Robert J. Thornton which was published in London's Philosophical Magazine, 1798:

"I have enclosed some sugar of the first boiling got from the juice of the wounded maple...Twas sent from Canada, where the natives prepare it from said juice; eight pints yielding commonly a pound of sugar. The Indians have practiced it time out of mind..."
(Thornton cited in Vogel, 1987).

There are several native legends that relate to the discovery of maple syrup. One talks of a time when maple syrup ran thick and pure from maple trees. After discovering this, villagers got lazy and started spending their days drinking syrup instead of hunting and fishing. A mischief-maker, known by names such as Glooskap and Ne-naw-bo-zhoo, sees that the villagers are taking the syrup for granted. He fills the trees with water from the river so as to dilute the sap. From that day forward, villagers have been required to boil down the sap to enjoy the pure form of maple syrup (Chamberlain, 1891).

Another legend tells of a chief's wife. The chief decides to go hunting for the day and grabs his tomahawk from the maple tree he had left it in the night before. Throughout the day sap leaks from the wound and collects in a basket that happens to be at the base of the tree. In a rush to get some water boiling for dinner, the chief's wife grabs the bucket full of sap and proceeds to cook their evening meal. The food flavoured with maple was greatly enjoyed and the discovery shared with all (Lawrence & Martin, 1993).

Ininatigs's gift of sugar is another story. It tells of a family's hardship during a long, cold winter. Food supplies had been depleted and the family was on the verge of starvation. From out of the forest comes a voice. It is the voice of Ininatig, the man tree. He tells the family to cut him and carefully collect the liquid flowing from his wounds. By boiling this liquid the family could make syrup and sugar that would sustain them and save their lives (Wittstock, 1993).

The final legend involves a hungry hunter who is watching the antics of a red squirrel in a grove of maple trees. The squirrel seemed to be biting holes in the branches and eating the emerging sap. The hunter may have collected some sap and heated it, possibly multiple times, to sustain him through a period of hunger (Lawrence & Martin, 1993). A study by Heinrich (1992) shows that red squirrels (*Tamiasciurus hudsonicus*) 'tap' sugar maple trees. They bite on the branches creating small wounds. Observations show that red squirrels do not eat the sap right away but wait for some of the water to evaporate and concentrate the sugar. Perhaps the maple tree's secret was discovered by someone who decided to try an icicle. The sap running from broken branches generally freezes to produce these icicles. During the freezing process, some water evaporates leaving a vaguely sweet taste (Hauser, 1998).

THE EVOLUTION OF MAPLE SYRUP PRODUCTION

First Nation people used to tap maple trees by creating a V-shaped wound in the tree. A piece of wood or bark was placed at the bottom of the wound to allow the sap to flow away from the tree into a wooden container placed at the base (Lawrence & Martin, 1993). Birch bark containers or wooden pots were used for heating the sap. As these types of containers could not withstand fire, hot stones were dropped into the containers as a means of heating the sap. Stones were replaced as needed until the sap boiled down to the desired consistency. Another method used was freezing. Sap would be left overnight in shallow containers to freeze and the resulting layer of ice that formed on top would be taken away, leaving the concentrated syrup underneath (Nearing & Nearing, 1950).

The iron kettle came with the arrival of European settlers (Fig. 7). These kettles greatly increased the quality and quantity of sap that could be produced (Whitney & Upmeyer, 2004). The use of multiple kettles was eventually adopted for boiling sap. As the sap achieved a desired consistency it could be transferred to the next kettle and so forth until it reached a finished state. This method helped to prevent burning and off-setting the flavour of the syrup (Nearing & Nearing, 1950).

Trees continued to be tapped with the traditional V-shaped slash for up to 80 years after the arrival of European settlers. The creation of these large wounds would significantly harm the tree and usually decrease its sap producing capacity considerably (Whitney & Upmeyer, 2004). Augers eventually replaced the use of axes to bore less harmful holes in the trees. Although techniques such as cutting branches and roots to collect sap were attempted, the trunks have remained the traditional location for tapping. Buckets were eventually attached to trees as a means to prevent high winds from blowing the dripping sap out of the buckets' range (Nearing & Nearing, 1950) (Fig. 8).

Figure 7: Kettles for boiling sap[3.]

Figure 8: A bucket for collecting sap[2.]

Collection and transportation of sap was labour intensive. Sugar shacks were virtually non-existent and most boiling occurred out in the sugar bush. Most maple syrup producers would plan to spend the entire season out in their sugar bush. Small shelters would occasionally be constructed to protect the fire and boiling sap from the elements (Fig. 9). A central fire would be constructed and sap transported by hand or with horse and sleigh to this central location (Nearing & Nearing, 1950).

Figure 9: A sugar shack at night[2.]

MODERN MAPLE SYRUP PRODUCTION

Maple syrup producers in Ontario must meet the requirements of Regulation 386 of the *Farm Products Grades and Sales Act* if they are going to sell their products locally. To sell outside of Ontario, producers must comply with the Maple Products Regulations found in the *Canada Agricultural Act* (Chapeskie & Hendersen, 2007). The CFIA is the governing body for maple syrup production. This agency is responsible for ensuring that maple syrup producers make and sell both a safe and high quality product.

The quality of maple syrup in Ontario is governed by a three-tier grading system which is based on colour and taste. The first grade, Canada No. 1, describes a category of syrup ranging in colour from extra light to medium (Heiligmann et al. 2006). This grade of maple syrup has a mild flavour and is often used as a condiment. Syrup that gets a Canada No. 2 grade has an amber colour class. It is often used in cooking due to its strong flavour (Chapeskie & Hendersen, 2007). Canada No. 3 is a dark syrup and the maple flavour may be off-set by a caramel or sappy taste. Only pure maple syrup, with a sugar content of at least 66%, can be graded in Canada (Heiligmann et al. 2006).

A product's colour class is assigned depending on the amount of light that can pass through it. The grade is given according to flavour. Commonly lighter syrups have a very mild taste whereas darker syrups have a strong candied flavour. Soil characteristics, timing and handling all contribute to differences in colour and taste among syrups. Most producers agree that sap collected earlier in the season will produce a higher quality product lighter in colour and milder in flavour compared to that made from sap collected later in the season (Hortvet, 1904).

Today there is a wide variety of technology to help alleviate the work and cost associated with maple syrup production while ensuring a high quality product. Plastic tubing has greatly decreased labour costs required for transporting sap from trees to the holding tank (Lawrence & Martin, 1993) (Fig. 10). Sap can move through the tubing by gravity or it can be pumped through. Vacuum pumps were adopted as a means of increasing sap production during times of imperfect weather conditions when sap flow is slow (Coons, 1992). Some producers continue to use buckets for sap collection but usually only those with small operations. Buckets must be collected daily to prevent microbial growth and labourers are generally friends or family members (Lawrence & Martin, 1993).

Figure 10: Sap lines[1] (left) and buckets[3] (right).

The adoption of sheet metal was a turning point in the history of maple syrup production. Metal replaced wooden spouts and pails. The use of large flat-bottomed pans replaced the old iron kettles. After much experimenting with these pans a primitive evaporator began to emerge (Lawrence & Martin, 1993). The modern-day evaporator is essentially a large, two-chambered pan (Fig. 11). The first chamber has a ridged bottom that maximizes the surface area for heating sap quickly and efficiently. Sap is directed through the chamber in a serpentine pattern. The final chamber has a flat bottom to prevent the sap from burning. When the syrup has reached the desired consistency it is passed through a filter and left to cool. Reverse osmosis machines were adapted to help concentrate the sap before boiling. These machines helped to reduce boiling time, thereby saving on energy costs associated with the long hours required for syrup production. They separate water from the soluble sugars found in maple sap through a membrane and by working on a pressure gradient (Heiligmann et al. 2006).

Figure 11: Evolution of flat-bottomed pans[2] to modern day evaporators[3.]

3.2.2
Economic and Cultural Significance

ECONOMIC VALUE

Maple syrup is only produced in Canada and the northern part of the United States. This is due to the relationship between sap flow and weather conditions. Canada is the leading producer of maple syrup with the majority of production coming from four provinces: Quebec, Ontario, New Brunswick and Nova Scotia. Ontario has approximately 2600 maple syrup producers (Leuty, 2009).

Ideal weather conditions in 2009 resulted in a record year for the maple syrup industry, with a total revenue of $353.8 million in Canada. Of this amount Ontario contributed $25.6 million. In 2008, Canada totaled $211.9 million with Ontario contributing $15.4 million (Statistics Canada, 2009).

The ability to produce maple sugar was of great value to the early settlers. It was too costly to import sugar and many families had to do without. The timing of the sap run was ideal for the farmer because it would not overlap with the crop growing season. Time could be spent collecting and boiling large amounts of sap for syrup and sugar production. After enough product was made and set aside for family use the rest could be sold for a profit (Whitney & Upmeyer, 2004).

Maple syrup production is not the necessity it once was for settlers. However, it is still an important product in Ontario. The economic value of maple syrup production benefits rural communities. It allows rural families to create an income and it contributes to tourism. Indeed, maple syrup is embedded in the image of Canada and represents a major asset for branding the country's tourism, food and agricultural sectors internationally. A trip to the sugar shack in the spring is a long-standing tradition in many families. The rustic feel of a traditionally run sugaring operation is a major attraction to the tourist (Hinrichs, 1995). From the viewpoint of a producer, making maple syrup allows one to make use of the land while developing a rural livelihood (Hinrichs, 1998).

HERITAGE VALUE

The maple leaf is meaningful for Canadians as individuals (Fig. 12). The maple leaf appears not only on the National Flag of Canada but also on the Canadian penny and on both the Ontario and Quebec coat of arms. In 1996 the maple tree officially became Canada's national arboreal emblem. It is no wonder that Canadians hold a sentimental place for the maple tree and its products when its leaf holds such an integral part of the country's identity (DCH, 2008).

Maple syrup production is a traditional part of Canada's heritage (Fig. 13). It is one of the earliest agricultural activities to exist in Ontario (Coons, 1992). It is associated with festivities, renews family bonds and brings communities together. The sugar season occurs in the spring and represents a time of renewal, a time to leave behind the feelings of isolation that a cold winter can create and a time of gathering to renew friendships. Perhaps it is the fact that syrup operations were, and still commonly are, family run businesses that lends romance to the industry.

Figure 12: A national emblem[3.]

Running a sugar bush represents a lifestyle that many long to experience – even if only for a day at the sugar shack (Whitney & Upmeyer, 2004).

Many maple syrup producers in Ontario sell their product directly to the consumer. In today's society, maple syrup is no longer the sole source of sugar in a household. It is considered a luxury item. Buying syrup directly from the vendor holds an appeal. It allows one to briefly connect with the past and celebrate the Canadian heritage. Many operators tend to shy away from an overabundance of new technology. They want to keep their operations looking traditional because it attracts customers who want to experience their rural heritage (Hinrichs, 1995).

Figure 13: Creating family traditions[2.]

4.0
WOODLOT MANAGEMENT

Managing a hardwood stand has many benefits for the landowner or woodlot manager. Whether the goal is to manage for timber harvest, maple syrup production or nature conservation, it is important to become familiar with the age of the forest and species composition. This can be done by completing a forest inventory. Forest inventories can be done by the landowner or by a hired consultant. The following two sections outline some basic management concepts depending on whether the goal of the woodlot is for timber harvest or maple syrup production. Managing a woodlot helps to keep the forest healthy. In turn, a healthy forest is generally less susceptible to invasion by exotic plants, insects and disease (Hilts & Mitchell, 1999).

4.1
Management for Timber Harvest

Written by Fraser Smith, M.Sc., Forestry, Ontario Federation of Anglers and Hunters

Stand structure describes the distribution of tree ages and size classes within a forest stand (Chapeskie et al. 2006). Stand structure helps to determine what has occurred in a stand previously, and what silvicultural actions should take place to best manage the forest for optimal health and long-term productivity. Broadly, there are two major categories of stand structure: even-aged and uneven-aged. Even-aged forests are composed of trees that are all similar in age, usually all within 10 years. Even-aged forests often experience stand-replacing disturbance patterns such as fires, after which most trees regenerate. This forest type is more typical of softwood stands, but can also be seen in the sun-loving pioneer species such as aspen (*Populus* spp.) and birch (*Betula* spp.). Managers of even-aged forests strive to open the canopy to allow sufficient light to reach these shade intolerant species and promote regeneration (Lane, 2007).

Uneven-aged forests have a broad range of size classes and ages. Generally, these forests are prone to small-scale disturbance patterns that affect individual or small groups of trees. They are composed of shade-tolerant or mid-tolerant species that regenerate in heavy or partial shade. Ideally, these forests have a large number of juvenile trees, a medium amount of middle-sized trees, and a small number of very large, old trees. This age distribution is characterized by a decreasing number of stems with increasing age and size. It fosters the development of vigorous young saplings that compete for light and grow straight and tall (Lane, 2007).

Selection harvesting is a management system where individual trees or small groups of trees are cut in intervals of 8 to 20 years. Selection management is designed to mimic the small, frequent disturbances such as wind, ice storms, lightning, and disease that are characteristic of the hardwood forests of southern Ontario (Burke et al. 2011). Each cut may harvest up to one third of the stand while maintaining a largely intact canopy that promotes regeneration of tolerant to mid-tolerant species. The aim of selection harvest is to maintain an uneven-aged stand with a diverse range of species and stand structure. This range of species and structure is most appropriate for mid-tolerant hardwood stands and promotes stand health while maintaining productivity (Lane, 2007).

The shelterwood system describes a management approach where a mature forest is harvested in two or more passes over a period of 5 to 60 years (Burke et al. 2011). Each of these cuts or "thinning" passes aims to carefully open up the canopy of mature trees and provide the increased space and light in the understory for natural regeneration of mid-tolerant trees to thrive (OMNR, 2004). The shelterwood system mimics disturbance patterns that affect only part of a stand such as ground fires, insects, and disease. The shelterwood system is most appropriate for species adapted to those disturbances such as white pine *(Pinus strobus)*, white spruce *(Picea glauca)* and red oak *(Quercus rubra)*. First, a preparatory cut thins the stand but leaves large vigorous trees with the ability to produce a large productive crown. Next, roughly 20 years after the preparatory cut, the regeneration cut removes approximately half of the originally retained trees. This cut allows light to reach the forest floor and for seedling regeneration to increase. Once regeneration has reached an appropriate level (usually 3 to 15 years later), one or two removal cuts are performed to harvest some of the remaining mature trees. This gives the now established saplings full sunlight and encourages vigorous growth (Burke et al. 2011).

The shelterwood system is most often applied in white pine forests, however it is sometimes applied in tolerant hardwood forests to promote turnover from a heavily degraded site. While the shelterwood system is considered even-aged, there are generally two to three distinct age classes growing together. These distinct age classes, or cohorts, represent those trees established during one of the thinning cuts and are intended to follow those natural disturbance patterns found in these stands. The shelterwood system should only be carried out using an appropriate prescription and employing a certified tree marker (OMNR, 2004).

The clearcut system describes an intensive management strategy where the majority of a stand of mature trees is harvested in one pass and forest regeneration is initiated in a short time-frame. This system is suited to those areas where the most common disturbance patterns are stand-replacing such as fire, flood, and large windstorms. The dominant tree species in Ontario's boreal forest, such as black spruce (*Picea mariana*), Jack pine (*Pinus banksiana*), and aspen (*Populus* spp.), regenerate best under the open conditions created by these disturbances. Since these species require full sunlight without competing shade, the clearcut system is designed to emulate these natural disturbance patterns and facilitate rapid stand renewal. If these stands were to be harvested using a selection or shelterwood system, the structure and species composition of this forest would be fundamentally altered from the original forest. This in turn would lead to cascading effects for the ecology of the area, including wildlife that depend on these stands and their natural replacement. In Ontario, clearcut systems never remove all trees on a site. Mature trees are left either scattered individually across the site (called clearcut with seed trees) or in small patches (aggregated structural retention). Regeneration of these sites can be either natural or through planting (Burke et al. 2011).

Whatever reason a landowner has for harvesting their woodlot, keeping site damage to a minimum should always be a primary goal. Site damage from harvest activities can include residual tree injury, soil compaction and rutting, and introductions of exotic invasive plant species that can have lasting implications for the future of the stand. Keep in mind that disturbance intensity appears to be positively correlated with a forest's susceptibility to the establishment and spread of invasive species (Bell & Newmaster, 2002). To avoid harvest-related damage, all woodlot operations should adhere to careful logging practices. For a complete guide to minimizing harvest damage, the Ontario Woodlot Association has produced "A Landowner's Guide to Careful Logging" (Byford, 2009) which provides landowners with sound advice as they make decisions to protect the health and integrity of their woodlots. Landowners planning harvest operations should also be aware of the potential for invasive species introductions. Invasive species can be accidentally transported as seeds, plant fragments or in soil on recreational or harvest equipment. Every attempt should be made to clean equipment before transport, minimize soil disturbance, and follow careful logging practices.

4.2
Sugar Bush Management

Management helps to increase the health and productivity of a sugar bush. Trees in a forest are in constant competition with one another for light, space, water and nutrients. This creates stress on maple trees and does not allow for optimum growth. For example, trees that are in competition for light will put more energy into growing tall so as to reach the canopy. As a consequence, these trees remain small in diameter and have less potential for reaching an adequate size to be useful for sap collection (Richardson, 2003). Trees with large crowns are desired because they produce a larger quantity of sweet (i.e., more concentrated) sap as compared to maples with small crowns. Crown development in sugar maples is a function of space and light availability (Chapeskie et al. 2006). Management allows for improved growth of sugar maple crowns through thinning procedures. Certain trees are harvested from the sugar bush to ensure that adequate resources are available for crop trees, which will grow both faster and larger. Trees with larger diameters will also produce more sap because they can withstand a greater number of taps (Coons, 1992). Management enables a maple syrup producer to tap a higher number of trees in a smaller amount of time (Richardson, 2003).

Management depends on the size and age class of the forest. A smaller forest with 300 taps is managed differently than a forest with 10 000 taps. Thinning a small sugar bush must be carried out very carefully. If too many trees are removed the sugar bush will lose taps and decrease in productivity. Likewise, an even-aged forest would be managed differently than a forest containing a variety of age classes. In a sugar bush where all the trees are roughly the same age, regeneration is a primary concern since there will be no new trees to replace the old ones for quite some time. A sugar bush containing trees of a variety of ages is generally thought to be ideal because there will always be younger trees available to replace the old (Richardson, 2003).

The goal of sugar bush management should be to sustain a healthy forest while keeping the future in mind. Focusing only on today's sap production could shorten the life of a sugar bush considerably. Thus, one main component of management is regeneration. Maple trees are long-living but they will not produce an adequate amount of sap consistently and across the entire life span of a tree. New trees will eventually be required to replace the old. One problem with regeneration has to do with the amount of time it takes for a sugar maple to reach a size where it can be tapped. Seedlings in the understory require a certain amount of space and sunlight to grow. Thus, management practices should consider the undergrowth (Coons, 1992).

There is an ongoing debate as to whether diversity or monoculture is the better management strategy for a healthy sugar bush. In the past, managers have been advised to harvest all species, other than maple, in the sugar bush. This strategy would free up more space for maple trees to grow and create a good environment for sugar maple saplings to take hold. Managers are now being advised that a diversity of species makes a healthier sugar bush because monocultures are more susceptible to insect outbreaks and disease. Managers must decide: by allowing the growth of other species there will be less crop trees in the forest and the production may be smaller than in a monoculture. On the other hand, going with a monoculture increases the risk of insect and disease outbreaks (Lawrence & Martin, 1993).

There are many benefits associated with maintaining a diversity of trees in a sugar bush. Biodiversity enhances a range of ecological functions within a forest. It creates wildlife habitat that can support predators of sugar maple pests. Some sites within the sugar bush may not be suitable for maple growth. By allowing other species to grow in these areas there is the added benefit of a periodic timber harvest. Wood can be sold for a profit or used to fuel the evaporators. A diverse forest has also been known to be more resistant and resilient to insect outbreaks (Chapeskie et al, 2006).

Management generally includes a forest inventory and a management plan. A forest inventory includes a list of species, age and diameter of individual trees, and the overall number of trees (OMNR, 2006). The relative abundances of tree species are recorded, allowing the manager to determine what proportion of the forest comprises maple and the general biodiversity of the area. Tree diameter and overall health are recorded for individual species greater than 10cm in diameter. Density and basal area are obtained to determine whether thinning is required to reduce the amount of competition around maple trees (Chapeskie et al. 2006). The inventory allows the producer to make informed decisions when it comes to making the management plan. Monitoring should be an ongoing part of management. It allows the producer to deal with problems, such as damage due to invasive species as soon as they arise (OMNR, 2006).

To aid producers with management decisions such as thinning, stocking recommendations are available. Table 5 lists the recommended number of trees per hectare based on average trunk diameter. It also gives the producer an idea as to the average number of taps a sugar bush of a particular diameter class can support (Richardson, 2003). As stated earlier, the goal of management is to produce a more sustainable forest, with healthy and productive maple trees. It is important to understand that improper tapping can have negative effects on trees and sap production. For example, trees that are stressed from other causes such as drought may not be able to withstand the additional stress caused by tapping. The number of taps per tree should depend on the diameter and overall health of each individual tree (Richardson, 2004).

Table 5: Sugar bush stocking and tapping recommendations (adapted from Richardson, 2003; 2004).				
Tapping rule	Average diameter (cm)	Number of taps	Recommended trees/hectare	Number of taps/hectare
Normal (healthy trees)	< 10	0	> 680	0
	10 – 25	0	210 – 680	0
	26 – 37	1	150 – 209	150 – 209
	38 – 50	2	100 – 149	200 – 298
	51 – 63	3	66 – 99	198 – 297
	≥ 64	4	< 66	< 364
Conservative (unhealthy trees)	30-46	1	NA	NA
	≥ 47	2	NA	NA

Management should be adjusted to provide the greatest amount of revenue both in the short and long term. It must be flexible to account for unpredictable events such as severe weather or invasive species outbreaks, which can reduce the sugar bush's productivity (Chapeskie et al. 2006). The following chapters on invasive species will cover best management practices, early detection techniques and prevention strategies to alleviate the negative effects associated with invasive species.

SECTION TWO

5.0 Invasive Species Accounts

5.1 Exotic Plants

5.2 Exotic Insects and Pathogens

5.1
Exotic Plants

5.1.1
Norway Maple
(*Acer platanoides*)

Other common names:
Schwedler maple, Crimson king maple

Priority Rating: **HIGH**

Figure 14: Norway maple[1.]

IDENTIFICATION

LEAVES: Norway maple has dark green leaves with an opposite arrangement (Fig. 15). Each leaf has 5 pointed lobes (Kaufman & Kaufman, 2007). The tops of the leaves are a darker green as compared to the lighter, shiny undersides. A milky sap is emitted from leaf stalks when they are cut (Farrar, 1995).

Figure 15: Norway maple leaves[1] (left) and opposite leaf arrangement[1] (right).

FLOWERS: Yellow-green flowers grow in clusters at the end of branches (Fig. 16). Each flower has 5 petals and 5 sepals. The flowers appear at the same time as the leaves emerge in early spring (Kershaw, 2001).

FRUIT/SEEDS: The fruit, also called a key, consists of a winged seedcase with an angle of 180° between the wings (Fig. 17). Two seeds are developed per fruit. The wings are approximately 35 to 50mm long and the seedcases have a flattened appearance (Farrar, 1995)

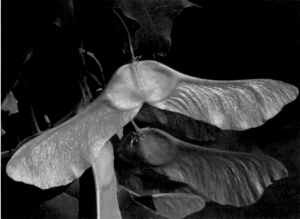

Figure 16: Norway maple flowers[4].   Figure 17: The fruit of Norway maple[5].

TRUNK: Norway maples are large trees that range in height from 12 to 21m (Kaufman & Kaufman, 2007; Kershaw, 2001). The bark of mature trees has deep grooves with interlacing ridges (Fig. 18). The bark is dark gray and lenticels are often prominent on young branches (Farrar, 1995).

Figure 18: The bark of Norway maple[6].

SIMILAR SPECIES

Sugar maple (*Acer saccharum*)

Sugar maple is a large shade tree that is very similar in appearance to Norway maple. There are several differences between the leaves and the keys that can help with identification. The leaves of Norway maple are of a much darker green than the yellow-green leaves of sugar maple (Fig. 19). The leaves of Norway maple only turn yellow in the fall whereas sugar maple leaves range in colour from yellow, orange and red. The angle between the wings of sugar maple keys is 120° whereas the angle between the wings of Norway maple keys is 180° (Farrar, 1995; Kershaw, 2001) (Fig. 20).

Figure 19: Comparing a sugar maple leaf[1] (left) to that of Norway maple[1] (right).

Figure 20: Comparing sugar maple keys[5] (left) to those of Norway maple[7] (right).

Black maple (*Acer nigrum*)

Black maple is a large shade tree. Generally the leaves of black maple have 3 lobes but they may have 5 lobes at times (Fig. 21). The smooth edged leaves with 5 lobes may appear very similar to those of Norway maples. However, the leaf undersides and stalks of black maple are hairy. Figure 22 shows how the keys of black maple have wings that are parallel to one another whereas those of Norway maple have a distinct 180° angle (Farrar, 1995; Kershaw, 2001).

Figure 21: Comparing black maple leaves[1] (left) to those of Norway maple[1] (right).

Figure 22: Comparing black maple keys[5] (left) to those of Norway maple[8] (right).

Red maple (*Acer rubrum*)

Red maple is a medium-sized shade tree. Red maple leaves have 3 to 5 lobes with many small, irregular teeth along the edges. The notches on either side of the central lobe have a distinctive V-shape whereas those of Norway maple have a gently curving U-shape (Fig. 23). The keys of red maple have an angle of 60° between the wings, whereas the wings of Norway maple keys are separated by an angle of 180° (Farrar, 1995; Kershaw, 2001) (Fig. 24).

Figure 23: Comparing a red maple leaf[1] (left) to that of Norway maple[1] (right).

Figure 24: Comparing the keys of red maple[7] (left) to those of Norway maple[6] (right).

Silver maple (*Acer saccharinum*)

Silver maple is a medium-sized shade tree. Silver maple leaves have 5 to 7 lobes that are distinctly separated by deep notches. The leaf edges have irregular teeth whereas the leaf edges of Norway maple are smooth (Fig. 25). Silver maple keys have an angle of 90° between the wings, which is much narrower than that found on Norway maple wings (Farrar, 1995; Kershaw, 2001) (Fig. 26).

Figure 25: Comparing a silver maple leaf[1] (left) to that of Norway maple[1] (right).

Figure 26: Comparing the keys of silver maple[5] (left) to those of Norway maple[4] (right).

Striped maple (*Acer pensylvanicum*)

Striped maple is a shrub or a small understory tree that only reaches heights of 10m. The leaves have 3 lobes and regular toothed edges whereas Norway maple has leaves with 5 lobes and smooth edges (Fig. 27). Figure 28 shows the differences between the keys of striped maple and Norway maple. Notice that the keys of striped maple only have a 90° angle between wings as opposed to the 180° angle found in Norway maple keys (Farrar, 1995; Kershaw, 2001).

Figure 27: Comparing a striped maple leaf[9] (left) to that of Norway maple[1] (right).

Figure 28: Comparing the keys of striped maple[10] (left) to those of Norway maple[4] (right).

Mountain maple (*Acer spicatum*)

Mountain maple is a shrub or a small understory tree that only grows about 5m tall. Mountain maple leaves may have a similar 5-lobed appearance to those of Norway maple. However, the edges are distinct. Mountain maple has irregular toothed edges whereas Norway maple has smooth leaf edges (Fig. 29). There is less than a 90° angle between the wings of mountain maple keys, while Norway maple keys have an angle of 180° between wings (Farrar, 1995; Kershaw, 2001) (Fig. 30).

Figure 29: Comparing a mountain maple leaf[1] (left) to that of Norway maple[1] (right).

Figure 30: Comparing the keys of mountain maple[1] (left) to those of Norway maple[7] (right).

A key to plants that may be confused with Norway maple (*Acer platanoides*)

1. Leaves with toothed edges

    2. Leaves with deep lobes (5-7 lobes) ....Silver maple (*Acer saccharinum*)

    2. Leaves with shallow lobes (3-5 lobes)

        3. Single-toothed leaves with teeth curved on one side ....Mountain maple (*Acer spicatum*)

        3. Irregular, double-toothed leaves with teeth straight on both sides

            4. Finely pointed and uniform teeth ....Striped maple (*Acer pensylvanicum*)

            4. Sharply pointed, irregular teeth...Red maple (*Acer rubrum*)

1. Leaves with smooth edges

        5. Leaf undersides and stalks hairy ....Black maple (*Acer nigrum*)

        5. Leaf undersides and stalks hairless

            6. Yellow-green leaves with 3-5 bluntly pointed lobes.....................Sugar maple (*Acer saccharum*)

            6. Dark green leaves with 5-7 sharply pointed lobes ....Norway maple (*Acer platanoides*)

BIOLOGY

TAXONOMIC HIERARCHY

Kingdom	Plantae
Subkingdom	Tracheobionta
Division	Magnoliophyta
Class	Magnoliopsida
Subclass	Rosidea
Order	Sapindales
Family	Sapindaceae
Genus	*Acer*
Species	*Acer platanoides*

ORIGIN & DISTRIBUTION

Norway maple is native to Europe where it is widespread and can be found growing naturally in mixed forests. Due to its popularity as a street tree in Europe it was only a matter of time before Norway maple became available for purchase as an ornamental in North America. It is thought to have first been introduced in 1756 in Philadelphia, Pennsylvania. Today, Norway maple can be found in six Canadian provinces, including Ontario, Quebec, Prince Edward Island, New Brunswick, Newfoundland and British Columbia (Nowak & Rowntree, 1990).

HABITAT

Norway maple grows well in both open and closed habitats. It is a popular street tree and is commonly found in urban areas. Due to its shade tolerance, Norway maple has spread into natural areas and can be found anywhere from urban woodlots to relatively undisturbed forests (Fig. 31). It grows better in mesic soils than in dry or very wet areas (Bertin et al. 2005; Meiners, 2005).

Figure 31: Fall colours of Norway maple in a forest[6].

REPRODUCTION

Norway maple's sexual reproduction drives its spread. The flowers are insect-pollinated and seeds are produced in large quantities. Seeds germinate readily to form extensive seedling banks. These seedlings wait in the understory until an opening is created in the canopy (Fig. 32). As sunlight penetrates to the seedlings below, they can quickly grow in height to fill the available space (Webb et al. 2001).

Figure 32: Norway maple seedlings in a forest understory[6].

LIFE CYCLE

Norway maple flowers early in the season, usually in April and May as the leaves expand (Nowak & Rowntree, 1990). Fruits are produced in the summer and mature in the autumn. Leaves senesce and turn yellow a couple of weeks later than native maples. Some winged fruits may stay on the tree throughout the winter (Kershaw, 2001).

SUCCESS MECHANISMS

Norway maple has a longer growing season as compared to native maples. Its leaves expand earlier and senesce later, thereby extending the growing season by as much as 3 weeks (Kloeppel & Abrams, 1995). This extra growing time may allow Norway maple to produce a larger and hardier seed crop. A superior seed crop allows for greater capacity to regenerate. The seeds germinate into shade tolerant seedlings that thrive in the understory, waiting for suitable conditions to grow into the canopy. Whenever light becomes available through an opening in the canopy the seedlings of Norway maple have the ability to rapidly grow in height. This rapid growth rate gives Norway maple a competitive advantage when it comes to canopy recruitment (Martin, 1999).

Not only does Norway maple produce a large quantity of seeds but each individual seed is hardy. Norway maple seeds are double and sometimes triple the weight of sugar maple seeds. A larger seed mass may benefit Norway maple by increasing its chances of survival and germination in a shaded understory. In fact, germination rates were observed to be higher for Norway maple as compared to sugar maple (Martin & Marks, 2006).

Norway maple may have an advantage in North America due to a lack of herbivores. One study documented less leaf and fungal damage to Norway maples in North America as compared to those found in Europe (Adams et al. 2009). Resources normally needed to repair damage done by herbivores can be put towards growth and reproduction. Even though Norway maple experiences some herbivory in its introduced range, studies have shown it to be more resilient to severe insect damage than native maples. Foliar insect damage was found to be greater for sugar maples as compared to co-occurring Norway maples in forests in New Jersey and Pennsylvania (Cincotta et al. 2009).

ECOSYSTEM IMPACTS

Norway maple invasions can suppress native hardwood regeneration (Fig. 33). In a 5ha woodlot in New York, concerns were raised that sugar maple was being replaced by Norway maple. Martin (1999) found that sugar maple (*Acer saccharum*) saplings were absent under Norway maple canopy trees. Norway maple saplings were found in greater abundance relative to other hardwood species and more than half of the saplings growing under sugar maple canopies were Norway maples.

Figure 33: Invasion of Norway maple saplings[6].

Similar effects on hardwood regeneration were observed in an 18ha forest preserve in New Jersey. Norway maple regeneration, in relation to total number of saplings, was found to be double that of American beech (*Fagus grandifolia*) and over five times that of sugar maple (Webb & Kaunzinger, 1993). Moreover, when Norway maple was present in a mixed oak forest in central New Jersey, the survival and growth of red maple (*Acer rubrum*), white elm (*Ulmus americana*) and red oak (*Quercus rubra*) were significantly reduced (Galbraith-Kent & Handel, 2008).

Norway maple invasions may inhibit the growth and occurrence of native wildflowers and shrubs. Norway maple casts a deeper shade as compared to native forest trees, which may eliminate or reduce shade intolerant species. Also, Norway maple's prolific reproduction allows for high seedling densities, which impart a high competitive pressure on other understory species. In a New Jersey forest preserve, fewer species were found growing under Norway maple canopies than under native sugar maple (*A. saccharum*) and American beech (*F. grandifolia*). In fact, Norway maple recruits occupied the majority of space under all three canopies (Wyckoff & Webb, 1996).

VECTORS & PATHWAYS

Norway maple can easily escape cultivation as its windborne seeds can disperse long distances. At times, seeds can disperse over 100 metres away from the parent tree (Bertin et al. 2005). Since Norway maple is commonly planted as a street tree (Fig. 34) many areas may be exposed to its seeds, especially urban woodlots (Anderson, 1999). Small mammals feed on Norway maple seeds and may contribute to its dispersal (Meiners, 2005).

Figure 34: Norway maple in an urban centre[6].

MANAGEMENT PRACTICES

PREVENTION STRATEGIES

· Use native maples in horticulture plantings;
· Remove any Norway maples from the property, especially large individuals that are capable of producing a large quantity of seeds;
· Minimize soil disturbance whenever possible.

EARLY DETECTION TECHNIQUES

· Learn how to properly identify Norway maple and be able to easily distinguish it from native maples;
· Monitor the woodlot frequently, paying particular attention to disturbed areas or places with recent openings within the canopy;
· Survey your local area for any large Norway maple trees that could be a potential seed source.

CONTROL OPTIONS

Hand-pulling: Small seedlings can be hand-pulled and weed wrenches can be used for saplings less than 3cm in diameter (Strobl & Bland, 2000). Soil disturbance should be minimized while pulling because it may promote the recruitment of new

Norway maple seedlings. Removal of small individuals in the understory should coincide with the removal of all mature seed-producing trees in the vicinity. Management efforts in the understory will eventually exhaust the seed bank and allow native species, such as sugar maple, to regenerate (Webb et al. 2001).

Cutting and Girdling: Cutting and girdling can be an effective non-chemical means of control for trees and saplings larger than 3cm in diameter. Cutting mature trees will eliminate the seed source and ease the burden of future management efforts. However, cutting down large trees will create an opening in the forest canopy, which may promote the growth of Norway maple saplings. To minimize this problem, ensure that management of seedlings and saplings in the understory coincide with canopy tree management. Divide large areas into manageable sections for control. Another option is to girdle large trees. It may take a few growing seasons for the tree to die. However, there will be no sudden openings in the canopy to encourage understory growth. Cut any re-sprouts from stumps as required (Webb et al. 2001; Clauson, 2011).

Herbicide application: Chemical control is effective in controlling Norway maple trees and to prevent re-sprouting. The cut-stump, basal bark and hack-and-squirt methods are all effective (Webster et al. 2006). Foliar application for understory saplings is generally not advised. Norway maple often grows in close proximity to sugar maple and other desirable hardwood species. Small seedlings and saplings can be hand-pulled. Alternatively, a cut-stump method can be used in conjunction with herbicide application to the cut surface of the stem after the saplings have been removed (Swearingen et al. 2010). Refer to section 2.3.2 for explanation of chemical application methods.

RECOMMENDATIONS FOR INTEGRATED CONTROL OF LARGE INVASIONS

Option #1: With chemical control

Target large seed producing trees first by applying herbicides using the basal bark, hack-and-squirt or cut-stump methods. The basal bark and hack-and-squirt methods may be easier than the cut-stump method in terms of labour as they do not require large trees to be felled. However, large dead standing trees may pose a hazard in some areas and may need to be felled anyway. Keep in mind that the cut-stump method will create large canopy openings that may promote invasion by other exotics in the vicinity. Monitoring such areas and controlling where needed, will give native species such as sugar maple time to fill in the canopy gaps (Swearingen et al. 2010).

After all seed producing trees are removed, focus can be put on the understory. Young seedlings under 3cm in diameter can be pulled. Anything larger can be cut followed by a herbicide application to the cut stem to prevent any re-sprouting. Norway maple often grows in the same areas as native sugar maple. Thus, applying herbicides using a foliar spray may cause undesirable damage (Strobl & Bland, 2000).

Option #2: Without chemical control

Large seed producing trees should be cut or girdled to prevent additions to the seed bank. Cut and girdled trees will likely re-sprout and will thus require frequent clipping. After all large trees have been controlled, management efforts can focus on smaller seedlings and saplings. As Norway maple takes several years to mature before seed production, understory control efforts can be scheduled every couple of years. Norway maple responds well to soil disturbance which is a natural result of management. Thus, allowing native saplings time to grow and become established may promote healthy competition with native plants (Galbraith-Kent & Handel, 2008).

Table 6: Management recommendations for Norway maple (*Acer platanoides*).		
Extent of infestation	Small invasions and satellite populations	Large invasions and dense populations
Recommended method of control	Hand-pulling seedlings and young saplings. Cutting trees that are too large to be hand-pulled.	Integrated control: (Combination of physical and chemical control).
Timing	Spring, summer and fall.	Cutting and hand-pulling can be done any time in the spring, summer and fall. Herbicide application should occur in the spring or fall while other native plants are dormant.
Frequency of control	Cut trees and saplings will likely re-sprout and require frequent clipping.	Cut trees and saplings will likely re-sprout and require frequent clipping. Plan to control Norway maple in the understory every couple of years.
Length of control	2-3 years.	5+ years.
Required restoration	Hand-pulling creates soil disturbance that benefits Norway maple recruitment. Consider planting native vegetation or transplanting with sugar maple seedlings.	Consider planting native vegetation in disturbed areas. Large dead standing trees may become a hazard and may need to be removed.

5.1.2
Tree-of-heaven
(*Ailanthus altissima*)

Other common names:
Varnish tree, Stinktree, Chinese sumac, Ailanthus, Copal tree,
Stinking sumac

Priority Rating: HIGH

Figure 35: Tree-of-heaven[11].

IDENTIFICATION

LEAVES: Tree-of-heaven has alternately arranged compound leaves. The compound leaves are composed of 11 to 41 leaflets (Fig. 36). Each leaflet has 1 to 4 glandular lobes near the base (Hu, 1979; Farrar, 1995).

Figure 36: The compound leaves[12] (left) and a single leaflet[1] (right) of tree-of-heaven.

FLOWERS: Tree-of-heaven is dioecious (i.e., each individual tree has either male or female flowers). These yellow-green flowers grow in large clusters called panicles (Fig. 37). Male trees generally produce more flowers, forming panicles that are 3 to 4 times larger than those found on female trees (Hu, 1979).

Figure 37: Tree-of-heaven flower panicles[4] (left) and individual flowers[4] (right).

FRUIT/SEEDS: Seeds are produced in winged fruits called samaras, each holding a single seed (Fig. 38). The samaras form dense clusters, with a mature tree producing over 300 000 seeds. Only female trees bear fruit (Bory & Clair-Maczulajtys, 1980).

Figure 38: Dense samara clusters[4] (left) and individual fruits[11] (right).

TRUNK: Tree-of-heaven is a fast growing, medium-sized tree. It can increase in height by 2 to 3m per season and range from 15 to 25m tall (Kershaw, 2001). The trunks of young trees are smooth and greenish-grey in colour (Fig. 39). As trees mature the bark turns a deeper grey and forms shallow, pale crevices (Farrar, 1995). Young branches are hairy and green, turning reddish-brown with age. Leaf scars are large and heart-shaped (Kowarik & Säumel, 2007).

Figure 39: Shallow crevices in mature bark[6] (left) and a heart-shaped leaf scar[1] (right).

SIMILAR SPECIES

Black locust (*Robinia pseudoacacia*)

Black locust has compound leaves with 7 to 19 leaflets that could be confused with those of tree-of-heaven. The leaflets of black locust have smooth edges whereas those of tree-of-heaven are lobed. Black locust leaves lack the glandular lobe at the base of the leaflet characteristic of tree-of-heaven (Fig. 40). Pairs of spines located along the stem may also help to identify black locust (Fig. 41). After being introduced from the eastern United States, black locust has become naturalized over much of southern Ontario (Farrar, 1995; Kershaw, 2001).

Figure 40: Comparing the compound leaves of black locust[5] (left) to those of tree-of-heaven[14] (right).

Figure 41: The characteristic spines of black locust[15].

Ash (*Fraxinus* spp.)

Several native species of ash in Ontario may be mistaken for tree-of-heaven. Ash trees have smaller compound leaves, with 5 to 11 leaflets, compared to the 11 to 41 leaflets of tree-of-heaven (Fig. 42). Another distinction is the arrangement of the compound leaves along the stem. Ash leaves have an opposite arrangement whereas tree-of-heaven displays an alternate arrangement (Farrar, 1995; Kershaw, 2001).

Figure 42: Comparing the compound leaves of black ash[8] (left) to those of tree-of-heaven[16] (right).

Poison-sumac (*Toxicodendron vernix*)

Poison-sumac is native to North America. It is a shrub or small tree with alternately arranged compound leaves. Each compound leaf has 7 to 13 leaflets with smooth edges whereas tree-of-heaven has 11 to 41 leaflets with glandular lobes close to the base (Fig. 43). Do not touch or burn poison-sumac as its oils and smoke can cause skin, eye and lung irritation (Farrar, 1995; Kershaw, 2001).

Figure 43: Comparing the compound leaves of poison-sumac[14] (left) to those of tree-of-heaven[5] (right).

Staghorn and smooth sumac (*Rhus typhina & R. glabra*)

Staghorn and smooth sumac are native to Ontario. They do not belong to the same genus as poison-sumac and since they are safe to touch they are commonly planted as ornamentals. These species of sumac have a similar number of leaflets (11 to 31) per compound leaf as compared to tree-of-heaven (11 to 41). However, the leaflets of staghorn and smooth sumac are sharply toothed unlike those of tree-of-heaven which are smooth with lobed bases (Fig. 44). Smooth sumac has hairless branches whereas those of staghorn sumac are covered in hair to the point where they appear fuzzy. Sumacs emit a characteristic milky sap when the leaf stalks or twigs are cut (Farrar, 1995; Kershaw, 2001).

Figure 44: Comparing the leaflets of staghorn sumac[5] (left) to those of tree-of-heaven[16] (right).

Mountain-ash (*Sorbus* spp.)

There are three species of mountain-ash in Ontario. American mountain-ash (*Sorbus americana*) and showy mountain-ash (*S. decora*) are native to Ontario while European mountain-ash (*S. aucuparia*) is exotic. They grow as shrubs or small trees and have pinnate, compound leaves consisting of 9-17 leaflets (Fig. 45). They can be distinguished from tree-of-heaven by the finely toothed edges of their leaflets (Farrar, 1995; Kershaw, 2001).

Figure 45: Comparing the compound leaves of mountain-ash[1] (left) to those of tree-of-heaven[6] (right).

Hickory (*Carya* spp.)

There are several species of hickory native to Ontario. Hickories have compound leaves with 5-11 leaflets (Fig. 46). The terminal leaflet is generally larger than the lateral leaflets. Hickory's leaflets have toothed edges while tree-of-heaven's leaflets have smooth, lobed edges (Farrar, 1995; Kershaw, 2001).

Figure 46: Comparing the compound leaves of hickory[5] (left) to those of tree-of-heaven[16] (right).

Butternut (*Juglans cinerea*)

Butternut is a medium-sized tree reaching 12 to 25m in height. Its compound leaves have 11 to 17 leaflets with toothed edges and are hairy underneath. The top three terminal leaflets are equal in size while the rest get progressively smaller from top to bottom along the central stalk (Fig. 47). Tree-of-heaven has leaflets that are generally equal in size with smooth lobed edges (Farrar, 1995; Kershaw, 2001). Butternut is native to Ontario and is currently considered a species at risk (OMNR, 2012b).

Figure 47: Comparing the compound leaves of butternut[8] (left) to those of tree-of-heaven[5] (right).

Black walnut (*Juglans nigra*)

Black walnut is a medium-sized tree, growing up to 30m tall. Black walnut is native to Ontario and is prized for its high value wood. The compound leaves have 14 to 22 leaflets with finely toothed edges and slightly hairy undersides (Fig. 48). The terminal leaflet is either absent or much smaller than the lateral leaflets. Tree-of-heaven's top and lateral leaflets are generally similar in size (Farrar, 1995; Kershaw, 2001).

Figure 48: Comparing the compound leaves of black walnut[1] (left) to those of tree-of-heaven[11] (right).

A key to plants that may be confused with tree-of-heaven (*Ailanthus altissima*)

1. Branches with spines..Black locust
(*Robinia pseudoacacia*)

1. Branches without spines

  2. Opposite compound leaves...Ash (*Fraxinus* spp.)

  2. Alternate compound leaves

    3. Leaflets with smooth edges...Poison-sumac
(*Toxicodendron vernix*)

    3. Leaflets with toothed or lobed edges

      4. Leaflets with sharp regular teeth

        5. Leaf stalks and twigs release milky sap when cut

          6. Branches very hairy..Staghorn sumac
(*Rhus typhina*)

          6. Branches hairless…..Smooth sumac (*Rhus glabra*)

        5. Leaf stalks and twigs do not release a milky sap when cut

          7. Leaflets on a compound leaf are all similar in size

            8. Leaflets with hairy undersides...........................European mountain-ash
(*Sorbus aucuparia*)

            8. Leaflets with smooth undersides

              9. Leaflets 3-5 times as long as they are wide with a tapering point.....American mountain-ash
(*Sorbus americana*)

              9. Leaflets 2-3 times as long as they are wide with an abrupt point......Showy mountain-ash
(*Sorbus decora*)

          7. Leaflets on a compound leaf are dissimilar in size

            10. Terminal leaflet larger than adjacent leaflets......................................Hickory (*Carya* spp.)

            10. Terminal leaflet equal in size or smaller than adjacent leaflets

              11. Three terminal leaflets equal in size...Butternut (*Juglans cinerea*)

              11. Terminal leaflet absent or smaller than the rest...........................Black walnut (*Juglans nigra*)

      4. Leaflets with lobes near the base ....Tree-of-heaven
(*Ailanthus altissima*)

BIOLOGY

TAXONOMIC HIERARCHY

Kingdom	Plantae
Subkingdom	Tracheobionta
Division	Magnoliophyta
Class	Magnoliopsida
Subclass	Rosidae
Order	Sapindales
Family	Simaroubaceae
Genus	*Ailanthus*
Species	*Ailanthus altissima*

ORIGIN & DISTRIBUTION

Tree-of-heaven is native to China. Seeds were supposedly shipped to Europe and planted in Paris in the early 1740's. In 1784 it was first introduced to North America in a garden in Philadelphia. Tree-of-heaven was highly valued as an ornamental plant due to its rapid growth and lush foliage. As a result, it was commonly planted in urban areas where it readily escaped cultivation (Fig. 49). Tree-of-heaven is found in southern Ontario but has the potential to expand north (Hu, 1979).

Figure 49: Tree-of-heaven growing alongside a building[15].

HABITAT

Tree-of-heaven is shade intolerant and has historically been documented to invade open, disturbed areas. It is considered a nuisance in urban areas where it grows close to buildings and through the cracks in sidewalks (Hu, 1979). Due to its shade intolerance, tree-of-heaven was not traditionally considered a threat to forests. However, recent studies have documented tree-of-heaven invasions in old- and second-growth forests (Kowarik, 1995; Knapp & Canham, 2000) (Fig. 50).

Figure 50: Tree-of-heaven occupying space in the canopy[11].

REPRODUCTION

Tree-of-heaven is dioecious (i.e., each tree is either male or female). Seeds are produced in winged fruits on female trees (Hu, 1979). A mature tree can produce more than 300 000 seeds

(Bory & Clair-Maczulajtys, 1980). Although tree-of-heaven reproduces mainly through seeds, it can also reproduce asexually by way of clones that readily sprout from the root and stem (Kowarik & Säumel, 2007).

LIFE CYCLE

Tree-of-heaven takes 3 to 5 years to mature. Only after this period will trees produce flowers and, consequently, produce seeds. Flowering occurs from mid-April through June and samaras are produced from August to October. These ripen from September until the end of October and germinate the following year (Kowarik & Säumel, 2007). In one study, a small percentage of seeds remained viable for a second growing season, implying that tree-of-heaven may establish a short-term seed bank (Kota et al. 2007). Further investigation into the longevity of such a seed bank is required.

SUCCESS MECHANISMS

Tree-of-heaven has the advantage of being able to reproduce sexually and asexually. A single tree can produce more than 300 000 seeds that are easily dispersed by wind (Bory & Clair-Maczulajtys, 1980) (Fig. 51). Tree-of-heaven's fast growth rate and preference for light allows it to quickly occupy gaps in the forest canopy created by management activities or natural causes (Knapp & Canham, 2000). Once canopy trees are established their root systems can branch out into the understory. Nutrients transferred from the parent to saplings emerging from its roots alleviate the stress imposed by the low-light environment (Kowarik, 1995).

Figure 51: Prolific seed production by tree-of-heaven[4].

Tree-of-heaven synthesizes secondary compounds that can be found in both the living tissue and the surrounding soil (Lawrence et al. 1991). These compounds can inhibit the establishment and growth of other plant species (Mergen, 1959; Heisey, 1990; Lawrence et al. 1991) and act as a defense against herbivores and pathogens (Heisey, 1990), thereby strongly enhancing tree-of-heaven's competitive ability against native species.

ECOSYSTEM IMPACTS

Tree-of-heaven may inhibit native hardwood regeneration through allelopathic effects and direct competition. Such effects could result in a shift in the species composition of the forest and thus change the dynamics of the forest community (Gómez-Aparicio & Canham, 2008b). Once established, tree-of-heaven can form dense patches (Fig. 52) and, due to its fast growth rate, directly compete with native vegetation for nutrients and canopy space (Knapp & Canham, 2000).

Figure 52: A dense population of tree-of-heaven[15].

VECTORS & PATHWAYS

Seeds are contained in winged capsules (samaras) that enable long distance, windborne dispersal. Seeds can easily be spread by wind currents into the interior of the forest from parent trees located at the forest edge (Landenberger et al. 2007). Water is another agent of dispersal for seeds and plant fragments that can produce clones (Kowarik & Säumel, 2008). Rodents may also help to disperse seeds by collecting and caching them for the winter (Kowarik & Säumel, 2007).

MANAGEMENT PRACTICES

PREVENTION STRATEGIES

· Do not dump yard wastes in natural areas. Seeds or stem fragments may be incorporated in the wastes and could easily germinate or re-sprout in refuse piles;
· Refrain from planting tree-of-heaven as an ornamental on your lawn. Seeds can disperse long distances and could easily enter a nearby woodlot or natural area.

EARLY DETECTION TECHNIQUES

· Learn how to properly identify tree-of-heaven at all life stages. Young saplings can easily be confused with other native understory species (Fig. 53). Tree-of-heaven is most easily identified by the characteristic lobes at the base of the leaflets (see above section on similar species);
· Monitor the woodlot frequently and pay particular attention to disturbed areas and forest edges.

Figure 53: Tree-of-heaven saplings[1] (left) are easily confused with sumacs[19] (right).

CONTROL OPTIONS

Hand-pulling: Hand-pulling is only practical for small seedlings. Larger saplings develop a taproot that is difficult to remove by hand (Hoshovsky, 1995). Although the use of tools such as a weed wrench may help to remove larger saplings, they can break the root system, leaving behind root fragments that can re-sprout. Moist soils make pulling easier and increase the likelihood that the entire root system will come loose. Clonal shoots arising from trailing roots may be difficult to remove as they are attached to other individuals. Moreover, removing the root system without leaving behind root fragments is nearly impossible. Care should be taken to remove as much of the root as possible to prevent re-sprouting (Swearingen & Pannill, 2009).

Cutting and girdling: Cutting and girdling are often ineffective means of control for tree-of-heaven because it can promote re-sprouting and make the invasion worse (Meloche & Murphy, 2006). Girdling will kill large trees, however, the roots will send up new clonal shoots. Cutting and girdling will only make the problem worse if frequent ongoing management is not an option. This is because frequent cutting will eventually exhaust the plant's reserves and kill the tree. To be successful, this method will require several years, with frequent repeated cuttings per year (Burch & Zedaker, 2003).

Excavation: Large trees and saplings can be cut and their entire root system excavated from the ground. However, digging out these stumps and roots is labour intensive and causes a great deal of soil disturbance, thus promoting re-invasion. Excavation is only practical in areas where there are only a few individuals. After management, holes should be filled and replanted with native vegetation or covered with mulch to help decrease the chance of re-establishment by tree-of-heaven and other exotics (Swearingen & Pannill, 2009).

Herbicide application: Herbicide application is an effective way of controlling tree-of-heaven invasions. It can help to kill existing trees while effectively preventing re-sprouting that is difficult to avoid with other non-chemical control methods (Burch & Zedaker, 2003). It is best to use a systemic herbicide when trying to control tree-of-heaven because they are absorbed by the plant tissues and transported below-ground to the entire root system. This is important because clonal shoots can continue to sprout even if the above-ground portion of the parent tree is dead. Use hack-and-squirt or cut-stump methods of herbicide application to large trees. Saplings may be treated using the cut-stump or basal bark method. Seedlings and saplings may be treated using a foliar spray (Miller et al. 2010).

RECOMMENDATIONS FOR INTEGRATED CONTROL OF LARGE INVASIONS

Option #1: With chemical control

Tree-of-heaven is often difficult to eradicate and control. Its abundant seed production coupled with vegetative spread makes frequent monitoring a necessity. In heavily invaded areas it may be more practical to target mature female trees, which can produce over 300 000 seeds per year. Once the large female trees have been removed, management efforts can focus on the male trees and the smaller saplings in the understory. Several years of monitoring may be required to catch any re-sprouts or germinating saplings from a potentially short-term seed bank (Miller et al. 2010).

Small seedlings can easily be pulled before they develop a tap-root whereas larger saplings may either be pulled by using a root wrench, excavation of their root systems or through a foliar herbicide application. In the case of mature trees it is important to target the female seed-producing trees first to reduce the addition of seeds into the area. The hack-and-squirt method may be applied to the large trees. Alternatively, the cut-stump method can be used keeping in mind the additional labour requirements of cutting and removing large trees from the area. In all situations, frequent monitoring will be needed to control any re-sprouts. A second application of herbicides may be needed to kill large trees or "stubborn" saplings (Miller et al. 2010).

Option #2: Without chemical control

Controlling large populations of tree-of-heaven without using herbicides will require repeated monitoring and management. Targeting large seed-bearing female trees will reduce the number of seedlings emerging the following year. Cutting these large trees will promote re-sprouting from the stump and roots. However, if these re-sprouts are frequently cut back the root reserves will eventually be exhausted. The initial tree felling should occur in the early summer, just after flowering, to minimize the proliferation of seeds. In addition, the root system is most vulnerable at this time because most of the energy has been spent on producing leaves and flowers. Promoting a healthy overstory that enhances the amount of shade will also discourage re-invasion (Pannill, 2000).

After all the large female trees have been removed, the invaded area should be split up into manageable sizes for control. Areas along the outer boundary of the invasion should be targeted first, working towards the centre of the most heavily invaded area. Large trees should be cut while small saplings should be pulled by hand. To completely destroy root reserves and prevent re-sprouting repeated control measures will be needed throughout the season and for multiple years (Hoshovsky, 1995).

The above-ground portion of tree-of-heaven should be put through a wood chipper or burned. For small invasions with a few individual trees a manager might choose to leave the slash as woody debris to enhance wildlife habitat. However caution should be taken due to tree-of-heaven's potential for allelopathy. In heavily invaded areas or where it could interfere with management activities, the wood can be turned into woodchips or firewood. Large slash piles may also be burned on site. Since even small root fragments can sprout into a new tree, the roots of tree-of-heaven should be carefully disposed of. It is recommended to bag or incinerate the roots (Hoshovsky, 1995).

Table 7: Management recommendations for tree-of-heaven (*Ailanthus altissima*).

Extent of infestation	Small invasions and satellite populations	Large invasions and dense populations
Recommended method of control	Hand-pulling, excavation and cutting.	Integrated control including hand-pulling, cutting and herbicide application.
Timing	Hand-pull all emerging saplings in the spring before they develop a large tap-root. Cut and excavate larger saplings throughout the year. Cut large trees in the early summer right after flowering for optimal results.	Hand-pull all emerging saplings in the spring before they develop a large tap-root. Cut large trees in the early summer right after flowering. Apply herbicides in the spring or fall when most native vegetation is dormant.
Frequency of control	Ongoing monitoring and control will be needed. Re-sprouts from cut trees will need to be controlled several times per year.	Ongoing monitoring and management will be needed to control tree-of-heaven invasions. Re-sprouts from cut trees will need to be controlled several times per year. Herbicides may need to be re-applied the following year.
Length of control	2-5 years.	5+ years.
Required restoration	Plant native species or apply mulch in areas where hand-pulling creates soil disturbance.	Plant native species or apply mulch in areas where hand-pulling creates soil disturbance.

5.1.3
Garlic Mustard
(Alliaria petiolata)

Other common names:
Hedge Garlic

Priority Rating: HIGH

Figure 54: Garlic Mustard[1]

IDENTIFICATION

GROWTH FORM: Garlic mustard has a two-year life cycle. During the first year, a small cluster of leaves called a basal rosette form (Fig. 55). During the second year, stems emerge from the basal rosette to produce flowers and seed. Flowering stems can reach 1.25m in height. All parts of the plant emit a garlic odour when crushed (Cavers et al. 1979).

Figure 55: First-year basal rosette[1] (left) and second-year growth[1] (right) of garlic mustard.

LEAVES: Basal rosette leaves are kidney-shaped with wavy edges (Rodgers et al. 2008). Deep veins give the leaves a wrinkled appearance. Each rosette has 2 to 12 leaves arranged in a whorl. These leaves remain green throughout the winter, even when buried in snow (Fig. 56). Second-year leaves grow from a stalk in an alternate arrangement (Fig. 57). They are triangular in shape with toothed edges (Cavers et al. 1979).

Figure 56: First-year basal leaves of garlic mustard[1].   Figure 57: Second-year leaves of garlic mustard[1].

FLOWERS: Flowers have 4 white petals, 4 green sepals and 6 stamen (Fig. 58). They grow in clusters, also known as racemes, at the top of each stem (Cavers et al. 1979).

Figure 58: Garlic mustard flowers[1].

FRUIT/SEED: Mature plants produce long, slender seedpods full of tiny black seeds (Kaufman & Kaufman, 2007) (Fig. 59).

Figure 59: Seedpod formation[1] (left) and mature seeds[1] (right) of garlic mustard.

ROOT: Taproots have an S-shaped pattern (Fig. 60) directly below the stem (Cavers et al. 1979).

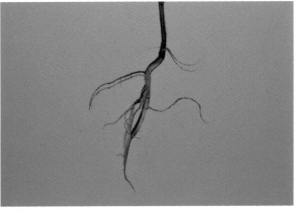

Figure 60: Characteristic S-curved root of garlic mustard[1].

SIMILAR SPECIES

Ground ivy (*Glechoma hederacea*)

The first-year basal leaves of garlic mustard can be confused with ground ivy leaves when the plants are not in flower (Fig. 61). Look closely for hair on the leaves. Ground ivy leaves are hairy whereas garlic mustard leaves are not. These plants cannot be confused when they are in flower because ground ivy has purple flowers (Fig. 62) whereas garlic mustard has white flowers (Newcomb, 1977; Dickinson et al. 2004).

Figure 61: Comparing the leaves of ground ivy[1] (left) to those of garlic mustard[1] (right).

Figure 62: Ground ivy flowers[1].

Violets (*Viola* spp.)

Violet leaves can be confused with the first-year basal leaves of garlic mustard when the plants are not in flower (Fig. 63). It is often very difficult to differentiate between violets and garlic mustard. Some guides point out that the wavy edges are less than 1mm long for violets whereas they are greater than 1mm long for garlic mustard. Perform a quick check by crushing the leaves to detect whether or not they emit a garlic odour. Although some violet species have white flowers they are not similar to those of garlic mustard (Newcomb, 1977; Dickinson et al. 2004) (Fig. 64).

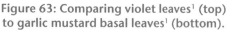

Figure 63: Comparing violet leaves[1] (top) to garlic mustard basal leaves[1] (bottom).

Figure 64: Violet flowers[20].

Kidney-leaved buttercup (*Ranunculus abortivus*)

Before flowering, the first-year basal leaves of garlic mustard can be confused with the basal leaves of kidney-leaved buttercup (Fig. 65). The leaves of kidney-leaved buttercup have a very flat appearance whereas the basal leaves of garlic mustard have deep veins that give them a wrinkled appearance. Kidney-leaved buttercup flowers are yellow (Fig. 66) in contrast to the white flowers of garlic mustard (Newcomb, 1977; Dickinson et al. 2004).

Figure 65: Comparing the basal leaves of kidney-leaved buttercup[1] (left) to those of garlic mustard[1] (right).

Figure 66: Kidney-leaved buttercup flower[1].

Wild ginger (*Asarum canadense*)

Wild ginger leaves may appear to be similar to garlic mustard basal leaves at first sight (Fig. 67). However, wild ginger leaves do not have the wavy edges that are characteristic of the basal leaves of garlic mustard. The flowers of wild ginger emerge close to the ground and are red (Fig. 68). Garlic mustard flowers are white and grow on the top of flowering stalks (Newcomb, 1977; Dickinson et al. 2004).

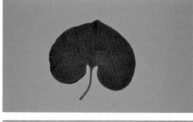

Figure 67: Comparing the leaves of wild ginger[1] (top) to those of garlic mustard[1] (bottom).

Figure 68: Wild ginger flower[1].

[73]

Toothwort (*Cardamine* spp.)

The flowers of toothwort are very similar in appearance to garlic mustard flowers. Both species have white flowers with four petals (Fig. 69). In contrast, these plants are easily identified by the characteristics of their leaves. Toothwort leaves are compound, consisting of three leaflets (Fig. 70), whereas garlic mustard leaves are simple (Newcomb, 1977; Dickinson et al. 2004).

Figure 69: Comparing the flowers of toothwort[1] (left) to those of garlic mustard[13] (right).

Figure 70: Comparing toothwort[1] (left) and garlic mustard[1] (right).

Catnip (*Nepeta cataria*)

Catnip leaves may be confused with the second-year leaves of garlic mustard. They are both triangular with sharp edges (Fig. 71). Close inspection will reveal that catnip leaves are very hairy while garlic mustard leaves are not. Catnip flowers do not resemble garlic mustard flowers (Fig. 72) as they are irregular in shape (Newcomb, 1977; Dickinson et al. 2004).

Figure 71: Comparing the leaves of catnip[1] (left) to the second-year leaves of garlic mustard[1] (right).

Figure 72: Catnip flowers[1]

A key to plants that may be confused with garlic mustard (*Alliaria petiolata*)

1. Compound leaves .... Toothwort (*Cardamine* spp.)

1. Simple leaves

   2. Leaf edges smooth .... Wild ginger (*Asarum canadense*)

   2. Leaf edges toothed

     3. Teeth rounded

       4. Leaves with hair .... Ground ivy (*Glechoma hederacea*)

       4. Leaves without hair

         5. Deep veins give leaves a wrinkled appearance .... Garlic mustard (*Alliaria petiolata*)

         5. Leaves appear flat .... Kidney-leaved buttercup (*Ranunculus abortivus*)

     3. Teeth sharp or pointed

       6. Leaves very hairy .... Catnip (*Nepeta cataria*)

       6. Leaves with little or no hair

         7. Teeth less than 1mm long .... Violet (*Viola* spp.)

         7. Teeth greater than 1mm long .... Garlic mustard (*Alliaria petiolata*)

BIOLOGY

TAXONOMIC HIERARCHY

Kingdom	Plantae
Subkingdom	Tracheobionta
Division	Magnoliophyta
Class	Magnoliopsida
Subclass	Dilleniidae
Order	Brassicales
Family	Brassicaceae
Genus	*Alliaria*
Species	*Alliaria petiolata*

ORIGIN & DISTRIBUTION

A native to Eurasia, garlic mustard was probably introduced to North America by early settlers. It was valued for its garlic flavour and healing properties (Huffman, 2005). The first documented evidence of garlic mustard in North America was found on Long Island, New York in 1868 (Anderson et al. 1996). Canadian records show that garlic mustard was found in Toronto, Ontario in 1879 where it has since spread to Quebec, New Brunswick, Nova Scotia and British Columbia (Cavers et al. 1979).

HABITAT

Garlic mustard is a shade tolerant species (Rodgers et al. 2008) that grows best in moist soils (Cavers et al. 1979). In its native range, garlic mustard occupies edge habitats such as those found on the borders of forests and rivers (Rodgers et al. 2008). In North America, garlic mustard also prefers these edge habitats. However, populations can be found anywhere from forest interiors to open fields (Cavers et al. 1979) (Fig. 73). Disturbed areas allow seedlings to establish where they can spread and invade undisturbed habitats (Kaufman & Kaufman, 2007).

Figure 73: Garlic mustard in the forest understory[1].

REPRODUCTION

Garlic mustard plants reproduce via seed production. Although a variety of insects help to pollinate the flowers of garlic mustard, these plants can also self-pollinate. This ensures that seeds will be produced by every flowering individual (Rodgers et al. 2008). Mature plants produce seedpods that hold 10 to 20 seeds and each plant can have anywhere from 1 to 150 seedpods (Cavers et al. 1979). Seeds have a thick outer layer that allows them to persist in the soil for up to 10 years (Rodgers et al. 2008).

LIFE CYCLE

Garlic mustard has a biennial (two-year) life cycle. Basal leaves develop during the first year. Flowers emerge in April during the second year of growth. Seedpods are formed shortly thereafter and seeds are dispersed throughout the summer and fall (Cavers et al. 1979).

SUCCESS MECHANISMS

Several aspects relating to garlic mustard's reproductive capabilities lend to its success as an invader. These include the ability to self-pollinate, to produce a large quantity of viable seed, and to form extensive seed banks. Many native plants need insect pollinators in order to produce seed. However, garlic mustard has the ability to self-pollinate. This gives garlic mustard the advantage of consistent seed production (Rodgers et al. 2008). Populations of garlic mustard can increase rapidly because these plants have a high reproductive potential (Drayton & Primack, 1999). An individual plant has the ability to produce over 3500 seeds and studies have shown that several populations in Ontario can produce 107 000 seeds within one square metre (Cavers et al. 1979). After dispersal, seeds remain dormant until ideal conditions prompt them to germinate. A thick outer seed coat (Cavers et al. 1979) allows seeds to remain viable for up to 10 years, forming a seed bank in the soil (Rodgers et al. 2008).

Garlic mustard has the ability to thrive in areas with a wide range of different light intensities. The basal leaves of garlic mustard remain green all year providing the plant with potential photosynthetic activity during late fall and early spring when other native herbs are dormant (Myers et al. 2005) (Fig. 74). Photosynthesis is important because it allows plants to convert solar energy into organic compounds for growth and reproduction. Being an evergreen species, garlic mustard obtains a competitive advantage over other species that can only photosynthesize during the summer months (Myers et al. 2005).

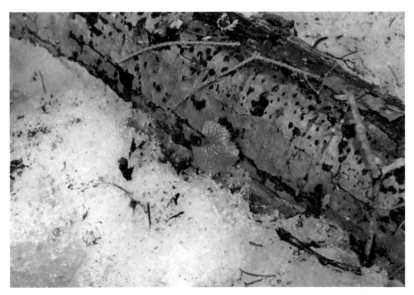

Figure 74: Garlic mustard's basal leaves remain green all year long[1].

Garlic mustard has a variety of secondary compounds that may decrease the likelihood of herbivore attack and suppress the growth of competing plants. Secondary compounds are found in the plant tissues and can react with water to form cyanide compounds. These compounds are toxic and help to discourage potential herbivores from feeding on the plants (Rodgers et al. 2008). In its native range, organisms have had time to co-evolve with these toxic compounds whereas North American species have not (Renwick, 2002).

Secondary compounds can potentially suppress the growth of competing native plants. This may be accomplished indirectly, by decreasing the amount of mycorrhizal fungi found in the soil (Barto et al. 2010). Unlike most native plants that rely on these beneficial fungi for nutrients, garlic mustard does not establish associations with mycorrhizal fungi. As such, by depressing mycorrhizal associations of native plants they can gain a competitive advantage (Wolfe et al. 2008).

ECOLOGICAL IMPACTS

Garlic mustard may change the species composition in mature hardwood forests. Greenhouse studies have shown that garlic mustard can dramatically affect the growth rate of dominant hardwood species such as sugar maple (*Acer saccharum*), red maple (*Acer rubrum*) and white ash (*Fraxinus americana*). Regeneration of these canopy tree species is repressed which in time could change the overall composition of a mature hardwood stand to that of an early successional community (Stinson et al. 2006). Further research in the field is needed to assess the effects of garlic mustard on the species composition of mature forests.

Diversity within a forest stand is important because it supports a healthy ecosystem. A diverse forest is less susceptible to the impacts of pest outbreaks and disease (Chapeskie et al. 2006). Garlic mustard actively decreases diversity through its superior competitive abilities and by preventing nutrient uptake by mycorrhiza-dependent species (Stinson et al. 2006). Dense stands can form in the understory, effectively decreasing the abundance of native wildflowers and potentially repressing hardwood regeneration (Fig. 75).

Garlic mustard invasions affect wildlife. Studies have shown that garlic mustard has a negative impact on certain species of butterfly. Native species such as West Virginia white (*Pieris virginiensis*) and mustard white (*Pieris napi oleracea*) have been observed to deposit their eggs on garlic mustard plants. Unfortunately, secondary compounds greatly lower the survival rate of hatching larvae (Rodgers et al. 2008). These butterflies usually oviposit on native toothwort (*Cardamine* sp.) found in forest understories. Garlic mustard populations can encroach upon toothwort habitat and gradually displace toothwort populations. With the absence of toothwort, these butterflies have little choice but to deposit their eggs on garlic mustard (Renwick, 2002).

Figure 75: Second-year garlic mustard plants towering over native vegetation[1].

VECTORS/PATHWAYS

Garlic mustard seeds usually fall within several metres of the parent plant. This allows for the growth of dense patches and the development of a large seed bank for established populations (Anderson et al. 1996). As populations have been observed along flood water paths it seems likely that flood waters can increase dispersal distance (Wilkens, 2000).

Long distance dispersal usually occurs with the help of other organisms. Humans are mainly responsible for the dispersal of garlic mustard seeds. Seeds can readily attach to clothing, shoes and tires. Seeds can get stuck to machinery such as heavy equipment used for creating roads or used for logging. Tires from all-terrain vehicles, tractors and trailers contribute to seed dispersal (Shartell et al. 2011).

Animals such as mice, raccoons and squirrels have been observed collecting seeds and moving them to roosting areas. Seeds often get stuck to the hooves of deer where they can be carried over long distances (Wilkens, 2000). While feeding, deer will often create areas of disturbance where garlic mustard can easily become established (Rodgers et al. 2008).

MANAGEMENT PRACTICES

PREVENTION STRATEGIES

· Prevent seeds from entering the woodlot by limiting access and washing all shoes and tires before entry;
· Do not let domestic animals roam freely if there are known garlic mustard populations in or around the woodlot;
· Try to minimize soil disturbance during woodlot management activities;
· Volunteer to help eliminate garlic mustard populations from nearby properties.

EARLY DETECTION TECHNIQUES

· Monitor the woodlot frequently paying attention to roadsides, flood water paths and disturbed areas;
· Learn how to identify both the basal rosette stage and second-year mature stage of garlic mustard.

CONTROL OPTIONS

Hand-pulling: Garlic mustard can be pulled from the ground with relative ease. Pulling from the base of the stalk will prevent the stem from breaking and allow a large majority of the root to be removed. Remove as much of the root as possible, with the upper half of the taproot being removed at the very least, to prevent re-sprouting (Fig. 76). All above-ground plant tissue should be placed in a bag and removed from the area. This is essential as pulled stems may have the ability to release viable seed. Care should be taken not to trample or pull native vegetation (NCC, 2007).

Figure 76: Hand-pulling garlic mustard plants[1].

In areas with small invasions or scattered satellite populations, the goal of hand-pulling should be to remove both first and second-year plants. In areas with larger invasions it will become impractical to try to remove all garlic mustard plants. In these areas, focus should lean towards removing all mature second-year plants while allowing the basal rosettes to remain. Removing the second-year plants will prevent seeds from producing and replenishing the seed bank. Management will need to continue for years until the seed bank is completely exhausted (Nuzzo, 1991).

Place all plant parts in a plastic or paper bag and dispose of in an appropriate landfill (Fig. 77). Garlic mustard is not a yard waste and should not be disposed of as such. Contact your local waste service provider and/or landfill manager to discuss disposal procedures. Ensure that no parts are left behind to produce roots or seed. Make sure that bags are properly sealed to prevent spread during transportation (Frey et al. 2005).

Figure 77: Garlic mustard disposal[1].

Flower-head removal: In small populations, removing flower heads can prevent seed production. However, constant vigilance is required as clipping encourages the growth of more flowers. This control method should only be used in very small populations as it involves frequent monitoring. One advantage of removing flower heads over hand-pulling is the absence of soil disturbance. When plants are pulled, they create extra space on the forest floor where garlic mustard can reinvade (NCC, 2007). Care should be taken when selecting this management option. It may prove difficult to ensure that all flowers have been removed. Missing a single reproductive individual could potentially negate the time and effort invested in control if seeds are allowed to replenish the seed bank (Frey et al. 2005).

Mowing or cutting: Manual control of dense patches can be accomplished by mowing or cutting. This is only appropriate in areas where large invasions have eliminated native vegetation.

Cutting can be done using weed whackers, scythes, and lawn mowers. The objective is to cut as close to the ground as possible. This control method will need to be conducted several times throughout the season as new shoots arise from the taproots (Drayton & Primack, 1999). There is a short window of opportunity in which the most damage can be done to individual garlic mustard plants using the cutting method. The roots of garlic mustard allocate the greatest amount of energy to the flower and fruiting stage, thus cutting the plants right after they produce flowers may leave the remaining roots in an energy deficient state (NCC, 2007). Cutting should be done before seeds are produced and throughout the season to prevent any late seedpod production. The main goal is to exhaust the seed bank, gradually eliminating the entire population (Strobl & Bland, 2000).

Herbicide application: Dense patches can be controlled chemically. Studies have shown that herbicides can decrease garlic mustard populations by as much as 91% (Rodgers et al. 2008). In order to decrease the amount of damage done to native vegetation it would be appropriate to use a spot-treatment method. This may increase the amount of labour required, however, it is essential to minimize any impacts to native plants (Landis & Evans, 2009). Herbicide application should only be done in the spring or fall when most native plants are dormant. A spring application has the advantage of eradicating both the first-year basal rosettes and the second-year flowering plants (Slaughter et al. 2007). However, a spring application may be inappropriate if the affected woodlot is valued for its early spring ephemerals (NCC, 2007). A fall application is generally preferred because a large majority of native plants have already entered into dormancy (Slaughter et al. 2007).

RECOMMENDATIONS FOR INTEGRATED CONTROL OF LARGE INVASIONS

Option #1: With chemical control

A plan should be created before the commencement of any management practice. Control efforts should focus on working from the outer boundaries of the invasion towards the centre. This will prevent seeds, a main dispersal agent for garlic mustard, from being spread to other areas of the hardwood stand. Be sure to inspect and clean footwear, clothing, tires and any other objects that could harbour seeds before moving to other areas (Nuzzo, 1991).

In the spring it is best to hand-pull, cut or mow dense patches of second-year plants shortly after they begin to flower but before they begin producing seedpods. Use caution in areas where there is desirable vegetation to prevent any unwanted damage. The goal is to prevent any seeds from replenishing the seed bank. Monitor the area throughout the summer and pull any late flowering individuals (NCC, 2007). Apply herbicides in the fall, after the majority of native vegetation has entered dormancy. Targeting the basal rosettes should reduce the number of second-year plants produced the following year. Repeat for 2 to 3 years or until the population has reached a manageable size to fully rely upon non-chemical control methods such as hand-pulling (Slaughter et al. 2007).

Option #2: Without chemical control

Hand-pull, cut or mow dense patches of second-year plants shortly after they begin to flower in the spring. Ensure this is done before the garlic mustard plants begin producing seedpods. Use caution in areas where there is desirable vegetation to prevent any unwanted damage. The goal is to prevent any seeds from replenishing the seed bank. Monitor the area and pull any remaining second-year plants throughout the summer. Focus on eliminating second-year plants to slowly exhaust the seed bank. As the population begins to decrease in size, basal rosettes may also be targeted to help speed up control (Nuzzo, 1991).

There is the potential to reintroduce native species to these disturbed areas which may jumpstart the restoration of the forest ecosystem. Results from a study by Murphy (2005) revealed that planting a native wildflower, bloodroot (*Sanguinaria canadensis*), helped to alleviate the spread of garlic mustard (Fig. 78). Further research is needed to determine which native species would be appropriate for such restoration efforts.

Figure 78: Planting a native species, bloodroot (*Sanguinaria canadensis*)[1].

Table 8: Management recommendations for garlic mustard (*Alliaria petiolata*).

Extent of infestation	Small invasions and satellite populations	Large invasions and dense populations
Recommended method of control	Hand-pulling and flower head removal.	Integrated control including physical control methods and herbicide application.
Timing	Hand-pulling: Spring (April-May). Flower head removal: Spring and early summer (April-June).	Integrated control: Physical control: Spring and summer. Herbicide application: Fall.
Frequency of control	Hand-pulling: Several times per year, up to five years or until the seed bank is exhausted. Flower head removal: Every few days until no more flowers are produced.	Manual removal in the spring and chemical control in the fall may be required for up to 5 years or until seed bank is exhausted.
Length of control	2-5 years.	5 + years.
required restoration	Plant native species in areas where hand-pulling creates soil disturbance.	Plant native species once seed bank has nearly been exhausted. Monitoring and hand-pulling any germinating garlic mustard seedlings will be needed.

5.1.4
Barberry
(Berberis thunbergii & B. vulgaris)

Other common names:
Japanese barberry, Purple Japanese barberry, Common barberry,
European barberry, Jaundice berry

Priority Rating: HIGH

Figure 79: Japanese barberry.

IDENTIFICATION

Two species of barberry currently invade Ontario hardwood stands: Japanese barberry (*Berberis thunbergii*) and common barberry (*Berberis vulgaris*). They are both deciduous shrubs with yellowish bark and spiny branches (Bailey, 1969).

Japanese barberry (*Berberis thunbergii*)

STEM & BRANCHES: The branches are brown with deep grooves and have alternately arranged simple thorns (Fig. 80). Japanese barberry shrubs range from 0.5m to 2m in height (Bailey, 1969).

Figure 80: Japanese barberry stem with simple thorns[1].

LEAVES: Japanese barberry has simple, oval leaves with smooth margins which taper at the base (Fig. 81). The leaves are found in clusters of approximately 2 to 6 leaves located above each thorn. Leaves range in colour from green to red to purple, depending on the cultivar (Kaufman & Kaufman, 2007).

Figure 81: Japanese barberry leaves[1].

FLOWERS: Pale yellow flowers emerge from the leaf axils, either as a solitary flower or in groups of 2 to 4 (Swearingen et al. 2010). They have 6 petals, 6 sepals and 6 stamen (Fernald, 1950) (Fig. 82).

Figure 82: Japanese barberry flowers[1].

FRUIT/SEED: The fruit is a bright red, oval berry containing several small seeds (Bailey, 1969) (Fig. 83).

Figure 83: Fruit of Japanese barberry[1].

Common barberry
(*Berberis vulgaris*)

STEMS & BRANCHES: The branches of common barberry are brownish-grey with deep grooves and have alternately arranged 3-pronged spines (Bailey, 1969) (Fig. 84). Common barberry shrubs range from 1 to 3m in height (Fernald, 1950).

Figure 84: Common barberry stem with 3-pronged spines[6].

LEAVES: Common barberry has simple, oval leaves with toothed margins which taper at the base (Fig. 85). They are found in clusters along the stem (Bailey, 1969). Leaves are green but turn red, orange or purple in the fall (Gucker, 2009).

FLOWERS: Clusters of 10 to 20 pale yellow flowers grow in racemes (Gleason & Cronquist, 1963). They have 6 petals, 6 sepals and 6 stamen (Fernald, 1950) (Fig. 86).

FRUIT/SEED: The fruit is a berry containing several small seeds (Bailey, 1969). As the fruits mature they change from green to bright red (Fig. 87).

Figure 85: Common barberry leaves[6].

Figure 86: Common barberry flower clusters[6].

Figure 87: Common barberry fruit[14].

SIMILAR SPECIES

Barberries are easily distinguished from other shrubs during the growing season when they have leaves. The oval, tapering leaves found in clusters along the stem are different than those of native shrubs in Ontario. However, the thorny branches may be confused with those of other shrubs when the leaves are absent during the colder months. Similar shrubs with thorns include buckthorn (*Rhamnus* spp.) hawthorn (*Crataegus* spp.), and gooseberry (*Ribes* spp.).

Buckthorn (*Rhamnus* spp.)

Several species of native and exotic buckthorn are found in Ontario. Buckthorn can be easily distinguished from barberry by the position of its thorns, which are opposite to one another while barberry has alternately arranged thorns (Fig. 88). The leaves of buckthorn are different than those of barberry; they have an opposite arrangement and do not taper at the base (Symonds, 1963) (Fig. 89).

Figure 88: Comparing the opposite thorns of buckthorn[14] (left) to the alternately arranged thorns of Japanese barberry[1] (right).

Figure 89: Comparing a buckthorn leaf[1] (left) to that of Japanese barberry[1] (right).

Hawthorn (*Crataegus* spp.)

There are many species of native hawthorn in Ontario. These hawthorns can sometimes be confused with barberries because they also have alternately arranged single thorns. However, their toothed leaves contrast with those of Japanese barberry, which have smooth edges (Fig. 90). Common barberry has 3-pronged thorns whereas hawthorns have singular thorns (Fig. 91). Unlike barberries, the buds of hawthorn are almost spherical and are not located above each thorn (Symonds, 1963).

Figure 90: Comparing the thorns and leaves of hawthorn[21] (top) to those of Japanese barberry[1] (bottom).

Figure 91: Comparing the singular thorns of hawthorn[16] (left) to the 3-pronged thorns of common barberry[6] (right).

A key to shrubs that may be confused with barberry (*Berberis* spp.)

1. Leaves are present (spring, summer, fall)

   2. Leaves with toothed edges...Common barberry (*Berberis vulgaris*)

   2. Leaves with smooth edges...Japanese barberry (*Berberis thunbergii*)

1. Leaves are not present (winter)

   3. Thorns found opposite to one another...Buckthorn (*Rhamnus* spp.)

   3. Thorns with an alternate arrangement

     4. Buds almost spherical..Hawthorn (*Crataegus* spp.)

     4. Buds not spherical

       5. Unbranched, single spine...Japanese barberry (*Berberis thunbergii*)

       5. Branched, 3-pronged spines ....Common barberry (*Berberis vulgaris*)

BIOLOGY

TAXONOMIC HIERARCHY

Japanese barberry (*Berberis thunbergii*)

Kingdom	Plantae
Subkingdom	Tracheobionta
Division	Magnoliophyta
Class	Magnoliopsida
Subclass	Magnoliidae
Order	Ranunculales
Family	Berberidaceae
Genus	*Berberis*
Species	*Berberis thunbergii*

Common barberry (*Berberis vulgaris*)

Kingdom	Plantae
Subkingdom	Tracheobionta
Division	Magnoliophyta
Class	Magnoliopsida
Subclass	Magnoliidae
Order	Ranunculales
Family	Berberidaceae
Genus	*Berberis*
Species	*Berberis vulgaris*

ORIGIN & DISTRIBUTION

Common barberry was introduced by early settlers due to its popular uses in dyes and jams. However, when it was discovered to act as a host for cereal stem rust (*Puccinia graminis*), control measures were put in place to eradicate the shrub from North

America (Kaufman & Kaufman, 2007). An eradication program was initiated in 1964 in Ontario and Quebec but complete eradication was never achieved. Since the 1980's populations have begun to increase due to alleviation of control measures (Clark et al. 1986).

Japanese barberry was brought into the country from Japan as an alternative to common barberry in the late 1800's. Although it is not a host for any agricultural crop diseases it has invaded forest understories. In spite of this outcome, some cultivars of Japanese barberry are still being sold as ornamental shrubs in Ontario (Zouhar, 2008).

HABITAT

Japanese barberry has high phenotypic plasticity, growing in a wide array of light and moisture conditions (Silander Jr. & Klepeis, 1999). It has been documented in riparian areas and in both open and closed-canopy habitats such as wetlands, old fields and forests (Zouhar, 2008). Japanese barberry can escape from cultivation and form dense stands in undisturbed forest understories (Ehrenfeld, 1997) (Fig. 92).

Figure 92: Japanese barberry growing in the forest understory[6].

REPRODUCTION

Barberry can spread via sexual and vegetative reproduction. Barberries produce a multitude of fruit. Seeds are dispersed as berries drop to the ground or are eaten by wildlife. Barberries reproduce vegetatively by way of tillers produced from the root system or when stems take root when they come into contact with the ground (Ehrenfeld, 1999).

LIFE CYCLE

Barberry seeds germinate in May. Mature shrubs produce flowers from April to June. Berries mature in late summer, usually at the end of August and early September. Unless eaten by wildlife, these berries will remain on the plants throughout the winter (Ehrenfeld, 1999) (Fig. 93).

Figure 93: Japanese barberry fruits are often seen in winter[14].

SUCCESS MECHANISMS

Barberry has high recruitment rates due to its ability to produce large quantities of seed. As stem densities increase in a barberry stand so does the rate of recruitment. The ability to employ a variety of reproductive methods (see above) increases barberry's ability to invade an area. Populations can expand quickly, taking up space and shading-out native understory species (Ehrenfeld, 1999).

Barberry produces leaves very early in the season before other native shrub species and well before canopy closure (Fig. 94). This results in longer photosynthetic activity compared to other co-occurring species (Silander Jr. & Klepeis, 1999) and helps these invasive shrubs to become established in the forest understory before light levels become sub-optimal as the canopy closes (Cheng-Yuan et al. 2007).

Figure 94: Japanese barberry in early spring[6].

ECOLOGICAL IMPACTS

Barberry forms dense stands in hardwood forest understories (Fig. 95). Such stands cover large areas and compete with native plants for space, nutrients and light (Zouhar, 2008). One study revealed a positive correlation between Japanese barberry stands and black-legged tick (*Ixodes scapularis*) populations. Indeed, areas invaded by Japanese barberry supported a greater number of tick hosts (Elias et al. 2006). Black-legged ticks are detrimental to human health as they can transmit a variety of diseases such as Lyme disease (*Borrelia burgdorferi*) (Magnarelli et al. 2006).

Figure 95: Japanese barberry invasion[22].

Barberry populations can change forest soil characteristics by increasing pH levels and nitrification rates (Ehrenfeld et al. 2001). These edaphic effects may inhibit the restoration of native flora and alter the forest's successional patterns after the removal of this invasive plant (Kourtev et al. 1999; Zouhar, 2008).

VECTORS & PATHWAYS

Barberry has bright red berries, which are attractive to wildlife. Turkeys, grouse and various songbirds consume the berries. Berries may thus be transported to other places where the birds eat the fruit pulp and discard the seeds. Seeds may also be eaten and passed through the digestive tract to later be discarded, often quite far from their origin (Silander Jr. & Klepeis, 1999). Animals such as chipmunks, mice and deer may also play a role in seed dispersal (Ehrenfeld, 1997; 1999).

Common barberry cannot be imported or sold within Canada due to its ability to act as an alternate host for cereal stem rust disease (*Puccinia graminis*) (Fig. 96). However, twelve cultivars of Japanese barberry have been approved for sale in Canada because they have been found to be resistant to the disease. Sold as ornamental shrubs, these cultivars frequently escape from cultivation due to bird-mediated dispersal. Humans can aid in seed dispersal when seeds get stuck under shoes or in tire treads (CFIA, 2008).

Figure 96: The symptoms of cereal stem rust (*Puccinia graminis*)[23].

MANAGEMENT PRACTICES

PREVENTION STRATEGIES

· Barberry is considered an invasive plant and should not be planted in the garden. Use native alternatives or species that are not considered invasive;
· Prevent seeds from entering the woodlot by limiting access and washing shoes and tires before entry.

EARLY DETECTION TECHNIQUES

· Learn how to identify both Japanese and common barberry;
· Regularly monitor the woodlot for new invasions and pay particular attention to road sides and trails where invasive plants can first establish;
· Talk with neighbours about what they grow in their gardens and the threats associated with growing invasive plants.

CONTROL OPTIONS

Hand-pulling, excavation and cutting: Although hand-pulling is a common method for controlling small populations of invasive plants, hand-pulling barberry shrubs is impractical due to their large size. Excavation with root wrenches allows roots to be dug up from the soil which can be effective but time consuming and labour intensive, unless the population is very small. Ensure that all stem fragments are collected as shoots can easily re-sprout. Cutting is suggested in areas where dense populations of barberry create access problems. Other methods of control will need to be administered to the exposed stumps to prevent re-sprouting (Silander Jr. & Klepeis, 1999; Ward et al. 2009).

Directed flame treatment: Applying a directed flame to the base of the stump is effective and minimizes disturbance, especially when compared with excavation. Using a propane torch and applying flame for 20 seconds to the base of the stem can effectively kill small shrubs in a single application (Ward et al. 2009). However, larger shrubs may require follow-up treatments. The directed flame method should only be attempted when the forest floor is wet or damp to prevent the risk of a fire (Ward et al. 2010). Consult with your local fire department before using the directed flame method.

Herbicide application: Herbicides may be applied as a foliar spray or using the basal bark or cut-stump methods. The latter methods are preferable as they reduce herbicide drift to nearby native vegetation. Basal bark treatments are effective and generally less labour intensive than the cut-stump method. Ensure that chemical treatments are performed in both the spring and fall for effective control of barberry invasions (Silander Jr. & Klepeis, 1999).

RECOMMENDATIONS FOR INTEGRATED CONTROL OF LARGE INVASIONS

Option #1: With chemical control

Control of barberry populations should occur twice per year, once in the spring and once during the fall. The goal of control treatments in the spring is to remove as many barberry shrubs as possible, paying particular attention to large, mature plants. Control treatments in the fall can focus on newly germinating seedlings as well as on any individuals that were not removed in the spring.

Herbicides can be applied in the spring. For large invasions, apply herbicides as a foliar spray. Barberry leaves emerge earlier in the spring than those of co-occurring native plants. This is an ideal time to apply herbicides because there is a lower chance of non-target effects on native vegetation. Herbicide application may prove difficult in areas where barberry populations exist as dense shrub thickets. In this case, it may be easier to first cut the stems close to the ground which would allow better access to the area. Afterwards, herbicides can be applied to the cut stems. In the fall, control will consist of treating any remaining individuals, newly germinating seedlings and re-sprouting shoots. Basal bark treatments are effective in areas where populations are not so dense that access is achievable. Basal bark treatments can be more cost effective as less herbicide is required and there is little chance of incidental damage to other plants (Silander Jr. & Klepeis, 1999).

Option #2: Without chemical control

If chemical control is not possible or wanted, the directed flame method is often a successful means of control for barberry invasion. In dense patches where access is difficult, cutting first is suggested. This is followed by removal of the woody stems, thereby allowing the base of the stump to be exposed for application of a directed flame. In areas where access is not a problem, stems do not need to be cut as the flame can be directed to the base. Directed flame treatments in both the spring and fall can be a cost-effective and relatively simple means of controlling barberry populations. The directed flame method should only be used when the forest floor is wet or damp to prevent the risk of a fire (Ward et al. 2010). Remember to consult with the local fire department before using the directed flame method.

Table 9: Management recommendations for barberry (*Berberis* spp.).		
Extent of infestation	Small invasions and satellite populations	Large invasions and dense populations.
Recommended method of control	Excavation or directed flame.	Cutting followed by directed flame and/or chemical control.
Timing	Spring and fall.	Spring and fall.
Disposal	Remove woody debris to a brush pile for burning. Dead standing shrubs may be left on site or cut and removed.	Remove woody debris to a brush pile for burning. Dead standing shrubs may be left on site or cut and removed.
Frequency of control	Twice yearly.	Twice yearly.
Length of control	1-2 years.	1-3 years.
Required restoration	Plant native species in areas where excavation creates soil disturbance.	Active seeding or planting with native species may be needed.

5.1.5
Japanese Knotweed
(Fallopia japonica)

Other common names:
Japanese fleece flower, Mexican bamboo, Crimson beauty, Reynoutria

Priority Rating: HIGH

Figure 97: Japanese knotweed[1].

IDENTIFICATION

STEM: Japanese knotweed has large, bamboo-like, hollow stems with green, red and purple markings. Distinctive nodes can be seen along the entire stem (Weber, 2003) (Fig. 98).

Figure 98: Japanese knotweed stems[1].

LEAVES: Japanese knotweed has simple triangular leaves arranged alternately along the stem (Wilson, 2007) (Fig. 99).

Figure 99: Japanese knotweed leaves[1].

FLOWERS: Japanese knotweed produces numerous flowers arranged in clusters. Each flower has 5 white petals (Fig. 100). Flowers emerge in late summer and persist through the fall (Bailey, 1969).

Figure 100: Japanese knotweed flowers[1].

FRUIT/SEED: The fruits are 3-sided and winged, encasing a single brown seed (Weber, 2003) (Fig. 101). There have been conflicting results regarding the viability of Japanese knotweed seeds. As such, more research is needed to determine the extent to which the seeds produced by this invasive species contribute to its spread.

ROOTS: Japanese knotweed produces a very large and extensive rhizome from which multiple stems arise (Fig. 102). This creates dense patches that consist of a single individual (Bailey, 1969).

HEIGHT: Japanese knotweed is a tall growing plant that can often reach 4m in height (Wilson, 2007) (Fig.103).

Figure 101: The fruit of Japanese knotweed[4].

Figure 102: Japanese knotweed roots[19].

Figure 103: Japanese knotweed can be up to 4m tall[1].

SIMILAR SPECIES

Dock (*Rumex* spp.)

The stems of some *Rumex* species may look very similar to those of Japanese knotweed. Species such as great water dock (*R. orbiculatus*) have jointed stems that can grow up to 2m tall and may even appear red at times (Fig. 104). Both great water dock and Japanese knotweed have fruits that are 3-sided (Fig. 105). However, *Rumex* species generally have long, lance-shaped leaves whereas Japanese knotweed has triangular leaves (Newcomb, 1977).

Figure 104: Comparing the stems of dock[20] (left) to those of Japanese knotweed[4] (right).

Figure 105: Comparing the seeds of dock[20] (left) to those of Japanese knotweed[6] (right).

Giant Hogweed (*Heracleum mantegazzianum*)

Giant hogweed is an introduced species from Eurasia. Like Japanese knotweed, its hollow stems are green with small purple spots and can reach approximately 5m in height (Fig. 106). In steep contrast, giant hogweed has deeply lobed leaves

whereas those of Japanese knotweed are triangular and unlobed (Kaufman & Kaufman, 2007) (Fig. 107).

Figure 106: Comparing the stems of giant hogweed[6] (left) to those of Japanese knotweed[1] (right).

Figure 107: Comparing the leaves of giant hogweed[24] (top) to those of Japanese knotweed[1] (bottom).

Common cow parsnip (*Heracleum maximum*)

Common cow parsnip belongs to the same genus as giant hogweed. However, it is native to North America. As with both giant hogweed and Japanese knotweed, common cow parsnip has tall, hollow stems. Common cow parsnip has deeply lobed leaves in contrast to the triangular leaves of Japanese knotweed (Newcomb, 1977) (Fig. 108).

Figure 108: Comparing common cowparsnip[1] (left) and Japanese knotweed[1] (right).

Wild buckwheat (*Fallopia convolvulus*)

Wild buckwheat and Japanese knotweed have similar triangular leaves. However, wild buckwheat has a twining stem that grows as a vine whereas Japanese knotweed's tall and erect stems do not need the support of other plants or objects (Chambers et al. 1996) (Fig. 109).

Figure 109: Comparing wild buckwheat (left) and Japanese knotweed[1] (right).

A key to plants that may be confused with Japanese knotweed (*Fallopia japonica*)

1. Plants with twining stems ....Wild buckwheat (*Fallopia convolvulus*)

1. Plants with tall, erect stems

  2. Plants with lobed leaves

    3. Leaves deeply and palmately lobed (up to 51cm long) ....Common cow parsnip (*Heracleum maximum*)

    3. Leaves coarsely and unevenly lobed (up to 152cm long)........Giant hogweed (*Heracleum mantegazzianum*)

  2. Plants with entire leaves

    4. Lanced to elliptically-shaped leaves ....Dock (*Rumex* spp.)

    4. Triangularly-shaped leaves..Japanese knotweed (*Fallopia japonica*)

BIOLOGY

ORIGIN & DISTRIBUTION

Japanese knotweed is native to Asia. It was introduced in both Europe and North America as an ornamental plant (Beerling et al. 1994). Japanese knotweed was introduced in Europe in the mid-19th century and in North America in 1877 (Forman &

TAXONOMIC HIERARCHY

Kingdom	Plantae
Subkingdom	Tracheobionta
Division	Magnoliophyta
Class	Magnoliopsida
Subclass	Caryophyllidae
Order	Caryophyllales
Family	Polygonaceae
Genus	*Fallopia*
Species	*Fallopia japonica*

Kesseli, 2003). Canadian introductions were documented around the 1900's and today Japanese knotweed is commonly found across Ontario (Bourchier & Van Hezewijk, 2010).

HABITAT

Japanese knotweed is often associated with nutrient-rich soils (Beerling et al. 1994) and is commonly found in both open and closed-canopy habitats such as old fields and forests. It has also been shown to be particularly invasive in wetlands and along stream and riverbanks (Maerz et al. 2005) (Fig. 110).

Figure 110: Japanese knotweed in a riparian habitat[6].

REPRODUCTION

Japanese knotweed is dioecious (i.e., with male and female individuals). Vegetative reproduction is important for this species, with the tiniest root fragments being capable of producing new plants (Beerling et al. 1994). Sexual reproduction and consequent seed production has been documented but the results are inconsistent. Some studies report the formation of empty seedpods or attribute high mortality rates to germinating seedlings (Locandro, 1973), while others report large numbers of highly viable seeds (Forman & Kesseli, 2003). More studies are needed to understand sexual reproduction as a dispersal mechanism for this exotic species.

LIFE CYCLE

Shoots begin to emerge and spread early in the spring and quickly grow in height. Flowering occurs from September through October with fruit development taking place soon thereafter (Beerling et al. 1994). New seedlings can flower in their first growing season (Forman & Kesseli, 2003).

SUCCESS MECHANISMS

Japanese knotweed can form very dense patches. Over the years, dead stems and leaves build up a thick litter layer, which in combination with low light levels contribute to form an inhospitable environment for other plant species (Fig. 111). This effectively eliminates competition from native plant species and promotes Japanese knotweed invasion (Beerling et al. 1994).

Figure 111: Japanese knotweed invasion with a visible accumulation of dead stems[1].

Japanese knotweed has a large and vigorous root system. The rhizomes form an extensive underground network that allows the plant to persist even if the above-ground portion is severely damaged. Japanese knotweed can rely on the reserves stored in the rhizome to boost its growth rate in the spring. This allows them to tower over native understory species to reach the sunlight (Beerling et al. 1994).

ECOLOGICAL IMPACTS

Japanese knotweed forms dense thickets that can effectively shade out native understory species (Fig. 112). The root systems grow outwards each year, sending up clonal shoots that can quickly form very dense stands. These stands displace native species and reduce available habitat for wildlife (Weber, 2003; Beerling et al. 1994). For instance, one study has shown that invasion by Japanese knotweed has a negative effect on frogs, which depend on terrestrial habitats such as forests and old fields for foraging and breeding. Indeed, areas with dense Japanese knotweed stands were found to be unsuitable breeding sites for green frogs (Maerz et al. 2005).

Figure 112: A dense patch of Japanese knotweed[1].

VECTORS & PATHWAYS

Japanese knotweed disperses mainly vegetatively; even small pieces of root or stem can act as propagules and establish a new invasion. Yard wastes and soils containing plant fragments are thought to be the main vectors of Japanese knotweed's dispersal into natural areas. As Japanese knotweed populations tend to grow in riparian areas, it has been assumed that waterways play a key role as a short and long distance transportation pathway (Beerling et al. 1994). Seed dispersal may also contribute to the spread of Japanese knotweed (Forman & Kesseli, 2003). However, more research is needed on the viability of Japanese knotweed seeds.

MANAGEMENT PRACTICES

PREVENTION STRATEGIES

- Do not dump any type of yard waste in natural areas;
- Ensure that soil being brought into a woodlot does not harbour any invasive seeds or plant fragments. Ask the distributor if the soil is classified as weed-free;
- Do not accept or plant any unknown plant fragments in your garden. It may seem neighbourly to share gardening tips and plant slips. However, ensure that you know what you are planting before you do it.

EARLY DETECTION TECHNIQUES

- Learn how to identify Japanese knotweed and ensure it is not growing in neighbouring areas;
- Regularly monitor your woodlot paying attention to riparian areas where root fragments may have washed ashore.

CONTROL OPTIONS

Excavation: Excavation is only feasible for very small populations. This should only be attempted when the population is recent and the root system is still relatively small. All root fragments should be removed because they can readily re-sprout. Excavation causes a great deal of soil disturbance. As such, it is recommended to plant desirable species in place of the Japanese knotweed to prevent invasion by other exotics (Stone, 2010).

Cutting: Continuous cutting to eliminate the plant's energy belowground can be an effective control strategy when dealing with large Japanese knotweed invasions. Every 2 to 3 weeks from spring to fall, cut the stems close to the ground, remove all the above-ground parts using a rake and bag everything. In areas with dense stands, re-sprouts may be controlled using a mower or weed whacker. Ongoing management for several years may be required to completely eliminate an invasion (Weston et al. 2005).

Herbicide application: Japanese knotweed invasions can be controlled using herbicides. A licenced exterminator will need to apply the herbicides, as effective systemic herbicides are needed to kill the robust root system. Several different application methods may be used, including foliar application and cut-stem methods. Foliar application may be more effective early in the season when the plants are still low to the ground. Japanese knotweed can reach 4m in height, which can make foliar herbicide applications a difficult task. As a result, cutting the stems may be a more practical method of control. Japanese knotweed stems can be quite dense, so cutting them will enable better accessibility. Herbicides can then be applied to the cross section of the stem (Remaley, 2005).

RECOMMENDATIONS FOR INTEGRATED CONTROL OF LARGE INVASIONS

Option #1: With chemical control

Administer a foliar application in the spring when the plants are still short and the leaves are within reach. Monitor the area every couple of weeks and cut any re-sprouting individuals. Alternatively, a fall application can be done using the cut-stem method. The following spring, a foliar spray can be applied if re-sprouting is significant. In the event that only a few re-sprouts emerge, cutting or mowing can be employed every couple of weeks until the root reserves are exhausted (Remaley, 2005).

Option #2: Without chemical control

Cut all stems close to the ground and remove the above-ground biomass. Cutting is recommended every 2 to 3 weeks from spring to fall. This will eventually eliminate any energy reserves stored in the roots. Management actions will be required for several years to completely eliminate an invasion (Weston et al. 2005). Digging up root crowns may speed up the control process. However, be prepared to plant native vegetation in areas where the soil has been disturbed. This will reduce the likelihood of other exotics establishing in the disturbed site. A plastic tarp may also be used on small areas where dense stands persist. Cut and remove all plant parts and cover the area with the plastic. The plastic will need to remain in place for several years to ensure that the roots die (Stone, 2010).

Table 10: Management recommendations for Japanese knotweed (*Fallopia japonica*).

Extent of infestation	Small invasions and satellite populations	Large invasions and dense populations
Recommended method of control	Excavation and cutting.	Integrated control: (Combination of physical and chemical control).
Timing	Spring, summer & fall.	Cutting and hand-pulling can be done any time in the spring, summer and fall. Herbicide application should occur in the spring or fall while other native plants are dormant.
Frequency of control	Cutting should be done every few weeks from spring to fall.	Cut stems will likely re-sprout and require frequent clipping. Plan to control every couple of weeks.
Length of control	2-3 years.	5+ years.
Required restoration	Excavation creates soil disturbance that benefits exotic species. Consider planting native vegetation.	Restoration is not feasible until the invasion is under control. Allow native vegetation to colonize the area and control around these desirable species.

5.1.6
English Ivy
(*Hedera helix*)

Other common names:
Hardy English ivy

Priority Rating: HIGH

Figure 113: English ivy[12]

IDENTIFICATION

STEM: English ivy has two growth forms. As an immature plant, the stem is a woody vine whereas mature plants look like a shrub (Reichard, 2000) (Fig. 114).

Figure 114: Comparing the immature vining growth form[11] (left) to the mature shrub-like growth form[4] (right) of English ivy.

LEAVES: English ivy leaves are evergreen and grow in an alternate arrangement around the stem. The leaves on immature plants have 3 to 5 lobes whereas mature plants have lobeless cordate leaves (Fig. 115). They are dark green with lighter veins and a waxy coat (Kaufman & Kaufman, 2007).

Figure 115: Comparing immature[12] (left) and mature[15] (right) English ivy leaves.

FLOWERS: Clusters of yellowish-green flowers with 5 petals and 5 sepals are produced at the ends of the stems on mature plants (Swearingen et al. 2010) (Fig. 116).

FRUIT/SEED: The fruit consists of a berry containing 3 to 5 seeds. Berries grow in clusters and change from green to black when ripe (Miller, 2003; Gleason & Cronquist, 1963) (Fig. 117).

HEIGHT: Vines can climb up to 28m high if they have a supporting structure (Miller, 2003) (Fig. 118).

Figure 116: English ivy flowers[4].

Figure 117: Ripe English ivy berries[25].

Figure 118: English ivy growing on a supporting tree[26].

SIMILAR SPECIES

Poison ivy (*Toxicodendron radicans*)

Poison ivy usually grows as an erect or trailing shrub. However, it has been found growing as a climbing vine in parts of southern Ontario. As a vine, it may appear similar to English ivy with its leaves arranged in an alternate pattern. In contrast, poison ivy's leaves are compound, containing three leaflets, whereas the leaves of English ivy are simple (Fig. 119). The fruits of poison ivy consist of white berries whereas the berries of English ivy are nearly black (Chambers et al. 1996).

Figure 119: Comparing poison ivy[27] (left) to English ivy[15] (right).

Virginia creeper (*Parthenocissus quinquefolia*)

Virginia creeper is a woody vine with similar dark coloured berries to those of English ivy. However, Virginia creeper has compound leaves, each with five leaflets (Fig. 120). The leaves of Virginia creeper are toothed whereas English ivy has leaves with smooth margins (Petrides, 1972).

Figure 120: Comparing Virginia creeper[12] (left) to English ivy[12] (right).

Grape (*Vitis* spp.)

Frost grape (*Vitis vulpina*), summer grape (*V. aestivalis*), fox grape (*V. lubrusca*), and river bank grape (*V. riparia*) may be confused with English ivy. The easiest way to distinguish them from English ivy is to take a close look at the leaf margins. English ivy has smooth leaf margins whereas all of these grape species have toothed margins (Fig. 121). See the key to help differentiate between grape species (Petrides, 1972).

Figure 121: Comparing the leaves of a species of grape[1] (left) to those of English ivy[1] (right).

Canada moonseed (*Menispermum canadense*)

Canada moonseed may be confused with English ivy. Both species are trailing, woody vines with alternately arranged simple leaves with smooth edges (Fig. 122). One clear difference between these two species is that the petioles of Canada moonseed are attached to the base of the leaf whereas those of English ivy are attached to the end (Petrides, 1972) (Fig. 123).

Figure 122: Comparing the leaves of Canada moonseed[1] (left) to those of English ivy[12] (right).

Figure 123: Canada moonseed petiole attachment[20].

A key to plants with climbing stems that may be confused with English ivy (*Hedera helix*)

1. Plants with compound leaves

   2. Leaves with three leaflets...Poison ivy (*Toxicodendron radicans*)

   2. Leaves with five leaflets..Virginia creeper (*Parthenocissus quinquefolia*)

1. Plants with simple leaves

   3. Leaves with toothed (serrate) edges

      4. Leaves without lobes...Frost grape (*Vitis vulpina*)

   4. Leaves with lobes

      5. Leaf undersides are white..Summer grape (*Vitis aestivalis*)

   5. Leaf undersides not white

      6. Leaf undersides densely hairy...Fox grape (*Vitis lubrusca*)

      6. Leaf undersides slightly hairy along veins..................River bank grape (*Vitis riparia*)

   3. Leaves with smooth (entire) edges

      7. Petioles attached to leaf undersides...........................Canada moonseed (*Menispermum canadense*)
         (peltate leaves)

      7. Petioles attached to leaf margins...............................English ivy (*Hedera helix*)

BIOLOGY

TAXONOMIC HIERARCHY

Kingdom	Plantae
Subkingdom	Tracheobionta
Division	Magnoliophyta
Class	Magnoliopsida
Subclass	Rosidae
Order	Apiales
Family	Araliaceae
Genus	*Hedera*
Species	*Hedera helix*

ORIGIN & DISTRIBUTION

English ivy has been used as an ornamental ground cover since the early 1700's when it was introduced from Europe, western Asia and northern Africa (Swearingen et al. 2010). Today it is still commonly sold as a garden plant throughout Ontario (Fig. 124).

HABITAT

English ivy can grow in a wide range of habitats in either full shade or sunlight (Swearingen et al. 2010). However, it thrives in open-canopy

Figure 124: English ivy being sold as a ground cover species[1].

forests (Miller, 2003). Deciduous forests are a prime habitat for English ivy invasion as their evergreen leaves benefit from full access to the sun before the tree canopy establishes in the spring (Fig. 125). Populations are often found in forests close to urban areas as they frequently escape from gardens (Reichard, 2000).

Figure 125: English ivy growing in an open-canopy forest[25].

REPRODUCTION

English ivy spreads vegetatively and by seeds. The species has a juvenile and a mature life stage. Juvenile plants grow as woody vines and do not produce flowers or fruits (Reichard, 2000). Maturity can take up to ten years and is often initiated by access to full sunlight conditions. In the mature stage the plant takes on a shrub-like growth form and begins to produce flowers and seeds. Stem fragments are able to root and produce new plants (Swearingen & Diedrich, 2006).

LIFE CYCLE

English ivy is a perennial evergreen vine. Mature plants flower throughout the summer and produce fruit in the fall. The pale green berries turn dark purple as they ripen and may stay on the plant throughout the winter (Miller, 2003).

SUCCESS MECHANISMS

The vining habit of English ivy coupled with its fast vegetative spread gives this species a competitive edge over other native plants. It can quickly climb over any supporting structure towards sunlight, smothering other plants and limiting their access to sunlight (Dlugosch, 2005).

The evergreen life-strategy allows English ivy to photosynthesize and grow earlier than native deciduous plants (Fig. 126). This jumpstart growth in the spring gives English ivy a competitive edge over other plants. As the forest canopy closes English ivy has the added benefit of shade tolerance. Therefore, not only can this plant thrive in shaded environments but it can also quickly climb to reach more preferable light levels (Swearingen & Diedrich, 2006).

Figure 126: The evergreen leaves of English ivy[15].

ECOLOGICAL IMPACTS

English ivy can form a dense carpet on the forest floor. They climb over native understory species, depriving them of sunlight and, as a result, exclude native species (Fig. 127). Germinating seedlings cannot compete with such a dense vegetative ground cover, which may cause a decrease in hardwood recruitment. With little to no recruitment, the species composition of the forest may shift (Dlugosch, 2005).

English ivy can climb over supporting structures such as trees and reach heights of 28m (Fig. 128). As these vines climb up the trunks of hardwood trees and onto their branches they

effectively prevent the sunlight from reaching the tree's leaves, causing a decrease in its vigor (Miller, 2003). In heavy invasions, English ivy has the ability to kill the host tree (Swearingen & Diedrich, 2006). These vines also create added weight that can cause trees to collapse during high winds or snow storms (Swearingen et al. 2010). The vining habit of English ivy creates pockets of water close to the tree trunks, which often causes fungal growth and decay (Kaufman & Kaufman, 2007).

Figure 127: A carpet of English ivy in the forest understory[15].

Figure 128: English ivy climbing into the forest canopy[16].

English ivy can carry a generalist bacterial plant pathogen (*Xylella fastidiosa*), which is the causing agent of leaf scorch. This pathogen affects the xylem of hardwood species. Infected trees show signs of scorched leaves and stunted growth (McElrone et al. 1999) (Fig. 129).

Figure 129: Symptoms of bacterial leaf scorch[90].

VECTORS & PATHWAYS

English ivy can be purchased throughout Ontario and is commonly found as an ornamental ground cover in urban gardens (Miller, 2003). The dark coloured berries on mature English ivy plants are attractive to birds. These fruits contain glycosides and other compounds which cause the seeds to quickly pass through the digestive track or cause the birds to regurgitate. In this way seeds can be dispersed over long distances and into natural areas. Some spread may also be due to the dumping of yard wastes into natural areas as new plants can easily grow from stem and root fragments (Swearingen et al. 2010).

MANAGEMENT PRACTICES

PREVENTION STRATEGIES

· Do not dump yard wastes in or close to forested areas;
· English ivy is considered an invasive plant and should not be planted in the garden. Use native alternatives or species that are not considered invasive (Fig. 130).

EARLY DETECTION TECHNIQUES

· Learn how to identify English ivy;
· Regularly monitor the woodlot for invasive species;
· Talk with neighbours about what they grow in their gardens and the threats associated with growing invasive plants;
· Ensure that yard wastes are properly disposed of.

Figure 130: English ivy is a common ground cover and border plant for gardens[25].

CONTROL OPTIONS

Hand-pulling: Small patches and satellite populations can be controlled by hand-pulling. From a kneeling position, individual vines should be uprooted as far as one can reach. Continue moving and uprooting vines until they all have been removed from the area (Soll, 2005). Be careful to collect as much of the root system as possible because even the smallest root fragments have the ability to re-sprout. Vines should be bagged and disposed of in an appropriate landfill. Monitor the area for approximately 2 to 3 years to ensure that no re-sprouting has occurred (Swearingen & Diedrich, 2006).

Herbicide application: Apply herbicide with a surfactant as a foliar spray to English ivy running along the ground. The surfactant is needed to help the herbicide penetrate the waxy layer of English ivy leaves. Apply herbicide to leaves until just wet and try to avoid any dripping (Miller, 2003). For English ivy that is climbing up trees, it is best to cut the vine and apply the herbicide to the stump (Swearingen & Diedrich, 2006). If done properly, herbicide treatments can eliminate the majority of English ivy invasion in the first treatment. Follow-up treatments will be needed to completely eradicate the population (Soll, 2005).

RECOMMENDATIONS FOR INTEGRATED CONTROL OF LARGE INVASIONS

Options #1: With chemical control

Plan to apply herbicide in the fall when other native vegetation is dormant. Choose a period when rain is not forecasted for at least several days. Perform spot herbicide application in dense patches of English ivy while hand-pulling scattered individuals or patches close to desirable vegetation. Hand-pulling can be done before or after herbicide application depending on the severity of the invasion. In areas with dense patches of English ivy and only a small number of native plants, herbicides can be applied in the fall, being careful to spray around any desirable vegetation. English ivy growing beside desirable vegetation should not be sprayed and should be hand-pulled at a later date. Hand-pulling any remaining English ivy plants can be scheduled for the following spring (Soll, 2005).

Depending on the effectiveness of the initial control measure, follow-up treatments may include a second herbicide application. It may take several months before any effects from the initial herbicide application are visible. If dense patches remain, a follow-up foliar spray or spot application may be needed (Soll, 2005). For small patches, manual removal of the entire plant is appropriate. Carefully pull up all roots and bag the plant for disposal to ensure that roots do not re-sprout. Monitor the area for approximately 3 to 5 years after the initial treatment (Swearingen & Diedrich, 2006). Planting native vegetation in the infested area after the initial treatment is recommended. This will promote natural re-growth and may increase natural resistance against the establishment of invasive plants (Soll, 2005).

Option #2: Without chemical control

Hand-pulling should be scheduled for the spring with a follow-up in the fall. However, most English ivy plants should be removed in the first hand-pulling. Be sure to collect as much of the root system as possible. Do not leave any root fragments behind as they can easily re-sprout. Being thorough during the first hand-pulling will make future management activities easier or potentially unnecessary (Swearingen & Diedrich, 2006). Vines should be bagged and disposed of in an appropriate landfill. Return in the fall to pull any remaining English ivy plants and monitor the area for approximately 3 to 5 years after the initial control (Miller, 2003).

Table 11: Management recommendations for English ivy (*Hedera helix*).

Extent of infestation	Small invasions and satellite populations	Large invasions and dense populations
Recommended method of control	Manual control: hand-pulling.	Integrated control: hand-pulling & herbicide application.
Timing	Spring, summer and fall.	Spring and fall.
Disposal	Bag all parts of the plant and dispose at an appropriate landfill.	Bag all hand-pulled plants and dispose at an appropriate landfill.
Frequency of control	Initial pull should remove as many plants and plant fragments as possible. Return several times per year to pull any missed plants or re-sprouts.	Manual removal in the spring and herbicide application in the fall may be required for up to 3 years depending on extent of the infestation. As infestation gets smaller manual removal should replace chemical control.
Length of control	2-3 years.	2-5 years.
Required restoration	Plant native species in areas where hand-pulling creates soil disturbance.	Plant native species in areas where hand-pulling creates soil disturbance.

5.1.7
Himalayan Balsam
(*Impatiens glandulifera*)

Other common names:
Purple jewelweed, Policeman's helmet, Indian balsam, Ornamental jewelweed

Priority Rating: **HIGH**

Figure 131: Himalayan balsam[1]

IDENTIFICATION

LEAVES: The leaves of Himalayan balsam are often found whorled around the stem in groups of three (Fig. 132). Some leaves may also be found as pairs in an opposite arrangement. The leaf edges are sharply toothed and lanceolate or elliptical in shape (Beerling & Perrins, 1993).

Figure 132: Himalayan balsam leaves[1].

FLOWERS: The flowers of Himalayan balsam are irregular and trumpet-shaped (Fig. 133). They range in colour from dark pink to white and grow in clusters of 3 to 12 flowers (Beerling & Perrins, 1993) (Fig. 134).

Figure 133: Himalayan balsam flowers[1]   Figure 134: Colour variation in the flowers of Himalayan balsam[6].

FRUIT/SEED: Seeds are found within green capsules (Fig. 135). When ripe, these capsules burst open at the slightest touch to disperse 4 to 16 seeds (Beerling & Perrins, 1993).

STEM: The stems are reddish-green and hollow (Fig. 136). They can grow as large as 5cm in diameter (Beerling & Perrins, 1993).

HEIGHT: In North America, this herbaceous herb can grow up to 3m tall, towering over other native vegetation in the understory (Tabak & von Wettberg, 2008) (Fig. 137).

Figure 135: Himalayan balsam seedpods[1].

Figure 136: The hollow stem of Himalayan balsam[1].

Figure 137: Himalayan balsam towering over native vegetation[1].

SIMILAR SPECIES

Himalayan balsam can be confused with native members of the "touch-me-not" family that have irregular flowers and "exploding" seedpods. The easiest way to identify Himalayan balsam is to look at the arrangement of the leaves on the stem. Himalayan balsam is the only species of *Impatiens* in Ontario with whorled or opposite leaves.

Spotted touch-me-not (*Impatiens capensis*)

Spotted touch-me-not is a native plant in Ontario commonly found in wet areas. The flowers have a similar shape to those of Himalayan balsam. However, they are orange with tiny red spots (Fig. 138). The leaves have irregular toothed margins and an alternate arrangement along the stem (Dickinson et al. 2004) (Fig. 139).

Figure 138: Comparing the flowers of spotted touch-me-not[1] (top) to those of Himalayan balsam[1] (bottom).

Figure 139: Comparing the leaves of spotted touch-me-not[1] (top) to those of Himalayan balsam[1] (bottom).

Pale touch-me-not (*Impatiens pallida*)

Pale touch-me-not is a native species with similar irregular flowers to those of Himalayan balsam. These flowers are pale yellow in contrast to the pink or white flowers of Himalayan balsam (Fig. 140). The leaves have an alternate arrangement along the stem with regular toothed margins (Dickinson et al. 2004).

Figure 140: Comparing the flowers of pale touch-me-not[15] (left) to those of Himalayan balsam[1] (right).

A key to plants that may be confused with Himalayan balsam (*Impatiens glandulifera*)

1. Plants with irregular flowers

   2. Plants with orange or yellow flowers

      3. Orange flowers with red spots .... Spotted touch-me-not (*Impatiens capensis*)

      3. Pale yellow flowers .... Pale touch-me-not (*Impatiens pallida*)

   2. Plants with pink, purple or white flowers .... Himalayan balsam (*Impatiens glandulifera*)

1. Plants without flowers present

      4. Alternate leaves

         5. Irregular toothed margins .... Spotted touch-me-not (*Impatiens capensis*)

         5. Regular toothed margins .... Pale touch-me-not (*Impatiens pallida*)

      4. Whorled or opposite leaves .... Himalayan balsam (*Impatiens glandulifera*)

BIOLOGY

TAXONOMIC HIERARCHY

Kingdom	Plantae
Subkingdom	Tracheobionta
Division	Magnoliophyta
Class	Magnoliopsida
Subclass	Rosidae
Order	Geraniales
Family	Balsaminaceae
Genus	*Impatiens*
Species	*Impatiens glandulifera*

ORIGIN & DISTRIBUTION

Himalayan balsam is native to the western Himalayas. It has become an invasive plant in North America, Europe and New Zealand where it was most likely introduced as an ornamental garden plant due to its large, attractive flowers. The first records of Himalayan balsam in North America are from Connecticut in 1883 (Tabak & von Wettberg, 2008). It has since been introduced to Ontario as a garden plant.

HABITAT

Himalayan balsam can grow in a wide variety of habitats. It has become a particularly troublesome invader along riparian areas, wetlands and forest understories in Europe (Tabak & von Wettberg, 2008), where dense stands have been reported in both mixed and deciduous forests. In Ontario, Himalayan balsam is prevalent in riparian areas (Fig. 141) and has the potential to become a problem in hardwood forests where localized disturbances allow this species to establish and spread (Perrins et al. 1993; Ammer et al. 2011).

Figure 141: Himalayan balsam growing alongside a stream[29].

REPRODUCTION

Himalayan balsam reproduces by seed. The flowers are able to self-pollinate. However, this is rarely needed as the large colourful flowers are attractive to insect pollinators such as bees and wasps (Bartomeus et al. 2010). Individual plants have the potential to produce an average of 800 seeds. These seeds are contained in pods that "explode" upon maturity when touched, allowing seeds to disperse several metres away from the parent plant. Seeds can survive in the soil for up to 18 months. No vegetative reproduction has been documented for Himalayan balsam (Perrins et al. 1993; Beerling & Perrins, 1993).

LIFE CYCLE

Himalayan balsam is an annual plant (i.e., it completes its life cycle in one growing season). Seedlings germinate and emerge in the early spring and quickly grow into tall flowering plants. Flowering begins in July and the formation of seedpods can occur as early as mid-July (Beerling & Perrins, 1993). Seedpods ripen and become sensitive to the touch from August to October (Ammer et al. 2011).

SUCCESS MECHANISMS

Himalayan balsam`s high reproductive potential contributes to its success as an invader. Prolific seed production allows populations to quickly increase in size while self-pollination allows for increased dispersal and establishment of this species. Transportation of a single seed to a new area can result in an invasion because Himalayan balsam does not solely rely on cross-pollination (Bartomeus et al. 2010; Perrins et al. 1993).

Factors that give Himalayan balsam a competitive advantage are synchronous seed germination and high vegetative growth rate. Seeds germinate in the early spring and all within a few days of each other. After seed germination the seedlings gain height and biomass in a very short amount of time. Native plants in the forest understory generally have a slower growth rate and do not exhibit synchronous germination. The presence of a large number of tall plants prevents native seedlings from acquiring the necessary amounts of light and energy to grow (Fig. 142). Very few native seedlings can survive under such low light conditions in the early spring (Beerling & Perrins, 1993; Andrews et al. 2009).

ECOLOGICAL IMPACTS

European habitats have been experiencing the negative effects of Himalayan balsam invasion since the 1850's, while its first introduction into North America occurred approximately 30 years later (Tabak & von Wettberg, 2008). Thus, most studies documenting the ecological impacts of Himalayan balsam have been done in Europe (Perrins et al. 1993; Maule et al. 2000; Andrews et al. 2009). These studies can help us predict the effects Himalayan balsam may have on hardwood forests in Ontario. As with other invasive plants, Himalayan balsam forms dense stands (Fig. 143) that compete and exclude native vegetation from the area (Andrews et al. 2009). This competition may reduce forest biodiversity and have an impact on hardwood regeneration (Pyšek & Prach, 1995). However, more research is needed to fully understand the impacts of Himalayan balsam on North American hardwood stands.

Figure 142: Himalayan balsam attaining great height[4].   Figure 143: A dense stand of Himalayan balsam[1].

VECTORS & PATHWAYS

Dispersal is initiated when the seedpods burst open, expelling seeds within several metres of the parent plant. Long-distance dispersal can occur when plants are close to streams or rivers. The seeds are buoyant and can be carried downstream (Tabak & von Wettberg, 2008). Humans are probably the main source of long-distance seed dispersal. Seeds can easily get stuck in clothing folds, shoes or on vehicle tires. Some dispersal may also be caused by the use of Himalayan balsam as a garden plant (Perrins et al. 1993).

MANAGEMENT PRACTICES

PREVENTION STRATEGIES

· Himalayan balsam can easily become established in areas where soil has been disturbed. Limit soil disturbing activities in the woodlot and plant native vegetation in areas where soil disturbance is unavoidable;
· If a river or stream runs through the woodlot, ensure that populations of Himalayan balsam are controlled upstream to prevent seed dispersal;
· Talk with neighbours about the potential consequences of using Himalayan balsam as a garden plant and suggest some native alternatives.

EARLY DETECTION TECHNIQUES

· Learn how to identify Himalayan balsam;
· Monitor the woodlot frequently paying attention to disturbed areas and along waterways;
· Become familiar with Himalayan balsam in neighbouring gardens.

CONTROL OPTIONS

Hand-pulling: Although hand-pulling may prove to be time consuming, the shallow root system of these plants makes pulling relatively easy. Hand-pulling is appropriate for areas where Himalayan balsam is mixed with desirable vegetation. Take hold of the stem as close to the ground as possible to prevent the stem from breaking. The root systems of some of the larger plants may prove difficult to remove. The roots may be dug up using a hand trowel to prevent any re-sprouting (Kelly et al. 2008). Himalayan balsam has a very shallow root system

which allows plants to be easily pulled from the soil. Even with a shallow root system, hand-pulling Himalayan balsam will create soil disturbance. Consider planting native vegetation to prevent re-colonization or invasion by other problematic species (Kelly et al. 2008).

Cutting and mowing: Cutting or mowing in areas with dense populations of Himalayan balsam can prevent these plants from producing seed. Using a weed whacker on dense patches of Himalayan balsam is a relatively quick method of removal. Make sure the plants are cut as close to the ground as possible, ideally below the lowest node, to prevent re-sprouting. This can be done several times between April and June before the plants have produced seedpods as this will scatter seeds thereby increasing the area of invasion (Havinga, 2000). Be sure to schedule a cutting towards the end of June to prevent late growing plants from reaching the fruiting stage. Ensure that stems are cut as close to the ground as possible to prevent re-sprouting (Kelly et al. 2008).

Herbicide application: Chemical control by a licenced exterminator is another way of managing large invasions of Himalayan balsam. Herbicides should be applied as a foliar spray after flowering but before seedpod development. Any plants that are sprayed after flowering should not have enough energy to produce viable seed. This approach should effectively prevent seed production and result in a smaller population the following year (Kelly et al. 2008).

RECOMMENDATIONS FOR INTEGRATED CONTROL OF LARGE INVASIONS

Option #1: With chemical control

Control efforts should be done between April and June before seedpods begin to develop. This timing is important because seedpods will explode at the slightest touch, releasing seeds and contributing to the seed bank (Kelly et al. 2008). Seeds are only known to survive in the soil for a maximum of 18 months so control measures should only be needed for 2 consecutive years (Beerling & Perrins, 1993).

In areas with large populations of Himalayan balsam a combination of manual and chemical control may be required. Herbicides can be applied as foliar sprays to dense patches. In areas where herbicides cannot be used, such as areas close to water, cutting down large invasions can help reduce seed production. Hand-pulling should be employed in areas where Himalayan balsam is intermingled with desirable vegetation. Consider planting native species in areas where hand-pulling has created soil disturbance or where control has left bare areas (Kelly et al. 2008; Havinga, 2000).

Option #2: Without chemical control

The best way to control small invasions of Himalayan balsam is to hand-pull individual plants. Hand-pulling should be done between April and June before seedpods begin to develop. This timing is important because seedpods will explode at the slightest touch, releasing seeds and contributing to the seed bank (Kelly et al. 2008). If timed appropriately, only one pull will need to be scheduled per year. By waiting until plants have begun to produce flowers, any seedlings that germinate thereafter should not have enough time to mature and produce seed before winter (Ammer et al. 2011). Pulled plants should be bagged and disposed of in an appropriate landfill or left to decompose on a tarp. In areas with large populations, use a weed whacker or lawn mower. Cuttings should be done several times per season to prevent any addition to the seed bank. After several years, the seed bank should be exhausted and populations should start to diminish (Kelly et al. 2008; Havinga, 2000).

Table 12: Management recommendations for Himalayan balsam (*Impatiens glandulifera*).

Extent of infestation	Small invasions and satellite populations	Large invasions and dense populations
Recommended method of control	Manual control: hand-pulling.	Manual control, cutting/mowing, hand-pulling, chemical control, and herbicide application.
Timing	April-June.	Manual control: April-June. Chemical control: May-early June (immediately after flowering).
Disposal	Bag all parts of the plant and dispose at an appropriate landfill or leave to decompose on a tarp.	Plant material may be left on site.
Frequency of control	Initial pull should remove as many plants as possible. If timed appropriately, only one pull per year will be needed.	Cutting or mowing should be down several times per year between April and June. Herbicides may be applied once per year between May and early June.
Length of control	1-2 years.	2-3 years.
Required restoration	Plant native species in areas where hand-pulling creates soil disturbance.	Plant native species in areas with soil disturbance or where controlled patches have left bare areas

5.1.8
Common Buckthorn
(*Rhamnus cathartica*)

Other common names:
European buckthorn, Carolina buckthorn, European waythorn, Hart's thorn

Priority Rating: **HIGH**

Figure 144: Common buckthorn[1]

IDENTIFICATION

LEAVES: Common buckthorn leaves are usually found in an opposite arrangement but at times can be alternate. They are oval in shape with toothed margins (Fig. 145). Each leaf has 3 to 4 pairs of veins that curve towards the leaf tip (Wieseler, 2005; Kershaw, 2001).

Figure 145: Common buckthorn leaves[1].

FLOWERS: Common buckthorn is dioecious, which means that each plant produces either male or female flowers (Fig. 146). Flowers are greenish-yellow in colour with 4 petals. They are arranged in a cluster at the leaf axils (Kershaw, 2001). Each cluster will often have 2 to 6 flowers (Wieseler, 2005).

Figure 146: Pistillate or female flowers[1] (left) and staminate or male flowers[1] (right) of common buckthorn.

FRUIT/SEED: The fruit is a berry containing approximately four seeds. As the berries mature they change from green to red to black (Fig. 147). They are arranged in clusters (Kershaw, 2001).

TRUNK & BRANCHES: The bark has characteristic spots called lenticels (Fig. 148). Branches and twigs are commonly spine-tipped (Kershaw, 2001).

Figure 147: Immature green (top) and ripe black (bottom) common buckthorn berries[1].

Figure 148: Common buckthorn trunk with characteristic lenticels[1] (top) and a spine-tipped twig[1] (bottom).

HEIGHT: Common buckthorn is a multiple-stemmed shrub or single-stemmed small tree that can reach up to 6m tall (Kershaw, 2001) (Fig. 149).

Figure 149: Common buckthorn growing as a small tree[1].

SIMILAR SPECIES

Glossy buckthorn (*Frangula alnus*)

Glossy buckthorn has similar leaf venation patterns to that of common buckthorn. However, the leaves have smooth edges and 5 to 10 pairs of veins. This is in contrast with common buckthorn, whose leaves have toothed edges and 2 to 4 veins per side (Fig. 150). Other differences include the glossy leaves and spineless twig tips of glossy buckthorn (Kershaw, 2001).

Figure 150: Comparing the leaves of glossy buckthorn[14] (left) to those of common buckthorn[1] (right).

Red-osier dogwood (*Cornus sericea*)

The leaves of red-osier dogwood have a similar venation pattern to those of common buckthorn. However, the leaf edges are smooth and not toothed as those of common buckthorn (Fig. 151). Red-osier dogwood has a characteristic bright red stem that is distinctive from other shrubs (Kershaw, 2001).

Figure 151: Comparing the leaves of red-osier dogwood[1] (left) to those of common buckthorn[1] (right).

Alternate-leaved dogwood (*Cornus alternifolia*)

As with red-osier dogwood, the leaf edges of alternate-leaved dogwood are smooth, which is in contrast to the toothed edges of common buckthorn's leaves. Common buckthorn has 3 to 4 vein pairs while alternate-leave dogwood has 5 to 6 vein pairs (Fig. 152). Although the leaves of common buckthorn are usually found in an opposite arrangement, they can at times have the same alternate arrangement typical of alternate-leaved dogwood (Farrar, 1995)

Figure 152: Comparing the leaves of alternate-leaved dogwood[1] (left) to those of common buckthorn[1] (right).

Alder-leaved buckthorn (*Rhamnus alnifolia*)

A close relative of common buckthorn, alder-leaved buckthorn, is very similar in appearance. Both species have leaves with toothed edges and arcuate venation. However, common buckthorn has 3 to 4 vein pairs whereas alder-leaved buckthorn has 6 to 7 vein pairs (Fig. 153). The best way to distinguish these species from one another is to count their vein pairs (Chambers et al. 1996).

Figure 153: Comparing the leaves of alder-leaved buckthorn[14] (left) to those of common buckthorn[1] (right).

A key to woody plants with leaves similar to common buckthorn (*Rhamnus cathartica*)

1. Leaves with toothed edges

    2. Leaves are glossy ....Glossy buckthorn (*Frangula alnus*)

    2. Leaves are not glossy

        3. Leaves in an opposite arrangement..Red-osier dogwood (*Cornus sericea*)

        3. Leaves in an alternate arrangement..Alternate-leaved dogwood (*Cornus alternifolia*)

1. Leaves with smooth edges

    4. Leaves with 6-7 pairs of veins...Alder-leaved buckthorn (*Rhamnus alnifolia*)

    4. Leaves with 3-4 pairs of veins ....Common buckthorn (*Rhamnus cathartica*)

BIOLOGY

TAXONOMIC HIERARCHY

Kingdom	Plantae
Subkingdom	Tracheobionta
Division	Magnoliophyta
Class	Magnoliopsida
Subclass	Rosidae
Order	Rhamnales
Family	Rhamnaceae
Genus	*Rhamnus*
Species	*Rhamnus cathartica*

ORIGIN & DISTRIBUTION

Common buckthorn is native to Europe and Asia. It was introduced into North America in the early 1800's as an ornamental shrub (Knight et al. 2007) and it was highly valued for its aesthetic appearance as an hedge plant (Kershaw, 2001). Common buckthorn escaped from cultivation and spread across southern Ontario through the 1900's (Kurylo et al. 2007). After being discovered as an alternate host for various crop pests such as oat crown rust (*Puccinia coronata*; Fig. 154), a ban was put on its importation and sale within Canada (CFIA, 2008).

Figure 154: Crown rust on an oat leaf[30].

HABITAT

Common buckthorn can be found occupying forest edges and open areas in its native range (Knight et al. 2007). In North America it can be found in both open and closed habitats such as fields, forests and disturbed sites (Mascaro & Schnitzer, 2007). Common buckthorn is a shade tolerant species that can readily invade forest understories (Kurylo et al. 2007; Knight et al. 2007) (Fig. 155).

Figure 155: Common buckthorn invading the edge of a forest[1].

REPRODUCTION

Common buckthorn is dioecious, which means that each plant produces either male or females flowers. Only female plants produce fruit and seed (Wieseler, 2005). It may take 9 to 20 years before common buckthorn can reproduce. After that it can reproduce every year. Reproduction is sexual and flowers require insect pollinators (Knight et al. 2007). Seeds can persist for at least 2 years in the soil after common buckthorn has been removed from an area (Delanoy & Archibold, 2007).

LIFE CYCLE

Seeds usually disperse in late fall and remain dormant until germination the following summer. The leaves of common buckthorn are deciduous but they generally appear earlier and fall later than those of native trees and shrubs. Leaves generally emerge in April and May followed by flowering in May and June. Fruits ripen in September and may remain on the plant during the winter months (Knight, 2005) (Fig. 156).

Figure 156: Common buckthorn berries in January[14].

SUCCESS MECHANISMS

A fast growth rate has been shown to be advantageous for common buckthorn in North America. In the early spring it produces leaves much earlier than co-occurring native plants. This enables exposure to full sunlight before the forest canopy closes, resulting in a jump-start in energy reserves. This, in conjunction with keeping its leaves longer than their native competitors in the fall, results in an overall longer photosynthetic period, which may contribute to its success in the forest understory (Knight et al. 2007).

Emodin is a secondary compound found in the leaf tissues and unripe berries of common buckthorn. Emodin is thought to play a role in protection against pathogen attack and herbivory. Emodin present in unripe berries may make them unpalatable to birds and other wildlife early in the season. As fruits ripen, their concentration of emodin decreases. This allows fruits to mature before they are consumed by wildlife which is thought to play an important role in seed viability and dispersal (Izhaki, 2002).

ECOLOGICAL IMPACTS

Common buckthorn is a competitive shrub that is capable of becoming a dominant understory species (Knight et al. 2007) (Fig. 157). Early leaf production and a fast growth rate allow these shrubs to tower over and smother understory plants. Dense shade from established thickets creates inadequate growing conditions for native species, thereby reducing hardwood recruitment (Delanoy & Archibold, 2007; Mascaro & Schnitzer, 2007).

Figure 157: A thicket of common buckthorn saplings in a forest understory[1].

Common buckthorn invasions can change soil characteristics and forest floor communities. The leaves contain high levels of nitrogen which is incorporated in the forest floor as they decompose. Studies have shown that earthworms are attracted to sites invaded by common buckthorn. High levels of earthworm colonization can lead to increased litter decomposition rates and thus to major changes in the dynamics of both food webs and nutrient cycling (Heneghan et al. 2007; Knight et al. 2007).

As common buckthorn becomes established in the forest understory it can effectively exclude co-occurring native shrubs, resulting in large monospecific thickets (Knight et al. 2007). Songbirds may be forced to nest in these thickets due to the displacement of native shrubs. A study by Schmidt and Whelan (1999) documented increased predation rates on American robin (*Turdus migratorius*) nests found in common buckthorn thickets as compared to those nests found on native shrubs. More studies are needed to determine the impact of common buckthorn on songbird populations.

VECTORS & PATHWAYS

Common buckthorn spreads via the dispersal of seeds. These seeds are borne in fruits that either drop to the ground or are eaten by wildlife. The berries can float and may be washed away by flood waters or carried down streams and rivers. Since birds can fly long distances before seeds pass through their digestive tracks, they are presumably the primary means of common buckthorn dispersal into hardwood forests (Gale, 2000).

The importation or sale of common buckthorn is prohibited in Canada due to its ability to act as an alternate host for oat crown rust (*Puccinia coronata*) and other crop pests such as potato and soybean aphids (CFIA, 2008; Knight, 2005). Although it can no longer be sold as an ornamental shrub, humans may still act as dispersal agents when seeds get stuck on shoes and clothing or in the treads of tires.

MANAGEMENT PRACTICES

PREVENTION STRATEGIES
· Prevent seeds from entering the woodlot by limiting access and washing all shoes and tires before entry;
· Increase awareness in your community about the consequences of common buckthorn invasions. Promote management to help control common buckthorn.

EARLY DETECTION TECHNIQUES
· Learn how to identify common buckthorn;
· Regularly monitor the woodlot for new species and pay particular attention to roads and trails where invasive plants can easily establish.

CONTROL OPTIONS

Hand-pulling: Common buckthorn can appear as a shrub with multiple stems or as a tree that can reach 6m in height (Kershaw, 2001). Hand-pulling is only practical for small saplings. Wet soil makes hand-pulling easier. As such, it is best to plan for manual control after a heavy rainfall. Small seedlings that are less than 1m tall can be pulled but gloves should be worn to prevent injury from the thorny branches (Gale, 2000). For saplings that are larger than 1m in height, mechanical levers such as root wrenches will be needed to pry up the root system from the soil. This may prove to be very labour intensive and should only be attempted for small invasions.

Cutting and excavation: Large trees may have to be cut and the roots dug out using a shovel (Gale, 2000). The root systems must be removed because shoots will emerge from root crowns and stumps (Pergams & Norton, 2006). Since mechanical removal will cause significant soil disturbance, restoration efforts will be required. Fill in the holes left by the removal of common buckthorn with soil and re-vegetate with native species (Moriarty, 2005).

Herbicide application: Herbicides should be applied in the early spring or late fall when most native vegetation is dormant to minimize any potential non-target effects. Applying herbicides to the basal bark will leave dead standing trees. These trees can be left standing, allowing native vegetation to grow around them, or they may be removed depending on the management planned for the area (Moriarty, 2005). Stems may also be cut down and removed, but in this case herbicides need to be applied to the stump to prevent re-sprouting. This method may be time consuming and labour intensive because common buckthorn can have numerous stems and grow in dense thickets (Delanoy & Archibald, 2007).

RECOMMENDATIONS FOR INTEGRATED CONTROL OF LARGE INVASIONS

Option #1: With chemical control

Areas with large thickets of common buckthorn will require time, effort and money to manage. To help reduce initial costs and ensure practicality, only female plants should initially be targeted for control. This will prevent seed production as male plants do not bear fruit. Preventing seed production helps to control the populations and will help to decrease recruitment, thereby leading to a more manageable scenario. Control should occur in the fall to reduce detrimental effects on nesting birds. The dark coloured berries will be very prominent in the fall, making identification of female plants easier (Delanoy & Archibald, 2007).

Although seed production is eliminated once all mature female plants are removed, seedlings may continue to emerge from an established seed bank. These seedlings may be pulled or treated with a basal herbicide treatment. When the invasion has become somewhat manageable, male plants may be removed in a similar fashion to that used for the females. Seeding or planting native species may be required to restore the native plant community (Delanoy & Archibald, 2007).

Integrated control should be implemented when facing dense patches of common buckthorn in areas with desirable vegetation. Hand-pulling small saplings decreases the amount of herbicide required. However, herbicides will be needed to kill larger trees that cannot be pulled or dug out from the ground without major soil disturbance or mechanical help. Alternatively, herbicides may be applied to the freshly cut stump to prevent any shoots from sprouting and to eliminate the need to dig out a large root system (Delanoy & Archibald, 2007).

Option #2: Without chemical control

Managing large common buckthorn invasions without the use of herbicides will require a greater amount of time and effort. Target the large berry producing female trees to help control seed production (Delanoy & Archibald, 2007). These large trees and shrubs can be cut and left on site or placed in a brush pile for burning. The stumps will continue to re-sprout and will require frequent clipping or removal of the entire root system. Keep in mind that removing large stumps will cause soil disturbance that could promote reinvasion by common buckthorn or other invasive plants (Moriarty, 2005).

After all the large common buckthorn trees and saplings have been removed, management efforts can focus on pulling the understory seedlings and saplings. Pulled plants may be placed in a slash pile for burning or left on site, ensuring that the roots are fully exposed to promote desiccation. Ongoing monitoring will be needed to control any seedlings emerging from a potential seed bank (Delanoy & Archibald, 2007).

Table 13: Management recommendations for common buckthorn (*Rhamnus cathartica*).

Extent of infestation	Small invasions and satellite populations	Large invasions and dense populations
Recommended method of control	Manual and mechanical control: hand-pulling and excavation.	Integrated control: hand-pulling and herbicide application.
Timing	Spring, summer and fall.	Fall herbicide application. Hand-pulling can occur in spring, summer or fall.
Disposal	Woody debris may be left on site or removed to a brush pile or burned.	Dead shrubs and woody debris may be left on site or removed to a brush pile or burned.
Frequency of control	Initial pull should remove as many trees and shrubs as possible. Return several times per year to pull any missed plants or new sprouts.	Initial pull should remove as many trees and shrubs as possible. Return several times per year to pull any missed plants or new sprouts. Use herbicidal control once every fall.
Length of control	2-3 years.	2-5 years.
Required restoration	Plant native species in areas where hand-pulling and excavating creates soil disturbance.	Plant native species in areas where hand-pulling and excavating creates soil disturbance.

5.1.9
Periwinkle
(*Vinca minor*)

Other common names:
Common periwinkle, Lesser periwinkle, Myrtle, Running myrtle

Priority Rating: **HIGH**

Figure 158: Periwinkle[1]

IDENTIFICATION

STEM: Periwinkle is a trailing vine growing as a carpet over the forest floor (Fig. 159). The stems contain a milky substance (Jenkins & Jackman, 1941) and can become slightly woody with age making them difficult to break by hand (Miller, 2003).

LEAVES: Evergreen leaves are ovate in shape with a pointed tip (Fig. 160). These shiny, dark green leaves can be found in an opposite arrangement along the stem (Kaufman & Kaufman, 2007) (Fig. 161). The leaf edges of periwinkle are smooth (Gleason & Cronquist, 1963).

Figure 159: Periwinkle is a trailing vine[1].

Figure 160: Periwinkle leaves[1].

Figure 161: Opposite leaf arrangement[1].

FLOWERS: Flowers have 5 petals and range in colour from blue to purple (Fig. 162). Solitary flowers are produced on short stems arising from leaf axils (Bailey, 1969).

FRUIT/SEED: The fruit is a follicle that contains 3 to 5 black seeds. Seeds are produced occasionally however this type of reproduction is rare compared to vegetative spread (Stone, 2009).

Figure 162: Periwinkle flowers[1].

SIMILAR SPECIES

Creeping snowberry (*Gaultheria hispidula*)

Creeping snowberry is an evergreen plant with creeping stems. It can easily be distinguished from periwinkle by its alternate leaves with bristled edges. Periwinkle has opposite leaves with smooth edges (Fig. 163). Creeping snowberry leaves are also much smaller (<1cm long) than those of periwinkle (2.5 to 7.6cm long) (Chambers et al. 1996).

Figure 163: Comparing creeping snowberry[32] (left) and periwinkle[1] (right).

Wintergreen (*Gaultheria procumbens*)

Wintergreen does not have trailing stems but still may be confused with periwinkle by its glossy, evergreen leaves. However, these leaves are alternate with toothed margins as opposed to the opposite, smooth-edged leaves of periwinkle (Fig. 164). Crushing the leaves of wintergreen will release a minty odour (Chambers et al. 1996).

Figure 164: Comparing wintergreen[20] (left) and periwinkle[1] (right).

Common bearberry (*Arctostaphylos uva-ursi*)

Common bearberry is similar to periwinkle in that it has trailing stems and evergreen leaves with smooth edges. It can be distinguished from periwinkle by its alternately arranged leaves (Dickinson et al. 2004) (Fig. 165).

Figure 165: Comparing common bearberry[17] (left) and periwinkle[1] (right).

Twinflower (*Linnaea borealis*)

Twinflower has creeping stems with opposite evergreen leaves similar to those of periwinkle. However, the leaves of twinflower are hairy with toothed edges while the leaves of periwinkle are hairless with smooth edges (Dickinson et al. 2004) (Fig. 166).

Figure 166: Comparing twinflower[20] (left) and periwinkle[1] (right).

Winter creeper (*Euonymus fortunei*)

Winter creeper shares several similarities with periwinkle. Its opposite evergreen leaves and trailing habit are similar to those of periwinkle as is its invasive nature in the forest understory. It is native to Japan, China and Korea. Winter creeper has leaves with toothed edges as opposed to the smooth edges of periwinkle leaves (Kaufman & Kaufman, 2007) (Fig. 167).

Figure 167: Comparing winter creeper[12] (left) and periwinkle[1] (right).

Partridge-berry (*Mitchella repens*)

Partridge-berry can be easily confused with periwinkle. A trailing habit, opposite evergreen leaves with smooth edges, and light green veins are all characteristics that these two species share. The easiest way to identify these species is to look at the leaf tip. Partridge-berry leaves have a very rounded tip whereas the leaves of periwinkle have pointed tips (Chambers et al. 1996) (Fig. 168).

Figure 168: Comparing partridge-berry[1] (left) and periwinkle[1] (right).

[147]

A key to evergreen plants that may be confused with periwinkle (*Vinca minor*)

1. Plants with alternate leaves

  2. Leaves with bristled edges

    3. Small leaves (less than 1cm long) .... Creeping snowberry (*Gaultheria hispidula*)

    3. Large leaves (2-5cm long) .... Wintergreen (*Gaultheria procumbens*)

  2. Leaves with smooth edges .... Common bearberry (*Arctostaphylos uva-ursi*)

1. Plants with opposite leaves

    4. Leaves with toothed (serrate) edges

      5. Leaves covered with hair .... Twinflower (*Linnaea borealis*)

      5. Leaves without hair .... Winter creeper (*Euonymus fortunei*)

    4. Leaves with smooth (entire) edges

      6. Leaves with rounded tips .... Partridge-berry (*Mitchella repens*)

      6. Leaves with pointed tips .... Common periwinkle (*Vinca minor*)

BIOLOGY

TAXONOMIC HIERARCHY

Kingdom	Plantae
Subkingdom	Tracheobionta
Division	Magnoliophyta
Class	Magnoliopsida
Subclass	Asteridae
Order	Gentianales
Family	Apocynaceae
Genus	*Vinca*
Species	*Vinca minor*

ORIGIN & DISTRIBUTION

Periwinkle was introduced by European settlers in the early 1700's (Swearingen et al. 2010). A native to Eurasia, it was valued as an easy-to-grow ornamental groundcover (Winterrowd & Stagg, 1993). Today it is still commonly sold as a garden plant throughout the province (Miller, 2003).

HABITAT

Periwinkle is a versatile plant that can grow in open sunny areas to closed canopy forests (Swearingen et al. 2010). It is a common garden plant that has escaped cultivation to be found in open areas such as meadows and fields, edge habitats such as roadsides and along trails, and in forested areas (Fig. 169). It is commonly seen growing as a dense cover in shaded areas (Miller, 2003; Stone, 2009).

Figure 169: Periwinkle growing alongside a road[1] (left) and trail[1] (right).

REPRODUCTION

Reproduction is mainly vegetative through stem runners. When these runners touch the soil at the leaf nodes they have the ability to take root (Jenkins & Jackman, 1941). Seeds are produced occasionally. However, this type of reproduction is rare compared to vegetative spread (Stone, 2009). These plants can easily establish from stem fragments (Winterrowd & Stagg, 1993).

LIFE CYCLE

Periwinkle is a perennial vine (Bailey, 1969) that flowers in the early spring (Gleason & Cronquist, 1963). The majority of flowers appear in April and May with occasional flowers appearing throughout the summer months. Seed-filled follicles are produced from May to July. Seeds are dispersed as the follicles dry out and crack. Periwinkles are evergreen and thus keep their leaves throughout the winter (Miller, 2003).

SUCCESS MECHANISMS

Although the seed dispersing capabilities of periwinkle are low, these plants can propagate relatively quickly. Plants can send out twining stems in all directions that can take root wherever there is an empty space on the forest floor (Darcy & Burkart, 2002). Since these plants are free-rooting, even small stem fragments have the ability to grow into a dense mat (Fig. 170). Such plant fragments can become established throughout the spring and summer months (Winterrowd & Stagg, 1993).

Periwinkle can effectively compete with native vegetation in the forest understory. This competitive advantage may be due to allelopathy, light suppression or a combination of both. A laboratory study suggested that periwinkle had allelopathic effects on the growth rate of tree seedlings. However, more studies are needed to fully understand these effects (Darcy & Burkart, 2002).

Periwinkle is an evergreen vine that has the ability to grow over other plants. This growth habit gives the plant the best access to sunlight. The native plants growing underneath are at a disadvantage as they cannot get enough sunlight for photosynthesis (Darcy & Burkart, 2002).

Figure 170: Periwinkle forming a carpet on the forest floor[1].

ECOLOGICAL IMPACTS

Due to periwinkle's limited dispersal capabilities it is not always considered a major threat. However, once established this species may have negative effects on the woodlot. Control is often difficult due to the free-rooting nature of this species. Monitoring the woodlot for invasions by periwinkle is recommended.

Periwinkle has the ability to suppress hardwood regeneration. It forms a dense carpet (Fig. 171) that covers low growing species (Drake et al. 2003). Through light suppression and the possibility of allelopathic effects, seedling growth is inhibited. With the absence of regeneration, the species composition of the forest may gradually change (Darcy & Burkart, 2002).

Periwinkle may also have negative impacts on the understory fauna. One study showed a change in the spider community associated with the forest floor. Such changes have a ripple effect where impacts may be felt throughout the local food web (Bultman & DeWitt, 2008). More studies are needed to document such underlying effects.

Figure 171: Periwinkle growing as a carpet on the forest floor[1].

VECTORS & PATHWAYS

Humans are the main vectors of periwinkle spread. Periwinkle is still a common garden plant and it is sold in garden centres throughout Ontario (Fig. 172). It is unlikely that seeds are a dispersal agent as these plants rarely germinate from seed in North America. Most spread is due to the dumping of yard wastes in natural areas. These plants can easily propagate from the smallest root fragments, thus such yard wastes are a major factor in the spread of this species (Stone, 2009).

Figure 172: Periwinkle being sold as a ground cover[1].

MANAGEMENT PRACTICES

PREVENTION STRATEGIES

· Do not dump yard wastes in or close to natural areas;
· Periwinkle is considered an invasive plant and should not be planted in the garden. Use native alternatives or species that are not considered invasive.

EARLY DETECTION TECHNIQUES

· Learn how to identify periwinkle;
· Regularly monitor the woodlot;
· Become familiar with periwinkle populations in neighbours gardens and ensure that yard wastes are properly disposed of.

CONTROL OPTIONS

Hand-pulling: Hand-pulling can be labour intensive and is only suitable for small invasions or for outlying satellite populations. All plant fragments need to be collected and bagged as they can easily propagate. Areas where runners have rooted into the ground need to be pulled. Using a rake will help to collect the twining stems while raising the runners to reveal the root system. Digging tools may be required to ensure removal of the entire root system since any portion of the root left behind has the ability to re-sprout. As the stems can be slightly woody it is recommended to have pruning shears on hand (Swearingen et al. 2010).

Herbicide application: Chemical control is suitable for severe invasions. Herbicides should be applied as a foliar spray, enough to wet leaves but not so much as to cause dripping. The leaves of periwinkle plants have a waxy cuticle that does not readily absorb herbicides (Bean & Russo, 1988). The addition of a surfactant to the herbicide solution will increase absorption by the leaves and increase the likelihood of success.

Repeated treatments and spot applications are often necessary. Alternatively, the cut-and-spray method may be used to increase the chance of absorption through the wounded plant tissues (Drewitz, 2000).

RECOMMENDATIONS FOR INTEGRATED CONTROL OF LARGE INVASIONS

Option #1: With chemical control

The use of chemical control is recommended during the fall when most native plants are dormant. The most effective means of control may be the cut-and-spray method. This method combines both physical and chemical control. The stems are cut and herbicides applied immediately afterwards. The wounded stems will readily absorb the herbicide solution (Drewitz, 2000). Herbicides may also be applied as a foliar spray. A second application may be needed the following year if the initial application was unsuccessful. Periwinkle plants that are in close proximity to desirable vegetation may be hand-pulled to prevent any damage to native species. It is also good to keep in mind that a combination of manual and chemical control decreases the amount of herbicides entering the forest ecosystem while managing cost and labour requirements (Bean & Russo, 1988).

Option # 2: Without chemical control

Hand-pulling can have a minimal impact on native vegetation if care is taken not to trample any native species. However, frequent monitoring is required and it has the potential to be labour intensive. The initial pull should be focused on removing as many plants and plant fragments as possible. Bag all parts of the plant and dispose of them at an appropriate landfill. Return to the area several times per year to pull any missed plants or new sprouts. Hand-pulling often creates soil disturbance which is known to increase the likelihood of reinvasion. It may be beneficial to plant desirable native seedlings in areas where such soil disturbing activities have occurred (Swearingen et al. 2010).

Table 14: Management recommendations for periwinkle (*Vinca minor*).

Extent of infestation	Small invasions and satellite populations	Large invasions and dense populations
Recommended method of control	Manual control: hand-pulling.	Integrated control: cutting, hand-pulling and herbicide application.
Timing	Spring, summer and fall.	Fall.
Disposal	Bag all parts of the plant and dispose at an appropriate landfill.	Plant material may be left on site.
Frequency of control	Initial pull should remove as many plants and plant fragments as possible. Return several times per year to pull any missed plants or new sprouts.	Once yearly until invasion has been eliminated or has become small enough to manage with manual control.
Length of control	2-3 years.	2-5 years.
Required restoration	Plant native species in areas where hand-pulling creates soil disturbance.	Plant native species in areas where hand-pulling creates soil disturbance.

5.1.10
Dog-strangling Vine
(*Vincetoxicum rossicum* & *V. nigrum*)

Other common names:
European swallow-wort, Pale swallow wort, Louis' swallow-wort, Black swallow-wort

Priority Rating: **HIGH**

Figure 173: Dog-strangling vine[1]

IDENTIFICATION

There are two species of dog-strangling vine currently invading Ontario habitats. They are *Vincetoxicum rossicum* and *V. nigrum*. A third species, *V. hirundinaria* has not yet invaded North America and thus will not be discussed herein. However, it could potentially become a problem in the future (see extensive review by DiTommaso et al. 2005).

LEAVES: Both species have similar leaves that are ovate with smooth edges (Fig. 174). They occur in an opposite arrangement along the stem (DiTommaso et al. 2005).

Figure 174: Dog-strangling vine leaves[1].

FLOWERS: Both species of dog-strangling vine have flowers with 5 petals. *Vincetoxicum rossicum* flowers range in colour from pink to dark maroon (Fig. 175). They form clusters of 5 to 20 flowers that sprout from leaf axils (Fig. 176). *Vincetoxicum nigrum* flowers can be dark purple to almost black in colour and form clusters of 4 to 10 flowers (DiTommaso et al. 2005).

Figure 175: Comparison of flower colours for *Vincetoxicum rossicum*[1] (left) and *V. nigrum*[6] (right).

Figure 176: *Vincetoxicum rossicum* flower clusters[1].

FRUIT/SEED: Generally, two fruits in the form of follicles are produced per *V. rossicum* flower (Fig. 177) whereas *V. nigrum* flowers will only rarely produce two fruits per flower. Seeds are connected to a tuft of white hairs (Fig. 178) and are similar to those of native milkweed (DiTommaso et al. 2005).

Figure 177: *Vincetoxicum rossicum* follicles[1].

Figure 178: Dog-strangling vine seed dispersal[6].

SIMILAR SPECIES

Amur honeysuckle (*Lonicera maackii*)

Amur honeysuckle is a shrub that may be confused with young dog-strangling vine plants that have not yet started to climb or look like a vine. They both have opposite, oblong leaves with smooth edges (Fig. 179). Amur honeysuckle leaves have long pointed tips whereas dog-strangling vine has leaves with a much shorter tip (Kaufman & Kaufman, 2007).

Figure 179: Comparing Amur honeysuckle[1] (left) and dog-strangling vine[1] (right).

Morrow's honeysuckle (*Lonicera morrowii*)

The shape and edges of a morrow's honeysuckle leaf is very similar to that of a dog-strangling vine leaf (Fig. 180). However, one key feature of morrow's honeysuckle is that the underside of each leaf is covered in hair, whereas the leaves of dog-strangling vine are hairless (Kaufman & Kaufman, 2007).

Figure 180: Comparing morrow's honeysuckle[1] (left) and dog-strangling vine[1] (right).

Canada fly honeysuckle (*Lonicera canadensis*)

Another shrub with similar looking leaves to dog-strangling vine is the Canada fly honeysuckle (Fig. 181). The leaf edges of Canada fly honeysuckle are ciliate which means that they are fringed with tiny hairs (Fig. 182). These hairs can be seen on close inspection with a magnifying glass. The leaves of dog-strangling vine are hairless (Chambers et al. 1996).

Figure 181: Comparing Canada fly honeysuckle[1] (left) and dog-strangling vine[1] (right).

Figure 182: Ciliate leaves of Canada fly honeysuckle[1].

Tartarian honeysuckle (*Lonicera tatarica*)

Tartarian honeysuckle leaves are similar to those of dog-strangling vine in that they do not have any hair on their surface or edges. However, some of the older leaves on tartarian honeysuckle have a heart-shaped appearance at the base (Fig. 183). This is usually not seen on leaves found close to the end of the twigs so be sure to check farther down the stem (Kaufman & Kaufman, 2007).

Figure 183: Comparing the leaves of tartarian honeysuckle[1] (left) and dog-strangling vine[1] (right).

Bush honeysuckle (*Diervilla lonicera*)

On close inspection bush honeysuckle's leaves can easily be distinguished from those of dog-strangling vine by the appearance of the leaf margin (Fig. 184). The leaves of bush honeysuckle have a toothed margin whereas the leaves of dog-strangling vine are smooth along the edges (Chambers et al. 1996).

Figure 184: Comparing bush honeysuckle[20] (left) and dog-strangling vine[1] (right).

Dogwood (*Cornus* spp.)

Some dogwood species in Ontario may be confused with dog-strangling vine. Although dogwood species in Ontario are trees and shrubs, when young they may be mistaken for dog-strangling vine. The key to distinguish them is to look at the leaf veins (Fig. 185). The leaf veins of dogwood species curve to meet the leaf tip whereas dog-strangling vine leaves have veins that curve towards the outer margin (Chambers et al. 1996).

Figure 185: Comparing the leaves of dogwood[1] (left) and dog-strangling vine[1] (right).

Oriental & American bittersweet (*Celastrus orbiculatus & C. scandens*)

Oriental and American bittersweet are vines with alternate leaves. The leaves of both species have toothed margins whereas dog-strangling vine has smooth margins (Fig. 186). Oriental bittersweet leaves are nearly round with a blunt tip while American bittersweet has oblong leaves with pointed tips (Kaufman & Kaufman, 2007).

Figure 186: Comparing Oriental bittersweet[15] (left) and dog-strangling vine[1] (right).

Bittersweet nightshade (*Solanum dulcamara*)

Bittersweet nightshade is a climbing vine with alternate leaves and smooth margins. Many of the leaves have two leaflets at the base (Fig. 187). The flowers and fruit of bittersweet nightshade are dissimilar to those of dog-strangling vine (Fig. 188). Bittersweet nightshade has seeds encased in berries whereas dog-strangling vine has the characteristic seedpods belonging to the milkweed family (Dickinson et al. 2004).

Figure 187: Comparing the leaves of bittersweet nightshade[1] (left) to those of dog-strangling vine[1] (right).

Figure 188: Comparing the flowers of bittersweet nightshade[1] (left) to those of dog-strangling vine[1] (right).

Honeysuckles (*Lonicera* spp.) with climbing stems

Honeysuckles with a climbing habit can be very similar to dog-strangling vine. They all have an opposite leaf arrangement. Three honeysuckle species, hairy honeysuckle (*Lonicera hirsuta*), smooth honeysuckle (*L. dioica*) and coral honeysuckle (*L. sempervirens*), can be excluded by looking at the leaf pairs located at the end of the vine (Fig. 189). These leaf pairs are joined together at the base so that the two leaves appear to be a single leaf that encircles the stem (Chambers et al. 1996).

Japanese honeysuckle (*L. japonica*) is very similar to dog-strangling vine. It may be useful to look for a lighter coloured green on the bottom surface of its leaves (Fig. 190). However, it may be better to check for the milky sap from crushed leaves and stem characteristic of dog-strangling vine when trying to distinguish these species (Kaufman & Kaufman, 2007).

Figure 189: The fused leaves of trumpet honeysuckle[16].   Figure 190: Japanese honeysuckle leaves[12].

A key to plants that may be confused with dog-strangling vine (*Vincetoxicum* spp.)

1. Plants with a woody stem (shrub) and opposite leaves (for specimens where stems may not seem woody)

  2. Leaves with sharply pointed edges (toothed margins) .... Bush honeysuckle (*Diervilla lonicera*)

  2. Leaves with smooth edges (entire margins)

    3. Leaves with narrow, long-pointed tips .... Amur honeysuckle (*Lonicera maackii*)

    3. Leaves with short, blunt tips

      4. Leaves with hair on surface or edges (margins)

        5. Underside of leaf covered in fine hairs .... Morrow's honeysuckle (*Lonicera morrowii*)

        5. Underside of leaf hairless, edges ciliate .... Canada fly honeysuckle (*Lonicera canadensis*)

      4. Leaves with no hair on surface or edges (margins)

        6. Leaf veins curve to meet tip of leaf .... Dogwood (*Cornus* spp.)

        6. Leaf veins curve towards margins

          7. Leaves slightly heart-shaped at base .... Tartarian honeysuckle (*Lonicera tatarica*)

          7. Leaves tapered at base .... Dog-strangling vine (*Vincetoxicum* spp.)

1. Plants with a climbing stem (vine)

      8. Alternate leaves

        9. Leaves with smooth edges (entire margins) .... Bittersweet nightshade (*Solanum dulcamara*)

        9. Leaves with sharply pointed edges (toothed margins)

          10. Leaves nearly round with short tip .... Oriental bittersweet (*Celastrus orbiculatus*)

          10. Leaves oblong with pointed tip .... American bittersweet (*Celastrus scandens*)

      8. Opposite leaves

        11. Upper leaf pairs joined together at base

          12. Leaves with hair on surfaces .... Hairy honeysuckle (*Lonicera hirsuta*)

          12. Leaves with no hair .... Smooth honeysuckle (*Lonicera dioica*) & Coral honeysuckle (*Lonicera sempervirens*)

        11. Upper leaf pairs distinct (not joined)

          13. Underside of leaf a paler green colour ... Japanese honeysuckle (*Lonicera japonica*)

          13. Both leaf surfaces similar in colour .... Dog-strangling vine (*Vincetoxicum* spp.)

BIOLOGY

TAXONOMIC HIERARCHY

Dog-strangling vine (*Vincetoxicum rossicum*)

Kingdom	Plantae
Subkingdom	Tracheobionta
Division	Magnoliophyta
Class	Magnoliopsida
Subclass	Asteridae
Order	Gentianales
Family	Asclepiadaceae
Genus	*Vincetoxicum*
Species	*Vincetoxicum rossicum*

Dog-strangling vine (*Vincetoxicum nigrum*)

Kingdom	Plantae
Subkingdom	Tracheobionta
Division	Magnoliophyta
Class	Magnoliopsida
Subclass	Asteridae
Order	Gentianales
Family	Asclepiadaceae
Genus	*Vincetoxicum*
Species	*Vincetoxicum nigrum*

ORIGIN & DISTRIBUTION

Vincetoxicum rossicum is native to the Ukraine and Russia while *V. nigrum* is native to southwestern Europe (Milbrath, 2010). It is assumed that both species were introduced into North America as horticultural plants (DiTommaso et al. 2005). In Ontario, *V. rossicum* was first collected in Toronto in 1889 (Smith et al. 2006). Today, it can be found invading areas from London to Ottawa. *Vincetoxicum nigrum* was often confused with *V. rossicum* and the date of its introduction into Ontario is unknown. *Vincetoxicum nigrum* has a wider distribution in Ontario than *V. rossicum* with populations scattered throughout southern and eastern Ontario (DiTommaso et al. 2005).

HABITAT

Both species of dog-strangling vine favour areas exposed to full or partial sunlight (Smith et al. 2006) but will also grow in open forests (Kaufman & Kaufman, 2007). As with most invasive species, they will readily invade disturbed areas such as roadsides. Once established, long distance seed dispersal allows satellite populations to establish in natural areas (DiTommaso et al. 2005). Dog-strangling vine can thrive in a wide range of soils and differing light and temperature conditions (Smith et al. 2008; Sanderson & Antunes, in press).

REPRODUCTION

Dog-strangling vines reproduce sexually and vegetatively through clones sprouting from an underground rhizome (Lumer & Yost, 1995). Plants self-pollinate if insect pollinators are unavailable for cross pollination (DiTommaso et al. 2005). Seeds are polyembryonic which means that each individual seed can give rise to a maximum of four seedlings (Ladd & Cappuccino, 2005).

LIFE CYCLE

Dog-strangling vine is perennial. Flowers begin to emerge in the middle of May and last until late summer (Lumer & Yost, 1995). Green seedpods, similar to those produced by native milkweed, emerge at the end of June. These pods break open to release seeds from September through November. Dead brown vines remain entangled around supporting vegetation throughout the winter months (DiTommaso et al. 2005).

SUCCESS MECHANISMS

With increasing size, dog-strangling vine populations can completely suppress native seedlings (Cappuccino, 2004). In low light environments, such as forest understories, dog-strangling vine has the ability to climb over native vegetation (Fig. 191). This allows the plant to obtain light while effectively reducing that available to the lower growing vegetation. As populations become larger they reduce space and nutrients available for other plants (Smith et al. 2006).

The robust rootstalks of dog-strangling vine store water that may be used at times of drought. These rootstalks also provide an energy source that allows plants to grow early in the season giving them a head start over competing native vegetation (DiTommaso et al. 2005).

Dog-strangling vine populations can increase rapidly due to their high reproductive potential (Fig. 192). Individual plants produce large quantities of seed. Even under shaded conditions where seed productivity is at its lowest, plants can

Figure 191: Dog-strangling vine in a forest understory[1] (left) and climbing over native vegetation[1] (right).

produce as many as 28 000 seeds per square metre. Since seeds are polyembryonic, the number of seedlings produced may increase fourfold (Smith et al. 2006). Factors contributing to such a large seed production include the ability to self-pollinate and a long flowering season. Self-pollination ensures that each plant will produce seed (DiTommaso et al. 2005) while long-lived flowers allow for a greater fruit-set (Lumer & Yost, 1995).

Figure 192: Numerous seedpods in a dog-strangling vine invasion[1].

Another factor lending to this species success is the high survival rate of first-year plants. Due to polyembryony, each seed has more than one chance at occupying a site. Seedling emergence does not always occur at the same time. It may take up to 20 days before all seedlings have emerged from a single polyembryonic seed. As such, new seedlings can emerge to offset control practices (Ladd & Cappuccino, 2005).

Dog-strangling vine has no known natural enemies in North America. Only minimal damage has been reported by insects or disease (Milbrath, 2010). As with other members of the milkweed family, dog-strangling vine contains cardenolides which are toxic if consumed in large quantities (DiTommaso et al. 2005). Thus, grazing wildlife such as deer are unlikely to eat these plants (Milbrath, 2010).

ECOLOGICAL IMPACTS

Healthy regeneration is an important woodlot management goal. Dog-strangling vine can negatively impact forest regeneration by climbing over saplings (Fig. 193) and reducing access to available space, nutrients and light (DiTommaso et al. 2005). Dog-strangling vine form symbiotic relationships with endomycorrhizal fungi and studies have shown that the number and types of fungi in soils are altered by large invasions. Such changes in soil biota can have negative consequences on native plants (Smith et al. 2008).

Wildlife diversity is a value-added feature in a woodlot. For example, wildlife viewing often enhances the sugar bush experience for customers. Dog-strangling vine populations have been found to decrease the diversity of both insects and birds. Recently, this invasive species was associated to population decreases of the monarch butterfly, which is a species-at-risk. Monarch butterflies normally lay their eggs on native milkweed. Dog-strangling vine is a member of the milkweed family and may attract monarchs in areas where native milkweed is scarce. This is detrimental since monarch larvae are unable to fully develop on dog-strangling vine (Ladd & Cappuccino, 2005). Dog-strangling vine also displaces native milkweed, thereby decreasing available host plants needed for reproducing monarchs (DiTommaso et al. 2005).

Figure 193: Dog-strangling vine climbing over native vegetation[1].

VECTORS & PATHWAYS

Dog-strangling vine will likely enter a woodlot via wind-driven seed dispersal. Being part of the milkweed family, the seeds are similar to native milkweed, fringed with hairs that allow the seeds to be airborne on windy days (DiTommaso et al. 2005). Although most seeds are known to fall within only a few metres of their parent, it only takes one seed to become an established plant that can grow with the help of clonal spread or self-pollination. Seeds may also get caught in the fur of animals, on clothing or tire treads (Smith et al. 2006).

MANAGEMENT PRACTICES

PREVENTION STRATEGIES

- Prevent seeds from entering the woodlot by limiting access when possible;
- Wash all shoes and tires before entering the woodlot;
- Do not let domestic animals roam freely in late summer and fall when seed dispersal begins, especially if there are known dog-strangling vine populations in or around the woodlot;
- Minimize soil disturbance during woodlot management activities;
- Volunteer to help eliminate dog-strangling vine populations in properties nearby.

EARLY DETECTION TECHNIQUES

- Learn how to identify dog-strangling vine;
- Regularly monitor the woodlot, paying attention to any unknown vines.

CONTROL OPTIONS

Cutting: Cutting can be used as a means to prevent seed production. Clipping the plants at ground level and removing the stem and leaves is best done in late June. This timing is important because the plants will have used up the majority of their resources to produce flowers. Thus clipped vines will not have enough energy left over to re-sprout and produce seeds before the winter. Although these plants will survive, it is beneficial to prevent any seed addition to the seed bank until more effective management strategies can be employed (Averill et al. 2008).

Excavation: One way to manually control small populations of dog-strangling vine is to dig and excavate the whole root system. Do not try to pull the root up by hand as the stems easily break off, leaving root crowns and fragments in the soil that can readily re-sprout. Use spades or shovels to dig underneath the root system. Plants should be removed before they produce seed to prevent additions to the soil's seed bank. Place all plant parts in a plastic bag for disposal in an appropriate landfill (DiTommaso et al. 2005). Excavating should only be used on very small populations as it can be labour intensive and causes soil disturbance. Restoration efforts will be required to fill in the holes where root systems were removed. Restoration should also include re-planting the area with native vegetation to prevent re-invasion of the disturbed area (Lawlor & Raynal, 2002).

Herbicide application: In large invasions where native vegetation has been compromised, it is best to apply herbicides as a foliar spray (Lawlor & Raynal, 2002). Be sure to add a surfactant to help the herbicide penetrate the waxy leaf surface (Douglass et al. 2009). Avoid applying herbicides as a foliar spray to vines that have become intertwined with young trees (Lawlor & Raynal, 2002).

RECOMMENDATIONS FOR INTEGRATED CONTROL OF LARGE INVASIONS

Option #1: With chemical control

In areas with large invasions the use of chemical control is recommended. As plants succumb to the herbicide they can be replaced by a competitive native plant. Do not start re-planting until the population is sufficiently under control, as spot treatments or excavation may be needed to completely eliminate dog-strangling vine from the area. Performing such control measures around newly planted vegetation may prove to be too labour intensive if done before adequate control is achieved (Lawlor & Raynal, 2002).

A combination of manual and chemical control may be needed to control dense patches of dog-strangling vine intertwined with desirable vegetation. The first step to integrated control is an initial application of herbicide using a foliar spray for dense patches, cutting in areas where the vine is intertwined with desirable vegetation. Chemical control should be done in the spring at the bud stage to allow for manual control later in the season (Lawlor & Raynal, 2002).

Option #2: Without chemical control

Dog-strangling vine invasions are particularly difficult to control. Hand-pulling is not effective as the stems easily break-off, leaving behind a root system that will quickly re-sprout. Excavating the entire root system is often successful. However, this method can quickly become too labour intensive to be a feasible management strategy in areas with large invasions. The disturbance caused by digging also promotes the establishment of other invasive plants, often negating any positive effects of control. In areas where chemical control is not an option it is best to try and control the invasion instead of opting for complete eradication. Frequently cutting back the plants will prevent seed production and thus slow the spread of invasion. Planting competitive native species may also help control dog-strangling vine's invasive potential (Averill et al. 2008; Lawlor & Raynal, 2002).

Table 15: Management recommendations for dog-strangling vine (*Vincetoxicum* spp).

Extent of infestation	Small invasions and satellite populations	Large invasions and dense populations
Recommended method of control	Manual Control: excavation	Integrated Control: herbicide application and cutting.
Timing	May-early June.	Herbicide application: Spring. Cutting: Late June.
Disposal	Place all plant parts in a plastic bag and dispose of in an appropriate landfill. Ensure no roots are left behind to resprout.	Place all clipped plants in a plastic bag and dispose of in an appropriate landfill.
Frequency of control	Several times per year. After initial excavation return to collect any resprouting plants from root fragments that were missed.	Herbicide application and clipping once yearly for up to 5 years to ensure that all root systems have been killed and all seeds eliminated from the seed bank.
Length of control	2-3 years.	3-5 years.
Required restoration	Soil disturbance created during excavation must be addressed. Fill in holes and replant with native vegetation.	May require some re-planting to fill in gaps where dense patches of dog-strangling vine eliminated native vegetation.

5.1.11
Goutweed
(*Aegopodium podagraria*)

Other common names:
Bishop's goutweed, Bishop's weed, Ground elder, Goat's-foot, Snow-on-the-mountain

Priority Rating: **MODERATE**

IDENTIFICATION

Goutweed is native to Eurasia. It is a perennial plant with creeping stems. Compound leaves are in groups of 3, with 3 or fewer leaflets per group (Fig. 194). Leaflets often have irregular lobes. The leaves are found in an alternate arrangement along the stem (Kaufman & Kaufman, 2007). Escaped populations of goutweed generally have leaves that are of a solid green colour. Many cultivars have leaves with white borders around their paler green leaves. Both varieties may be seen in natural areas; however, the solid green colour is the most common. White flowers are produced in clusters on top of flowering stalks (Garske & Schimpf, 2005) (Fig. 195).

Figure 194: Two colour varieties of goutweed including solid green[1] (left) and a lighter, multi-coloured version[6] (right).

ENVIRONMENTAL &
ECOLOGICAL IMPACTS

Goutweed will usually establish around forest edges where it can access higher light levels. Once established the creeping stems can quickly spread through the forest understory (Fig. 196). Its aggressive growth pattern often displaces native understory plants, which may inhibit hardwood regeneration (Garske & Schimpf, 2005).

CONTROL

Goutweed has an extensive rhizome that must be removed or severely damaged to prevent re-sprouting. Hand-pulling can be an effective method of control if both the above and belowground portions of the plant are entirely removed. Leaving small root fragments behind will often lead to a new invasion. Mowing in areas with dense stands can be effective if frequently repeated throughout the season. Root reserves must be completely depleted to prevent new invasions. Covering the invaded area with a black tarp will prevent re-sprouting by eliminating access to sunlight. Pay particular attention to the tarp edges and hand-pull any sprouting individuals (Fig. 197). Eventually, root reserves will be depleted and the tarp can be removed. Applying herbicides as a foliar spray may kill goutweed but repeated applications are usually required (Garske & Schimpf, 2005; Kaufman & Kaufman, 2007).

Figure 195: Goutweed flowers[6].

Figure 196: Goutweed invasion in a forest understory[6]

Figure 197: Goutweed control[1].

5.1.12
Oriental Bittersweet
(*Celastrus orbiculatus*)

Other common names:
Asian bittersweet, Japanese bittersweet, Asiatic bittersweet, Round-leaved bittersweet

Priority Rating: **MODERATE**

IDENTIFICATION

Oriental bittersweet is native to Japan, China and Korea (Kaufman & Kaufman, 2007). It is a perennial woody vine. Leaves are round with toothed margins, ending in an abrupt tip. The leaves have an alternate arrangement along the stem. Oriental bittersweet is dioecious with separate male and female plants. Only female plants produce the distinctive berry-like fruits with 3 seed compartments (Fig. 198). These compartments are encased in a yellow capsule that opens as the fruit ripens (Swearingen, 2006). The exotic and the native bittersweet are often mistaken for one another, which makes control difficult. The leaves of American bittersweet (*Celastrus scandens*) are not as circular and the tips are not as abruptly pointed as in Oriental bittersweet leaves (Fig. 199).

Figure 198: Oriental bittersweet fruits[6]

ENVIRONMENTAL & ECOLOGICAL IMPACTS

As a vine, Oriental bittersweet can girdle trees and smother understory vegetation (Fig. 200). It can establish in a forest understory and remain relatively unobtrusive until a canopy gap appears. As light penetrates through the canopy, Oriental bittersweet will quickly grow and climb over native species to compete for available light (Greenberg et al. 2001). Oriental bittersweet competes with native American bittersweet for space and nutrients. As a result, American bittersweet is declining (Steward et al. 2003). Hybridization between the two species is also becoming a problem, as valuable genes may be lost. It is very important to ensure that American bittersweet is not damaged during management activities (Swearingen, 2006).

CONTROL

Hand-pulling is only practical in areas with a few scattered individuals. The entire plant, including the roots, should be removed to prevent re-sprouting. For large vines that have become tangled around valuable trees it is best to make two cuts in the stems so that the portion within reach is severed. The root system can either be removed to prevent re-sprouting or regular cuttings can be made throughout the season to exhaust the root reserves (Kaufman & Kaufman, 2007). A combination of manual and chemical control is recommended for large invasions. A licenced exterminator using the basal bark or cut-stem methods can apply herbicides. Repeated applications may be required to kill the vines. Monitor the area and cut any re-sprouts or perform a second herbicide treatment (Swearingen, 2006).

Figure 199: Comparing the leaves of American bitter-sweet[15] (left) to those of Oriental bittersweet[15] (right).

Figure 200: Oriental bittersweet girdling a tree[6] (left) and smothering native vegetation[35] (right).

5.1.13
Exotic Bush Honeysuckle
(*Lonicera* spp.)

Other common names:
Amur honeysuckle, Morrow's honeysuckle, Tartarian honeysuckle, and Bell's honeysuckle

Priority Rating: MODERATE

IDENTIFICATION

There are several invasive honeysuckles that can negatively impact a hardwood stand. They include amur honeysuckle (*Lonicera maackii*), morrow's honeysuckle (*L. morrowii*), tartarian honeysuckle (*L. tatarica*), and bell's honeysuckle (*L. x bella*). Invasive honeysuckles were introduced from China and Korea. All are shrubs with simple, opposite leaves and showy flowers (Fig. 201). These flowers are white or pink in the spring but slowly fade to yellow later in the season (Fig. 202). An abundance of bright red berries are produced in the fall (Kaufman & Kaufman, 2007) (Fig. 203).

Figure 201: Exotic bush honeysuckle leaves[1].

Figure 202: Exotic bush honeysuckle flowers[1]

ENVIRONMENTAL & ECOLOGICAL IMPACTS

Exotic bush honeysuckles produce leaves earlier than most native species in the spring. Early spring ephemerals evolved as a means of acquiring light before canopy closure. However, bush honeysuckles can out-compete these understory species by towering over them with even earlier emerging leaves. An aggressive growth rate and ability to form a dense shrub layer can exclude native understory species and affect hardwood regeneration (Kaufman & Kaufman, 2007) (Fig. 204). The bright red fruits are very attractive to birds, which leads to the avian dispersal of seeds. However, these fruits are nutrient-poor, which may have negative effects on migrating birds (Williams, 2005). Nest predation rates may also be higher for songbirds nesting in invasive bush honeysuckles. A study by Schmidt and Whelan (1999) found that American robin nests experienced greater rates of predation due to being less protected in invasive bush honeysuckles than in native shrubs such as hawthorns.

CONTROL

Hand-pulling is only practical for small seedlings or saplings. For larger shrubs, mechanical levers such as root wrenches are needed to pry up the root system. Shrubs can be left onsite as long as their roots are exposed and do not touch the soil. This will allow the roots to dry out and eliminates any chance of re-sprouting. Shrubs may also be cut and the roots dug out with a shovel. This can be very labour intensive and causes a large degree of soil disturbance. Clipping re-sprouts may eventually exhaust the root reserves. However, this approach requires constant vigilance and is only practical when dealing with a few individuals. Invasive bush honeysuckles can be controlled using herbicides. A licenced exterminator can apply the chemicals using the basal bark or cut-stump method (Williams, 2005).

Figure 203: Exotic bush honeysuckle berries[1]

Figure 204: Exotic bush honeysuckle in a forest understory[12]

5.1.14
Kudzu
(*Pueraria montana* var. *lobata*)

Other common names:
Japanese arrowroot, Nepalem

Priority Rating: MODERATE

IDENTIFICATION

Kudzu is a perennial vine with a semi-woody stem. The leaves are compound with 3 lobed leaflets that may also be entire (Fig. 205). The leaves have hairy margins and are arranged alternately along the stem. The flowers are pink to purple and grow in long clusters (Fig. 206). The seeds are encased in flat, hairy seedpods. Kudzu was introduced from Japan (Kaufman & Kaufman, 2007).

Figure 205: Comparing lobed[36] (left) and entire kudzu leaflets[12] (right).

Figure 206: The flowers[37] (left) and seedpods[36] (right) of kudzu.

ENVIRONMENTAL & ECOLOGICAL IMPACTS

Kudzu grows in large mats, using other plants as supporting structures. The dense foliage often kills native vegetation by reducing light levels. The vining growth strategy girdles trunks and stems and the rapid and prolific growth rate creates large amounts of biomass that can crush supporting plants and up-root trees. Kudzu grows along forest edges but once established might spread into the forest interior as it destroys native edge species (Bergmann & Swearingen, 2005) (Fig. 207).

Figure 207: Kudzu invading a forest edge[38].

CONTROL

Kudzu has an extensive and robust root system. Taproots can grow very large and weigh hundreds of pounds. The key to controlling an invasion of kudzu is to destroy the taproot through the exhaustion of nutrient reserves or through herbicide application (Kaufman & Kaufman, 2007). Large invasions should be cut and removed. However, since it is often impractical to remove the large taproots, repeated cutting is recommended. After this, close monitoring is required so that any new growth is immediately cut to prevent photosynthesis and prompt the roots to utilize energy to create new sprouts (Bergmann & Swearingen, 2005).

Herbicide application is another method of controlling kudzu invasions. Herbicides are best applied using the cut-stump method. Since kudzu stands are usually dense the stems must be cut so that the herbicide can reach the interior of the stand. Herbicides should be applied by a licenced exterminator immediately after the stems have been cut. Monitor the area and clip any re-sprouts or perform a second application of herbicides as required (Bergmann & Swearingen, 2005).

5.2
Exotic Insects & Disease

5.2.1
Emerald Ash Borer
(*Agrilus planipennis*)

Other common names:
EAB

Priority Rating: HIGH

Figure 208: Emerald ash borer[39].

IDENTIFICATION

ORGANISM

As an adult insect, the emerald ash borer (EAB) has a long, narrow body that ranges in length from 0.75 to 1.5cm. They are shiny with emerald green and metallic copper coloured hues (Fig. 209). Their black or copper eyes appear very large on their heads. The top of the abdomen is a bright metallic red colour that can be seen when the beetle is flying (Lyons et al. 2007) (Fig. 210).

Figure 209: Adult emerald ash borer[39].

Figure 210: Characteristic metallic red abdomen of the emerald ash borer[39].

HOST TREES

The only species directly affected by EAB belong to the ash genus (*Fraxinus* spp.) (Kimoto & Duthie-Holt, 2006) and even exotic ash trees are vulnerable to EAB (Lyons et al. 2007). Emerald ash borer insects are primarily attracted to stressed ash trees, however, in heavy infestations even healthy individuals are attacked (Poland & McCullough, 2006). Ash trees are characterized by their oppositely arranged, pinnately divided compound leaves consisting of 5 to 11 leaflets (Farrar, 1995)(Fig. 211). There are 16 species of ash in North America with 5 found in Ontario. The blue ash (*F. quadrangulata*) and pumpkin ash (*F. profunda*) are relatively rare, found mainly in southwestern areas of Ontario. Black ash (*F. nigra*) is common throughout Ontario, found mostly in wet, swampy areas. White ash (*F. americana*) and red ash (*F. pennsylvanica*) are common and economically valuable lumber species in Ontario (Kershaw, 2001).

Figure 211: Compound leaf of black ash (*Fraxinus nigra*)[8].

SIGNS & SYMPTOMS

EXIT HOLES

The emerald ash borer is host specific to species of the genus *Fraxinus*; all ash trees in North America are susceptible. After larval development is complete, adult beetles emerge from their host tree creating D-shaped exit holes (Fig. 212). These holes are approximately 3.5mm wide and 4mm long. Exit holes can be found on the trunk and branches of ash trees (Kimoto & Duthie-Holt, 2006).

Figure 212: D-shaped exit hole created by the emerald ash borer[40].

FEEDING GALLERIES & BARK DAMAGE

Larvae feeding on the inner sapwood create long curving tunnels called feeding galleries (Fig. 213). These S-shaped feeding galleries can cause vertical cracks on the trunk (Fig. 214). Galleries are generally 6mm wide and vary from 9 to 16cm long. On occasion, up to 30cm long galleries have been observed (Kimoto & Duthie-Holt, 2006).

Figure 213: Feeding galleries[41] created by emerald ash borer larvae

Figure 214: Bark damage caused by emerald ash borer feeding galleries[40].

ADULT FEEDING

Emerald ash borer beetles feed on ash leaves immediately after emerging from the tree trunk as adults. Adult feeding creates notches along the edges of the leaves (Lyons et al. 2007) (Fig. 215). Several leaf notches may be seen along the outer margin. Feeding adults are most active during the day. They may be found seeking shelter under the leaves or in bark fissures during cold or wet weather (McCullough et al. 2008).

Figure 215: Emerald ash borer feeding on an ash leaf[42].

BRANCH DIE-BACK & EPICORMIC SHOOTS

Feeding tunnels created by EAB larvae prevent the transport of sap in the tree, which usually results in death within 2 years. The top branches are usually the first to wilt. In response, ash trees produce new shoots along their lower trunk (Fig. 216), which can be used to detect EAB infestation (OMNR, 2010b).

Figure 216: Crown dieback and epicormic shoots on an infested ash tree[43].

SIMILAR SPECIES, SIGNS & SYMPTOMS

Other *Agrilus* spp.

Several other beetles belonging to the *Agrilus* genus are found in Ontario. Most appear very similar to EAB. Some examples, including the bronze birch borer (*A. anxius*) and the metallic wood-boring beetle (*A. cyanescens*) are shown in Figure 217. Although very similar in appearance, these species do not reproduce on ash trees. The only other species of *Agrilus* known to attack ash in Ontario is *A. subcinctus*; however this species is much smaller than EAB, has a black body and the abdomen has a copper shine. Always look for additional signs and symptoms to help identify potential EAB infestations (GISD, 2006).

Figure 217: Comparing *A. anxius*[44] (left) and *A. cyanescens*[44] (right).

Ash Yellows

The majority of ash species are susceptible to a disease called ash yellows. This disease is caused by a specialized group of bacteria (*Candidatus* Phytoplasma fraxini) that affects the phloem of the tree (Griffiths et al. 1999). The disease is spread by leafhoppers. Small sections of the crown will experience branch dieback as a result of phloem disruption (Fig. 218). In contrast, EAB infestations can cause branch dieback throughout the crown, eventually killing the tree (Sinclair & Griffiths, 1994).

Figure 218: Ash showing symptoms of ash yellows disease[45].

Feeding Galleries & Exit Holes

Various insect species can create similar tunnels and exit holes in ash trees that can be confused with those of EAB. Although the actual insects look nothing like EAB, their damage may appear similar. One example is the native red-headed ash borer (*Neoclytus acuminatus*). This red and yellow insect is quite distinct and its larvae feed on the sapwood of ash trees, creating feeding tunnels that can kill the tree. These tunnels are generally not as meandering as EAB's S-shaped galleries (Fig. 219). The exit holes are circular unlike the distinctive D-shaped exit holes made by EAB (Herms, 2007).

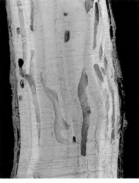

Figure 219: Red-headed ash borer, exit holes[46] and feeding galleries[18].

BIOLOGY

TAXONOMIC HIERARCHY

Kingdom	Animalia
Phylum	Arthropoda
Class	Insecta
Order	Coleoptera
Family	Buprestidae
Genus	*Agrilus*
Species	*Agrilus planipennis*

ORIGIN & DISTRIBUTION

EAB is a bark beetle native to Asia, where it can be found in China, Japan, Korea, Mongolia, Taiwan and Russia (Haack et al. 2002). It was first discovered in North America in 2002 in Michigan, and shortly thereafter in Ontario. However, evidence indicates that it went unnoticed since the early 1990's (Siegert et al. 2007). EAB is very difficult to detect, especially at the early stages of infestation. Any noticeable signs and symptoms are often attributed to other environmental stressors such as other insects, pathogens and weather events (Lyons, 2010). Since its detection in Michigan and Ontario in 2002, surveys have confirmed its presence in other states such as Indiana and Ohio (Cartwell, 2007).

LIFE CYCLE

The emerald ash borer has a four-stage life cycle including egg, larva, pupa and adult (Fig. 220). Adult females deposit their eggs on the trunk or branches of ash trees during the summer months. Each individual female can produce 50 to 90 eggs during their 3 to 6 week lifespan. Eggs hatch within 2 weeks and the larvae bore into the sapwood creating S-shaped feeding galleries. Larvae slowly develop through 4 instars and stop feeding by November. These pre-pupae overwinter within the sapwood. Pupation begins in the spring and lasts for about 3 weeks. After pupation, adult beetles create a D-shaped hole through which they emerge (Kimoto & Duthie-Holt, 2006; Poland & McCullough, 2006).

Figure 220: Life cycle of the emerald ash borer: egg[28], larva[39], pupa[39] and adult[43].

IMPACTS

EAB is destroying ash populations in Ontario. The larvae feeding on the inner sapwood of ash trees effectively cut off the transportation of sap within the tree (Fig. 221). Mortality usually occurs within 2 to 4 years after EAB establishes in large mature trees but may only take 1 year for small trees and saplings. The 5 species of ash in Ontario contribute to forest biodiversity and are a source of food and habitat for wildlife (Poland & McCullough, 2006). Ash is also a popular ornamental tree in urban areas and is an important commercial lumber and pulp species. Considering that ash mortality due to EAB is 100%, the environmental, aesthetic and economic impacts caused by this invasive species represent a major challenge to Ontario (Cartwell, 2007). As natural regeneration of ash decreases due to a diminishing seed bank, the natural regeneration of ash in EAB-infested areas seems unlikely (Kashian & Witter, 2011).

Figure 221: Larval tunneling damage causing tree mortality[39].

VECTORS & PATHWAYS

The emerald ash borer was most likely introduced into North America through international trade in wood packaging material. Once in North America, it could easily be spread either by humans, through the transportation of wood products, or by flight during the adult life stage. Adult beetles have the potential to fly up to 7km per day (Taylor et al. 2010) and can create small colonies in previously uninfested areas, in some cases far removed from the main advancing front (Liebold & Tobin, 2008). However, humans are the leading cause of long distance dispersal, mainly through the movement of firewood (Petrice & Haack, 2007).

MANAGEMENT PRACTICES

PREVENTION STRATEGIES

Promoting a healthy woodlot while increasing forest diversity will help to deter EAB infestations. Healthy woodlots are often comprised of a wide range of species of different ages and sizes. This helps to decrease the number of available hosts, thereby creating poorer conditions for EAB invasion (OMNR, 2010b).

In Ontario, a quarantine zone has been established by the CFIA, under the authority of the Plant Protection Act, to help control the spread of EAB. This quarantine restricts the movement of ash materials that could be vectors. These items include live or dead ash trees such as nursery stock, logs, leaves, lumber, wood and wood chips. In effect, it restricts the movement of any type of firewood (Poland & McCullough, 2006). This is important as studies have shown that EAB females will oviposit on ash trees after they have been cut (Anulewicz et al. 2008) and that EAB can successfully complete their life cycle on freshly cut material (Petrice & Haack, 2007). Indeed, preventive measures such as establishing quarantines do help to slow down the spread of EAB and other invasive forest pests (CFIA, 2011b).

EARLY DETECTION TECHNIQUES

Visual surveys and monitoring activities are crucial for EAB detection. When walking through the woodlot it is best to take a close look at a few individual ash trees. Check for signs and symptoms of EAB invasion such as exit holes, epicormic shoots, and weak or dying ash trees. Ensure that monitoring activities are a regular routine. It is often difficult to detect EAB before the infestation becomes severe. This is because EAB spends most of its life cycle underneath the bark (Cappaert et al. 2005). Also, when EAB populations are low, the small number of larvae tunneling in the inner sapwood has little effect on halting sap transportation (McCullough et al. 2008). Emerald ash borer establishment on uninfected trees have frequently been observed to occur in the upper canopy as opposed to the trunk. This is one more reason why EAB infestations are difficult to detect (Anulewicz et al. 2007).

Trap trees have been used as a means of detecting whether EAB is present in a woodlot. A trap tree is girdled with the intent of eliciting the release of stress related chemical signals that attract adult EAB (Poland & McCullough, 2010). Several studies have shown that EAB prefer weakened ash trees. However, they are equally capable of attacking healthy trees (McCullough et al. 2006; Poland et al. 2006).

Figure 222: Emerald ash borer trap tree[40].

Constructed traps made with a sticky surface can also be used to trap EAB adults. These traps utilize visual and olfactory cues to attract beetles. Colour is an important visual cue for EAB. Purple and green are the most attractive colours likely because they mimic reflections of the trunk and leaves of ash trees as seen by EAB (Lyons, 2010). Olfactory cues are attractive to EAB because they mimic the odour of stressed ash trees (Rodriguez-Saona et al. 2006; de Groot et al. 2008; Crook et al. 2008). Pheromones are also an olfactory cue that can be used as an attractant on the traps (Lyons, 2010).

CONTROL OPTIONS

Currently there are two ways of managing EAB infestations, including the removal of infested trees and the use of systemic insecticides. Infested trees can be cut down, chipped and burned (Fig. 223). Chipping and burning ensures that all life stages including the eggs, larvae, pupae and adults are destroyed. Trees should be cut down before the adults emerge in late May and June to prevent natural dispersal (Poland & McCullough, 2010). Although this method can be both destructive and costly it should be done as early as possible. Infested trees will eventually die and may need to be removed anyway due to their potential to become a hazard to people. Moreover, removing and destroying infested trees helps to prevent further spread. Considering that EAB populations are already abundant and since some infested trees may show little or no sign of infestation, complete eradication is currently unattainable (Cartwell, 2007).

Figure 223: Removing ash trees infested with emerald ash borer[43].

There is one systemic insecticide available for purchase in Canada that can be used in EAB control. TreeAzin was created by the Canadian Forest Service and BioForest Technologies Incorporated. This insecticide must be applied by a licenced exterminator and is only effective for a two-year period. Injecting ash trees with this insecticide will help to protect EAB free trees and may save some of those that are lightly infested (BioForest, 2012). Using TreeAzin for EAB control may be practical for use in woodlots with a very small percentage of ash trees or on ornamental trees in urban areas. Conversely, it can quickly become impractical in areas with large numbers of ash. The insecticide must be reapplied biannually in areas where EAB populations persist, which can be costly (Lyons, 2010).

5.2.2
Asian Long-horned Beetle
(*Anoplophora glabripennis*)

Other common names:
Asian longhorn beetle, ALB, Basicosta white-spotted longicorn beetle, Starry sky beetle

Priority Rating: **HIGH**

Figure 224: Asian long-horned beetle[49].

IDENTIFICATION

ORGANISM

Adult Asian long-horned beetles are black with a glossy coating that reflects blue. They range from 2 to 3.5cm long. Adult females have antennae that are as long as their body whereas adult males have antennae that are twice their body length (Fig. 225). These antennae are made up of 11 segments with an alternating white and black colour. Approximately 20 white or yellow spots (Fig. 226) are found on each wing cover (Ric et al. 2007).

Figure 225: Comparing a female[50] (left) and a male[50] (right) Asian long-horned beetle.

Figure 226: Asian long-horned beetle with yellow wing spots[50].

HOST TREES

The Asian long-horned beetle only attacks hardwood trees (i.e., deciduous trees). However, some hardwood species are more susceptible to the insect than others. They include maple (*Acer* sp.), birch (*Betula* sp.), poplar (*Populus* sp.), willow (*Salix* sp.), elm (*Ulmus* sp.), horsechestnut (*Aesculus* sp.), sycamore (*Platanus* sp.), mountain-ash (*Sorbus* sp.) and hackberry (*Celtis* sp.). Members of the maple genus seem to be the preferred host of Asian long-horned beetle in Ontario (Kimoto & Duthie-Holt, 2006; Hu et al. 2009).

SIGNS & SYMPTOMS

OVIPOSITION OR EGG PITS

Female Asian long-horned beetles use their mandibles to chew holes in the bark of hardwood trees. They deposit their eggs in these cavities (Kimoto & Duthie-Holt, 2006), also called ovipo-

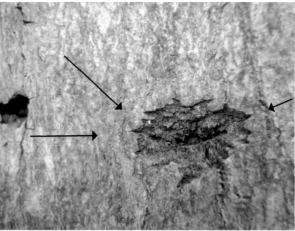

sition pits, which have characteristic mandible marks (Fig. 227) and range in size from 1 to 15mm (Ric et al. 2007).

EXIT HOLES

Adult beetles create circular holes as they emerge after larval development is complete (Fig. 228). Exit holes ranging in size from 6 to 12mm can be found anywhere on the tree trunk, branches and exposed roots (Kimoto & Duthie-Holt, 2006).

FEEDING GALLERIES & BARK DAMAGE

Larval feeding can cause separation between the bark and sapwood. As a result, the bark may appear raised, hollow or cracked (Fig. 229). After one year, the bark may begin to fall off the tree, leaving large exposed areas with the tunnels or feeding galleries visible (Ric et al. 2007).

Figure 227: Asian long-horned beetle oviposition pit with arrows pointing to mandible marks[51].

Figure 228: An exit hole created by an Asian long-horned beetle[52].

Figure 229: Bark damage[40] (left) and exposed feeding galleries[53] (right).

FRASS OR SHAVINGS

Tunneling and feeding larvae leave behind a mixture of sawdust and feces that is collectively called frass (Fig. 230). Frass can sometimes be seen protruding from exit holes or cracks in the bark and can accumulate at the base of trees or in the forks of branches (Kimoto & Duthie-Holt, 2006).

ADULT FEEDING

Asian long-horned beetles spend two weeks feeding and mating after they emerge from trees as adults. They feed on the outer tissues of branches, twigs and petioles (Fig. 231), and consume the primary and secondary veins of leaves (Ric et al. 2007).

Figure 230: Frass created by the Asian long-horned beetle[40].

Figure 231: Damage caused by adult Asian long-horned beetles feeding on branches[54] (left) and leaves[40] (right).

BRANCH DIEBACK & HARDWOOD MORTALITY

High population densities of Asian long-horned beetle can weaken and eventually kill hardwood trees. Branch dieback caused as a result of larval tunneling occurs from the top branches downward, eventually killing the tree (Fig. 232). Repeated infestations at lower population densities can produce similar results (Nowak et al. 2001).

Figure 232: Branch dieback[40] (left) and hardwood mortality[40] (right) resulting from Asian long-horned beetle infestations.

SIMILAR SPECIES, SIGNS & SYMPTOMS

Whitespotted sawyer (*Monochamus scutellatus*)

The whitespotted sawyer is native to North America. Females lay their eggs on conifers as opposed to the hardwood species that host the Asian long-horned beetle. The wing covers are black and appear rough in contrast to the blue-black glossy wing covers of the Asian long-horned beetle (Fig. 233). Female whitespotted sawyer beetles have white markings on their wing covers similar to those of Asian long-horned beetles whereas the males are completely black. The easiest way to differentiate between the two species is to look for a white or yellow spot between the top of the wing covers. Asian long-horned beetles do not have that distinctive spot (OMNR, 2010c).

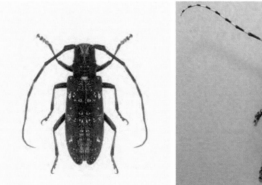

Figure 233: Comparing the whitespotted sawyer[55] (left) and the Asian long-horned beetle[56] (right).

Oviposition or Egg pits

Other insects, wildlife and people can cause damage to the outer bark of hardwood species that may appear similar to the pits created by Asian long-horned beetle. Look for mandible marks to determine if an Asian long-horned beetle caused the damage. These marks appear on the outer edges of the oviposition pit, giving the wound a jagged appearance. Oviposition pits are very small, ranging in size from 1 to 15mm (Ric et al. 2007).

Exit Holes

Several species create exit holes similar to those made by adult Asian long-horned beetles. Remember that Asian long-horned beetles only infest certain hardwood trees, not conifers. The gallmaking maple borer (*Xylotrechus aceris*) and the maple callus borer (*Synanthedon acerni*) are two examples of species that create exit holes similar to those of Asian long-horned beetle (Fig. 234). Pay attention to the size of the holes. Gallmaking maple and maple callus borers create exit holes that are less than 5mm in diameter whereas those made by Asian long-horned beetles are 6 to 14mm in diameter (Ric et al. 2007).

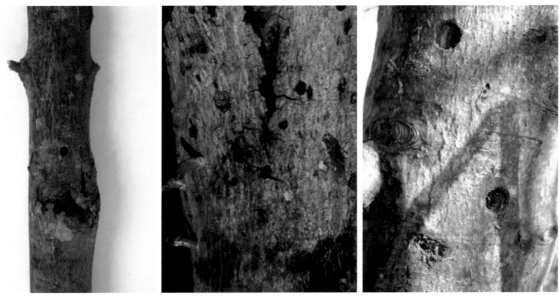

Figure 234: Comparing the exit holes of the gallmaking maple borer[57] (left), to those of the maple callus borer[57] (centre) and the Asian long-horned beetle[51] (right).

Feeding Galleries & Bark Damage

There is an abundance of other insect species that create tunnels similar to those made by the Asian long-horned beetle in hardwoods. It can be extremely difficult to identify the causative agent of feeding galleries just based on tunneling patterns. Note the similarities between the tunnels and larvae of Asian long-horned beetle and those of poplar borer (*Saperda calcarata*), carpenterworm (*Prionoxystus robiniae*), and red oak borer (*Enaphalodes rufulus*) in Figure 235. Always look for other signs and symptoms that can help identify the correct species. For further information, see the training guide to detecting the signs and symptoms of Asian-long-horned beetle injury written by Ric et al (2007).

Figure 235: (A) Comparing feeding tunnels made by poplar borer larvae[57] (left) with those made by the Asian long-horned beetle larvae[52] (right); (B) comparing the feeding galleries created by the carpenterworm[57] (left) with those made by the Asian long-horned beetle[40] (right); (C) comparing the feeding galleries created by the red oak borer[58] (left) with those made by the Asian long-horned beetle[51] (right).

Frass or Shavings

Frass or shavings are created by many insect borers. Frass can be found at the base of hardwood trees or protruding through holes and cracks in the bark (Kimoto & Duthie-Holt, 2006). Figure 236 shows how frass created by tunneling Asian long-horned beetle larvae can easily be confused with that created by other insects such as the white oak borer (*Goes tigrinus*).

Figure 236: Comparing frass of the white oak borer[57] (left) to that of the Asian long-horned beetle[51] (right).

BIOLOGY

TAXONOMIC HIERARCHY

Kingdom	Animalia
Phylum	Arthropoda
Class	Insecta
Order	Coleoptera
Family	Cerambycidae
Genus	*Anoplophora*
Species	*Anoplophora glabripennis*

ORIGIN & DISTRIBUTION

The Asian long-horned beetle is native to Asia. The first documented infestations in North America occurred in New York (1996), Chicago (1998), New Jersey (2002 & 2004) and Ontario (2003). Introduction was likely a result of having individuals at various life stages in solid wood packaging material used in international trade (Fig. 237). In Ontario, infestations were located between the cities of Toronto and Vaughan. The species was detected rapidly upon introduction and eradication efforts were immediately put into place. Approximately 17 000 hardwood trees were destroyed in the first year following detection and, although more infested trees have since been found and destroyed, the invasion appears to be under control (OMNR, 2010c).

Figure 237: Solid wood packing material is a vector for Asian long-horned beetle introduction[60].

LIFE CYCLE

The Asian long-horned beetle has a four-stage life cycle including egg, larva, pupa and adult (Fig. 238). In Ontario they require 2 to 3 years to complete their life cycle (Ric et al. 2007). Adult females deposit their eggs under the bark of hardwood trees. Each female can lay up to 80 eggs during an average adult life span of approximately 40 days (OMNR, 2010c). After hatching, larvae feed on the inner sapwood and may take 1 to 2 years to fully mature. They then enter the pupal stage, usually in June and July, and adult beetles emerge approximately 20 days later (Ric et al. 2007).

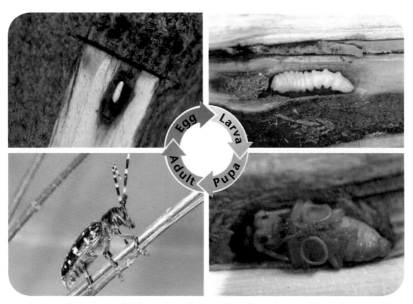

Figure 238: Typical life cycle of the Asian long horned beetle: egg[60], larva[52], pupa[60], and adult[49].

IMPACTS

The Asian long-horned beetle attacks healthy trees. The larvae feed on the inner sapwood creating a series of tunnels that effectively block the movement of sap. This can kill the tree depending on insect population densities and frequency of establishment. The tunnels created in the wood greatly decrease timber value (Cartwell, 2007)(Fig. 239). The insect's preference for maple trees is a serious threat to maple syrup operations. In addition, large numbers of dead or decaying hardwood trees affect the aesthetic value and biological diversity of a forest (Dodds & Orwig, 2011).

Figure 239: Galleries made by Asian long-horned beetle reduce timber value[51].

Until recently, all Asian long-horned beetle infestations occurred in urban areas. In 2008 a new outbreak was reported in Worcester, Massachusetts. This outbreak was particularly concerning because the infestation was encroaching into a hardwood forest. Dodds & Orwig (2011) used this outbreak to determine that Asian long-horned beetle can indeed disperse rapidly. Their findings have caused a great deal of concern. Asian long-horned beetle has the capability of permanently altering economically and ecologically important hardwood forests throughout North America.

VECTORS & PATHWAYS

The Asian long-horned beetle is problematic in parts of its native range, particularly in northern China. Populations exploded after a large number of suitable host trees, mainly in the *Populus* genus, were planted during a reforestation campaign on old farmlands. It is hypothesized that such rise in abundance greatly enhanced the probability of introductions into other countries (Hajek, 2007).

It is the general consensus that the Asian long-horned beetle arrived in North America in solid wood packing material. International trade is a common pathway of exotic species transportation to new countries. Regulations and inspections are mandatory. However, eggs, larvae and even adult beetles can be extremely difficult to detect and it is impossible to inspect every single product crossing the border (Smith et al. 2009). Adult beetles can disperse approximately 1 to 3km over their lifespan, contributing to the natural spread of established populations (Bancroft & Smith, 2005).

MANAGEMENT PRACTICES

PREVENTION STRATEGIES

The CFIA established a quarantine zone to control the population of Asian long-horned beetles found in the Greater Toronto area in 2003. Firewood, live trees, lumber and wood chips are prohibited from moving out of the regulated area (CFIA, 2012b). Woodlot owners can help prevent the spread of Asian long-horned beetles by increasing tree species diversity. This has helped suppress outbreaks in China (Hu et al. 2009). It is important to avoid introducing firewood and other wood products that may harbour eggs, larvae or adult beetles (Smith et al. 2009).

EARLY DETECTION TECHNIQUES

Early detection of Asian long-horned beetle infestations requires the regular monitoring of the woodlot by undertaking visual inspections of the bark and branches of random hardwood trees. Look for various signs and symptoms to avoid misidentifications (Turgeon et al. 2010).

CONTROL OPTIONS

The primary method of control and possible eradication of Asian long-horned beetle is to destroy infested trees and all potentially infested trees within a given radius (Fig. 240). Removal of all potential host trees within a 400m radius around the infested tree appears to have successfully controlled the outbreak in the Toronto area. The trees were cut and the wood chipped and burned to ensure that all eggs and larvae were killed (Cartwell, 2007). Approximately 28 700 trees have been removed to date from the infested area. The CFIA has offered compensation to property owners to replace any trees that were lost as a result of the eradication campaign (CFIA, 2012b).

Figure 240: Removing a tree infested with Asian long-horned beetle[61].

Since Asian long-horned beetle is established in North America the risk of re-introduction to a quarantined area is high. Thus, increased awareness is needed to help detect new infestations early. The earlier an infestation is detected the easier it is to eradicate and control. Woodlot owners should become familiar with the signs and symptoms of an Asian long-horned beetle infestation. Report any signs of Asian long-horned beetle to the CFIA and/or OMNR as soon as possible (OMNR, 2010c).

5.2.3
Chestnut Blight
(*Cryphonectria parasitica*)

Other common names:
Chestnut canker, Chestnut bark disease

Priority Rating: HIGH

Figure 241: Chestnut blight⁴.

IDENTIFICATION

CAUSAL ORGANISM

The fungal pathogen *Cryphonectria parasitica* is the causal agent of chestnut blight disease. Species belonging to the genus *Cryphonectria* are characterized by stromata (i.e., mass of fungal filaments and host plant tissues) that are partially submerged under the bark of the host tree (Kazmierczak et al. 2005). Orange asexual spores, called conidia, have a convex shape giving them a swollen appearance. Sexual spores, or ascospores, containing partitions created by a single septum also characterize species belonging to *Cryphonectria* (Gryzenhout et al. 2006). *Cryphonectria parasitica* produces an abundance of orange conidia and yellow ascospores that may at times be seen on the outer bark of the host tree (Fig. 242). Underneath the bark, the fungus has a fan-like growth form (Horst, 2008).

Figure 242: Orange fruiting bodies[62] (left) and yellow spores[41] (right) of the chestnut blight fungus.

HOST(S)

The two most susceptible host species to the chestnut blight fungus are the American (*Castanea dentata*) (Fig. 243) and European chestnut (*C. sativa*). This exotic disease has hit the American chestnut the hardest, whereas in its native range has only had a minor effect on four species of chestnut. These include Chinese chestnut (*C. mollissima*), Henry chinkapin (*C. henryi*), Japanese chestnut (*C. crenata*) and Seguin chestnut (*C. seguinii*), which have all developed a level of resistance to the disease. There is evidence that the fungus can also grow on other hosts such as oak, maple, sumac and hickory. However, it causes little to no damage to these hosts (Diller, 1965).

Figure 243: American chestnut leaves[62] (left) and fruit[5] (right)

SIGNS AND SYMPTOMS

CANKERS

The infection caused by the chestnut blight fungus promotes the formation of callus tissue and cankers (Fig. 244). These cankers cause the bark to split, creating cracks that can vary in size from several centimeters to upwards of a metre (Agrios, 2005). Cankers may appear orange or yellow due to the presence of fungal fruiting bodies and spores (CFS, 2011).

Figure 244: Stem cankers on young[63] (left) and old[40] (right)
chestnut trees.

WILTING FOLIAGE

Wilting foliage is a sign of chestnut blight infection (Fig. 245). The chestnut blight fungus starts by infecting the bark and outer sapwood but eventually spreads over the entire circumference of branches and trunks, compromising the vascular system of the tree. Water and nutrients can no longer move from the roots to the leaves, which results in yellowing and wilting foliage (Anagnostakis, 1982).

Figure 245: Wilting foliage on an American chestnut infected with chestnut blight[41].

EPICORMIC SHOOTS

Epicormic shoots are often a sign of stress in deciduous species. As the chestnut blight fungus spreads around the circumference of the trunk it affects the vascular cambium, preventing water from reaching the upper branches and leaves. In response, the tree sends out epicormic shoots underneath the cankers and dead tissue (Fig. 246) (Anagnostakis, 1987).

Figure 246: Epicormic shoots growing below a chestnut blight-induced canker[41].

SIMILAR SPECIES, SIGNS & SYMPTOMS

There are several species of parasitic fungi belonging to the genus *Nectria* that can cause similar symptoms to those of chestnut blight. These species of *Nectria* infect hardwood trees and create target-like cankers or large areas of callus tissue (Fig. 247). Some *Nectria* species may infect chestnut trees but these cankers are rarely fatal (Brandt, 1964). Cankers and cracks may also form on the trunks and branches of American chestnut as a result of frost damage or sunscald. This damage usually occurs as a result of fluctuating temperatures (i.e., as the water freezes and thaws, exerting pressure on the outer bark) and callus tissue is produced by the tree in response to the damage (Swift et al. 2008).

Figure 247: Target-like cankers[41] (left) and excessive callus tissue (right)[41] on native hardwoods resulting from *Nectria* infection.

BIOLOGY

TAXONOMIC HIERARCHY

Kingdom	Fungi
Division	Ascomycota
Class	Sordariomycetes
Order	Diaporthales
Family	Valsaceae
Genus	*Cryphonectria*
Species	*Cryphonectria parasitica*

ORIGIN & DISTRIBUTION

The chestnut blight fungus was likely introduced into North America on nursery stock from Asia. It was first discovered in New York in 1904 when American chestnut trees started deteriorating (Diller, 1965). The disease spread very quickly and within a period of 50 years it was present across the entire range of the American chestnut. It is estimated that 3.5 billion American chestnut trees have been killed by this pathogen (Turchetti & Maresi, 2008). The first reports of the disease in Ontario occurred in the 1920's. Today, less than 700 trees have been documented in the Carolinian zone of southern Ontario, the American chestnut's natural range (Fig. 248). The majority of surviving trees occur in the forest understory as non-reproductive individuals (Tindall et al, 2004). Chestnut blight has also been introduced to Europe where it is causing similar devastation on the European chestnut. However, evidence of natural recovery from blight symptoms has been observed since the early 1950's (Brewer, 1995). For more information on natural recovery see discussion on hypovirulence in control options.

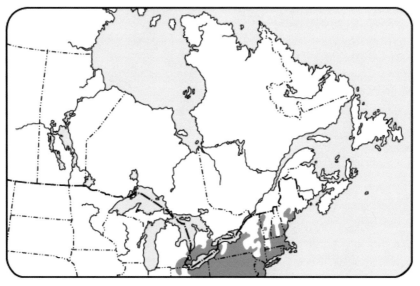

Figure 248: Natural range of the American chestnut (*C. dentata*)[64].

DISEASE CYCLE

The fungal pathogen *C. parasitica* overwinters within the sapwood of its host tree. In the spring, ascospores (sexual spores) and conidia (asexual spores) are released into the environment (Tattar, 1978). Ascospores are released and transported to new hosts via wind currents while conidia are transported with the help of rainwater, animals and insects (Kazmierczak et al. 2005). Spores are dispersed throughout the year, with wet weather enhancing dispersal ability (Sinclair & Lyon, 2005). Spores infect new hosts through wounds in the bark and, once there, germinate and develop filaments (i.e., hyphae) that invade the healthy tissue of the inner bark and cambium. A structure called a stroma is formed that houses the fruiting bodies in which spores are formed (Kazmierczak et al. 2005). Figure 249 demonstrates the disease cycle of chestnut blight.

Formation of fruiting bodies and spores[41].

Spores transported by wind, rain or other organisms to new hosts[66].

Cankers are formed at sites of infection[63].

Spores infect host trees through wounds in the bark[67].

Figure 249: Disease cycle of chestnut blight.

IMPACTS

The greatest impact resulting from the introduction of chestnut blight is its devastating effects on the American chestnut. Both the provincial and federal governments have listed the American chestnut as an endangered species (Environment Canada, 2011; OMNR, 2012b). The loss of the vast majority of large American chestnuts in southern Ontario has had an impact on forest biodiversity. Prior to the introduction of the disease, southern Ontario had as many as 2 million American chestnut trees. Today less than 700 trees have been documented in Ontario (Tindall et al. 2004). Chestnut blight does not kill the root system thus allowing the American chestnut to escape extinction by existing as small saplings in the forest understory (Fig. 250). However, there is little possibility of these saplings becoming established because they quickly become infected with age (Sinclair & Lyon, 2005).

Figure 250: American chestnut surviving in the forest understory[27].

VECTORS & PATHWAYS

Spores of the chestnut blight fungus are constantly being released from infected trees. Ascospores (sexual spores) are transported long distances via wind currents. Conidia (asexual spores) are transported shorter distances with the help of rainwater and animal or insect vectors (Manion, 1991). The fungus can survive even after the host tree has died. In fact, it has been observed growing on fallen logs. As such, the movement of firewood could contribute to the spread of this devastating disease (Diller, 1965). Other tree species, such as oaks, maples, sumacs and hickories, may also act as hosts allowing the fungus to remain viable in the forest even after the loss of the American chestnut as a primary host. These genera have varying degrees of susceptibility to the fungus; only the American chestnut appears to die as a result of the infection (Tindall et al. 2004).

MANAGEMENT PRACTICES

PREVENTION STRATEGIES

Keeping a diverse and healthy woodlot is the best means of alleviating the effects of chestnut blight. Strong and healthy chestnut trees have a better chance of resisting infection or recovering should they become infected (Boland et al. 2000). Competition from other forest trees, heavy frosts, and the presence of other insects and pathogens increase the damage caused by chestnut blight infections (Griffin, 2000). The American chestnut is shade intolerant and requires high light levels for optimal growth (Fig. 251). Since healthy trees may be less susceptible to infection, consider removing any trees that are directly competing with American chestnut. This will promote vigorous growth and contribute to the overall health of the tree (Boland et al. 2000).

Figure 251: A healthy American chestnut leaf[5].

It is good practice to limit the movement of firewood that may act as a vector for spreading the disease. Be especially careful during woodlot management activities not to damage or wound trees as chestnut blight spreads through airborne or organism-transported spores that can infect healthy trees through wounds in the bark (Boland et al. 2000).

EARLY DETECTION TECHNIQUES

It is important to know if American chestnut is present in your woodlot. Woodlot surveys are encouraged to identify the species composition of the forest. If American chestnut is present, it is recommended that these individuals are monitored for signs of chestnut blight infection. Becoming familiar with the American chestnut trees in your woodlot will help you to recognize any new signs or symptoms of infection (Boland et al. 2000). Pay particular attention to the small branches. Infection usually occurs in smaller branches before it spreads to larger, more prominent ones. Wilting foliage and branch dieback is another symptom to be on the lookout for (Sinclair & Lyon, 2005).

CONTROL OPTIONS

There are several ways in which the chestnut blight epidemic is currently being handled in Ontario, including the implementation of forest management practices, the incorporation of hypovirulence, and the development of blight-resistant genotypes.

American chestnut has not been completely eliminated from North America's forests because the rootstocks are not affected by the disease. Once infected, the aboveground portion of the tree will die off leaving an uninfected rootstock that will periodically send up new shoots. However, these emerging shoots are not immune to the disease and usually become blighted with age. Rootstocks may eventually succumb to the continuous pressure of diseased stems (Turchetti & Maresi, 2008). Thus, it is important to keep these understory saplings healthy by alleviating environmental stresses and promoting blight resistance through proper forest management (Sisco, 2012).

American chestnut is a shade intolerant species that benefits from thinning practices. Harvesting a small portion of the trees in the woodlot to create openings in the canopy and discourage competition among desirable species will allow the American chestnut to establish. Cultural practices such as removing infected twigs and branches are recommended to lower the fungal population in the area. These infected branches should be promptly bagged and incinerated (Boland et al. 2000). Remember that American chestnut is considered an endangered species protected by the Endangered Species Act, 2007. Consult a species-at-risk biologist from the OMNR before removing an American chestnut tree.

In the early 1950's, European chestnuts in Italy were observed to be healing from the chestnut blight symptoms (Brewer, 1995). The chestnut blight fungus contained a virus that made the blight pathogen less virulent to their hosts. This type of natural recovery has been termed hypovirulence (Barakat et al. 2009). American chestnut trees with hypovirulence exhibit superficial cankers that affect the outer bark while leaving the vascular cambium intact. This ultimately allows them to survive an otherwise deadly disease (Brewer, 1995). Hypovirulence has since been documented to occur in American chestnuts in several locations in North America (Griffin et al, 1983; Brewer, 1995) including Ontario, Canada (Melzer & Boland, 1999; Tindal et al. 2004). Researchers have been attempting to introduce the hypovirulent strains throughout the American chestnut's range, however with limited success. Natural dispersal of the hypovirulent strains is almost non-existent. This may be due to reduced spore production as well as the inability for certain virulent strains to fuse successfully with the hypovirulent strains (Manion, 1991; Griffin, 2000).

Research on genetic engineering and the creation of transgenic trees (i.e., American chestnut containing blight-resistant genes from Chinese chestnut) is currently underway. These potentially blight-resistant genes may help the American chestnut gain resistance. However, introducing transgenic trees to the forest ecosystem is a matter of debate (Hirsch, 2012).

Another method currently being investigated is interspecific hybridization. Creating blight-resistant Chinese/American chestnut hybrids using a method of backcross breeding is currently underway in Canada by the Canadian Chestnut Council (www.canadianchestnutcouncil.org) and in the United States by the American Chestnut Foundation (www.acf.org). The goal of backcross breeding is to create blight-resistant trees that are morphologically similar to the American chestnut. Hybrids of Chinese and American chestnut are bred over three generations with pure American chestnuts. This breeding method creates trees that will appear in every aspect similar to American chestnut with the added benefit of blight resistance (Diskin et al. 2006). It is expected that the small percentage of exotic genes will provide the same level of natural resistance as that observed in chestnut species that co-evolved with *C. parasitica* (Griffin, 2000). Field trials are currently underway to test the level of blight-resistance in natural forest ecosystems (Smith, 2012).

5.2.4
Beech Bark Disease Complex
(*Cryptococcus fagisuga* & *Neonectria* spp.)

Other common names:
BBD, Beech bark canker, *Neonectria* canker

Priority Rating: **HIGH**

Figure 252: Beach bark disease

IDENTIFICATION

CAUSAL ORGANISMS

Beech bark disease is caused by the combined effects of an insect and a pathogen. The beech scale insect (*Cryptococcus fagisuga*) is very small, only reaching lengths of approximately 1mm (Fig. 253). These tiny insects feed and lay their eggs on American beech (*Fagus grandifolia*) and European beech (*F. sylvatica*). The larvae form a protective white, waxy coating that hides them from view (Fig. 254). In heavy infestations this substance can cover large portions of the trunk (Wainhouse, 1980). Feeding by the scale insect kills cells in the outer bark tissues creating wounds in which pathogen infection can occur (Ehrlich, 1934).

Figure 253: Beech scale (*Cryptococcus fagisuga*)[41].

Figure 254: White larval secretions created by beech scale[68].

The primary fungal pathogen associated with beech bark disease is the invasive *Neonectria faginata*. A native fungus, *N. ditissima*, can also infect beech after scale colonization, however severe infections are rare in Ontario (McLaughlin & Greifenhagen, 2012). Both species form red fruiting bodies, called perithecia, which can be seen on the outer bark (Fig. 255). Spores are released from the perithecia and transported to new hosts via wind and rain (Houston & O'Brien, 1983).

Figure 255: Fruiting bodies of *Neonectria* species[69].

HOST(S)

Two species of beech are primarily affected by beech bark disease in Ontario: American beech (*Fagus grandifolia*), which is native to North America and European beech (*F. sylvatica*). American beech is shade tolerant and typically occurs in climax forests. Conversely, European beech is commonly planted as an ornamental in Ontario. The leaves of American beech have 9-14 vein pairs whereas European beech has 5-9 vein pairs (Fig. 256). The teeth on the margins of American beech are more prominent than those of European beech (Farrar, 1995).

Figure 256: Comparing the leaves of American beech[1] (left) to those of European beech[15] (right).

SIGNS & SYMPTOMS

WHITE, WAXY WOOL

The first sign of beech bark disease is the occurrence of beech scale, whose larvae secrete a white wool-like substance (Fig. 257). As insect populations increase the tree becomes covered with white larval secretions and in large infestations the main stem can appear almost entirely white (Wainhouse, 1980) (Fig. 258).

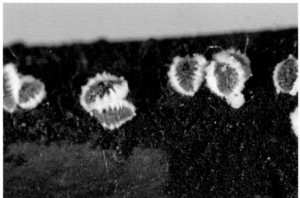

Figure 257: Scale insect producing a white, waxy wool[31].

Figure 258: American beech covered in larval secretions from beech scale[41].

NECROTIC SPOTS

Infection by *Neonectria* fungi causes necrosis of the bark and inner sapwood, which may produce a reddish-brown sap (Fig. 259). As the bark continues to decay and the infection spreads, beech scale populations decrease. The fungus eventually destroys the bark, cambium and outer sapwood, leaving trees vulnerable to other insects and diseases (Sinclair & Lyon, 2005).

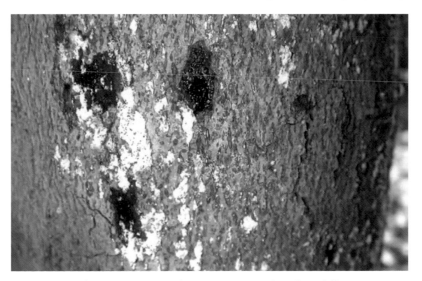

Figure 259: Necrotic spots on American beech[41].

CANKERS & CALLUS TISSUE

Cankers form on the main stem and branches as a result of beech bark disease (Fig. 260). A natural defense of the tree is to create callus tissue. However, after 2 to 3 years of infection, large pieces of bark begin to fall off, revealing areas of extensive decay (Sinclair & Lyon, 2005)

Figure 260: Cankers and callous tissue resulting from beech bark disease[71].

SIMILAR SPECIES, SIGNS & SYMPTOMS

Phytophthora **bleeding cankers**

Several species of fungal pathogens in the *Phytophthora* genus can create cankers similar to those caused in response to beech bark disease. These cankers produce a reddish-brown substance giving the appearance that the trunk is bleeding. These cankers may at times appear similar to the necrotic spots caused by beech bark disease (Fig. 261). Look for the white, wooly signs of the beech scale to help determine whether the necrotic spots are indeed a result of beech bark disease. Some *Phytophthora* bleeding cankers will cause tree mortality. Consult a professional arborist or forester should these types of canker appear (Pijut, 2006).

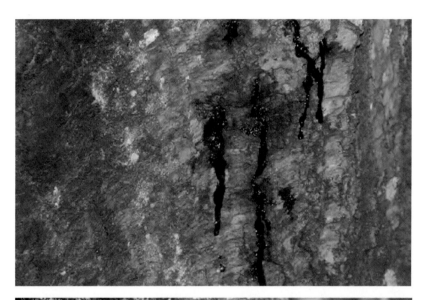

Figure 261: Comparing *Phytophthora* bleeding cankers[33] (top) and necrotic spots resulting from beech bark disease[41] (bottom).

BIOLOGY

TAXONOMIC HIERARCHY

Beech Scale Insect

Kingdom	Animalia
Phylum	Arthropoda
Class	Insecta
Order	Hemiptera
Family	Eriococcidae
Genus	*Cryptococcus*
Species	*Cryptococcus fagisuga*

Neonectria fungi

Kingdom	Fungi
Phylum	Ascomycota
Class	Sordariomycetes
Order	Hypercreales
Family	Nectriaceae
Genus	*Neonectria*
Species	*Neonectria ditissima*

Kingdom	Fungi
Phylum	Ascomycota
Class	Sordariomycetes
Order	Hypercreales
Family	Nectriaceae
Genus	*Neonectria*
Species	*Neonectria faginata*

ORIGIN & DISTRIBUTION

Beech scale was introduced to North America in the 1890's. It was first observed in Nova Scotia and is thought to have arrived on ornamental stock of European beech (Houston & O'Brien, 1983). In 1981, the first evidence of the beech scale in Ontario was found in Newmarket as a result of an investigation into the decline of beech trees in the area (Bisessar et al. 1985). However, it was not until 1999 that the beech bark disease complex was officially confirmed in Ontario. Today, beech bark disease is present across the majority of the native range of American beech (McLaughlin & Greifenhagen, 2012) (Fig. 262)

DISEASE CYCLE

In the summer months, adult scale insects lay their eggs on the outer bark of beech trees. Upon hatching the nymphs can disperse to new hosts via wind and animal vectors (McLaughlin & Greifenhagen, 2012). In the late summer and fall, the nymphs attach to the outer bark and start producing a protective woolly coating. These immobile nymphs hibernate over the winter and moult into adults in the spring (Shigo, 1972). While feeding, the beech scale insects create wounds in the host tissue, increasing the tree's susceptibility to pathogen infection. Fungal spores of *Neonectria* species are carried by wind or water from infected trees to new hosts where they can easily establish and germinate within tiny wounds in the bark (McLaughlin & Greifenhagen, 2012).

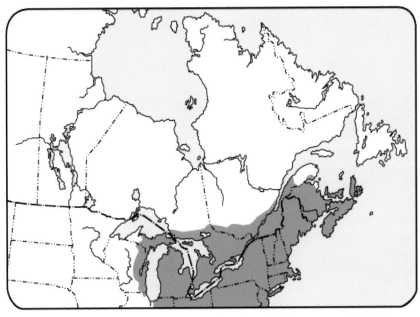

Figure 262: Natural range of American beech (*Fagus grandifolia*)[64].

Beech bark disease has three stages (Fig. 263). The first stage is called the advancing front. This is when scale insects become established in a forest stand and begin to reproduce on the outer bark of beech trees. The next stage or killing front is when the *Neonectria* species infect the tree, resulting in high levels of mortality. The aftermath forest consists of a few scattered large beech trees and many infected young saplings (Shigo, 1972).

Advancing front: Invasion by beech scale[68] (top).
Killing front: Disease complex causes tree mortality[41](top right).
Aftermath forest: Few surviving large beech trees, forest characterized by small saplings[41] (bottom right).

Figure 263: Stages of beech bark disease.

IMPACTS

American beech is an important food source for wildlife. It produces a large nut crop every 2 to 8 years and provides habitat for birds and mammals (Tubbs & Houston, 1990). By causing high levels of beech mortality beech bark disease results in the sudden loss of an abundant and important resource in forest food webs (Storer et al. 2005). Beech bark disease may also alter the species composition of the forest through indirect effects that inhibit the regeneration of native hardwood species. As large beech trees succumb to the disease they send up multiple saplings that can quickly form dense patches of beech saplings that compete with other regenerating species (Nyland et al. 2006).

American beech wood is used to make flooring and furniture. Therefore, compared to others, woodlots with a high percentage of beech trees may be at an increased risk of economical losses as a result of beech bark disease (Farrar, 1995). Beech bark disease often girdles the tree and causes structural weakening up to the point of collapse (Fig. 264). The tops of large beech trees have been observed to break off the main stem, an occurrence known as "beech snap". It can be a hazard to humans, especially in recreational areas (Heyd, 2005).

Figure 264: Tree mortality caused by beech bark disease[41].

VECTORS & PATHWAYS

The beech scale insect is the first stage of the disease complex. These tiny insects can disperse during what is called a crawler stage. At this stage the insects have some mobility and are largely aided by wind currents. Scale insects have been observed

to disperse up to 10m to a new host tree (Wainhouse, 1980). Humans are also thought to play a major role in the dispersal of scale insects by moving ornamental stock and firewood (McLaughlin & Greifenhagen, 2012). *Neonectria* spores are vectored through wind currents and water to new host trees where infection occurs at wound sites created by the feeding of scale insects (Shigo, 1972).

MANAGEMENT PRACTICES

PREVENTION STRATEGIES

Consider implementing preventative silvicultural techniques in uninfested woodlots by increasing tree species diversity. This can be accomplished through selective thinning practices (McCullough et al. 2005). American beech is a desirable species that contributes to diversity and is an important source of food and habitat for wildlife (Storer et al. 2005). As such, the complete removal of beech trees is not recommended. Choose to retain large healthy beech trees with smooth bark while harvesting those with signs of decay or injury, which are more likely to be infected (McCullough et al. 2005). Moving firewood increases the risk of introducing beech bark disease into new areas (Jacobi et al. 2011), especially from mid-summer to late fall when the scale insects are relatively mobile (Heyd, 2005).

EARLY DETECTION TECHNIQUES

Early detection requires regular monitoring and surveying the woodlot for signs of beech bark disease. The first signs of the advancing front are the characteristic white wooly substance produced by the beech scale insect (Shigo, 1972). Look for beech trees with rough bark as the scale insects seem to prefer the rougher texture, which may provide greater protection from enemies or the weather. Look at larger older trees; these seem to be the first to be colonized by scale insects (Koch & Carey, 2005). If the beech scale is present, the next sign to look for is the formation of necrotic spots and cankers. As the *Neonectria* fungus begins to destroy the tree scale insects die and the white wooly cover turns black. This is a sign that the killing front is advancing (Shigo, 1972).

CONTROL OPTIONS

Prevention strategies are available to help protect a forest from beech bark disease. However, there is no absolute way of ensuring that a woodlot will remain disease free. When faced with the advancing front of beech bark disease there are several ways in which to alleviate damage. Conduct a survey of the woodlot to identify the extent of beech scale infestation. High value trees may be washed off with water in an attempt to save the tree from fungal infection. However, this is only practical for a small number of trees as regular washings will be needed to prevent re-colonization (McCullough et al. 2005).

Identify potentially resistant trees that either have a very small amount of beech scale or none. These trees' genotypes should be protected since resistance is extremely rare. Approximately 1% of all the beech trees in North America are thought to be resistant to beech bark disease, thus it is important to keep resistant genes in the gene pool (McLaughlin & Greifenhagen, 2012). Research is underway to increase the number of disease-resistant trees in natural areas. However, breeding for resistance has proven difficult because beech does not reach a reproductive age for approximately 40 years, at which time they are nearly 120 feet tall. Despite these challenges, recent studies have shown that disease resistance is heritable (Koch & Carey, 2004) and that a high number of seedlings derived from resistant parents will also show signs of resistance (Koch et al. 2010).

Consider harvesting or thinning the woodlot to salvage heavily infected trees. Diseased saplings may undergo vigorous growth in response to higher light levels resulting from thinning practices. However, these saplings may compartmentalize cankers and grow with trunk defects that greatly decrease their timber value (Fig. 265). Removing these deformed saplings will provide room for other species to grow and contribute to the overall diversity of the woodlot (McCullough et al. 2005). Beech also has the ability to multiply via vegetative reproduction. Numerous saplings may emerge from underground roots associated with infected trees. These saplings should be removed as they will eventually become infected and create competition for other understory species (Smallidge & Nyland, 2009).

Figure 265: American beech growing with deformities[66].

5.2.5
Gypsy Moth
(*Lymantria dispar*)

Other common names:
European gypsy moth, Asian gypsy moth

Priority Rating: HIGH

Figure 266: Gypsy moth larva[72]

IDENTIFICATION

ORGANISM

Gypsy moths range from 2.5 to 3cm in length. Males have light brown wings with darker coloured markings. Females are much lighter in colour. They have creamy white wings with markings that can be either distinctive or faint (Fig. 267). Males have large grayish-brown feathery antennae (Benoit & Lachance, 1990) (Fig. 268). There are two exotic strains of gypsy moth present in North America, one from Europe and one from Asia. Only the European strain has been documented in Ontario. All females of the European strain are flightless (Nealis & Erb, 1993).

Figure 267: Comparing female (left) and male (right) gypsy moths[34].

Figure 268: Male gypsy moth with characteristic feather-like antennae[68].

Gypsy moth caterpillars go through several developmental stages (Fig. 269). During the 1st stage, called 1st instar, the caterpillar appears reddish-brown and is covered in fine black hairs. During the 2nd and 3rd instars the body turns to a mottled black and yellow colour. Orange and gray spots appear along the back. The later instars have a central stripe showcasing 5 rows of blue spots and 6 rows of red spots. Prominent tufts of hair cover the body (McManus et al. 1989).

Figure 269: Changes in appearance from early[74] (left) to later[75] (right) instar development of gypsy moth larvae.

HOST TREES

The European strain of gypsy moth present in Ontario has a wide host-range, which includes over 300 species of hardwood trees. However, the most commonly preferred trees are oak (*Quercus* sp.), willow (*Salix* sp.), aspen (*Populus* sp.) and birch (*Betula* sp.). Only the larvae cause damage to these host trees through feeding on the leaves (Tobin & Liebold, 2011). The Asian strain has an even wider host range than the European strain, feeding on both hard and softwood species (Régnière et al. 2009).

SIGNS & SYMPTOMS

EGG MASSES

Female gypsy moths create large, light brown egg masses, which can be found in sheltered areas such as sheds, under picnic tables, on vehicles, etc. (McManus et al. 1989) (Fig. 270). During outbreaks, multiple egg masses can be seen on the tree trunks and branches of hardwood trees. Each egg mass is approximately 3.5 x 2cm and can contain up to 1000 eggs (Nealis & Erb, 1993).

Figure 270: Egg masses of gypsy moth are found both outdoors[76] (left) and in sheltered locations[77] (right).

LARVAL FEEDING

Gypsy moth larvae, or caterpillars, in Ontario feed on the leaves of various hardwood species. They avoid the veins and mid-veins, creating leaves with a skeletal appearance (Fig. 271). However, during severe outbreaks, complete defoliation can occur. Larvae feed mostly at night and hide in communal areas during the day (Nealis & Erb, 1993).

Figure 271: Gypsy moth larvae feeding on leaves[78] (left) and congregating on a tree trunk[43] (right).

SIMILAR SPECIES, SIGNS & SYMPTOMS

Eastern Tent Caterpillar (*Malacosoma americanum*)

The eastern tent caterpillar is a native defoliating insect that has similar population outbreaks to those of the gypsy moth. Larvae of both species feed at night and hide during the day. However, eastern tent caterpillars construct silken tents in which they congregate and find shelter. Eastern tent caterpillars have a white stripe bordered in yellow with blue markings along their sides (Rabaglia & Twardus, 1990) (Fig. 272).

Figure 272: Eastern tent caterpillar[39] (left) and a silken tent[40] (right).

Forest Tent Caterpillar (*Malacosoma disstria*)

Forest tent caterpillars are native to North America. Similarly to gypsy moth, the larvae feed at night and congregate during the day, often in large clumps on tree trunks. The forest tent caterpillar has a row of alternating small and large white spots along their backs that give the impression of footprints (Fig. 273). Gypsy moth caterpillars have five blue and six red dots along their backs (Dodds & Seybold, 1996).

Figure 273: Forest tent caterpillar[79] (left) and a large congregation[44] (right).

BIOLOGY

TAXONOMIC HIERARCHY

Kingdom	Animalia
Phylum	Arthropoda
Class	Insecta
Order	Lepidoptera
Family	Lymantriidae
Genus	*Lymantria*
Species	*Lymantria dispar*

ORIGIN & DISTRIBUTION

The European strain of gypsy moth was introduced into North America in 1869. Several moths escaped from the office of an entomologist, Leopold Trouvelot, who was conducting crossbreeding research with silk worms in Massachusetts (Benoit & Lachance, 1990). Within 20 years severe defoliation brought the gypsy moth to public attention (Tobin & Liebold, 2011). It is unknown when the species established in Canada but the first outbreak requiring management occurred in Quebec in 1924 (Nealis, 2002). The European strain was first observed in Ontario in 1969 whereas the Asian strain has become established in western North America and has not been detected in Ontario (Nealis & Erb, 1993).

LIFE CYCLE

Gypsy moths have a four-stage life cycle, including egg, larvae, pupae, and adult (Fig. 274). In the fall female moths create large egg masses that contain up to 1000 eggs. Eggs overwinter in these masses and hatch the following spring. Larvae, or caterpillars, emerge from their eggs and begin feeding on leaves from May through June. After feeding, they enter the pupal stage in which the larvae undergo metamorphosis from a caterpillar to a moth. This process takes approximately 2 weeks. Upon emerging from cocoons the adult moths mate and each female creates a single egg mass (Nealis & Erb, 1993).

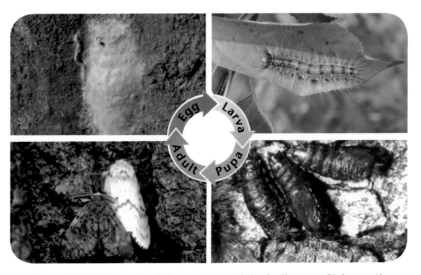

Figure 274: Life cycle of the gypsy moth including egg[76], larvae[40], pupae[47] and adult[48] life stages.

IMPACTS

The introduction of gypsy moth to North America had devastating effects on deciduous forests. Larvae can completely defoliate entire forest stands during an outbreak. Defoliation has been linked to both hardwood growth loss and mortality, with forest stands experiencing 25-30% mortality as a result of an outbreak (Fig. 275). In areas with already stressed trees mortality can reach 100% (Tobin & Liebold, 2011).

Figure 275: Defoliation caused by a gypsy moth outbreak[80].

Economic hardships ensue with the loss of hardwood trees. For instance, defoliation and mortality affect the value of timber products. In areas affected by gypsy moth outbreaks, quarantines are often implemented to prevent further spread. These quarantines have economic impacts associated with trade and the movement and sale of wood products. Tourism may also be affected as the aesthetic value of natural forested areas is compromised (Régnière et al. 2009).

VECTORS & PATHWAYS

Flightless adult females characterize the European strain of gypsy moth presently found in Ontario (Nealis, 2002). They release a pheromone to attract the males and do not disperse from the tree or structure in which they reached the pupal stage (Nealis & Erb, 1993). Dispersal occurs during the larval stage. Young caterpillars climb to the upper-most branches of the canopy and hang from long silken threads. Winds can then aid in their movement to new host trees, a type of passive dispersal known as ballooning (Hajek & Tobin, 2010).

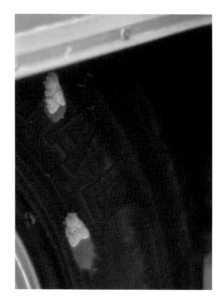

Figure 276: Female gypsy moths ovipositing on a tire[81].

Long distance dispersal occurs via human vectors (Fig. 276). Females deposit egg masses in sheltered locations near the ground, often in man-made structures. For instance, egg masses have been found in vehicles, campers, tents and lawn furniture (Régnière et al. 2009), with firewood being one of the leading causes of long-distance dispersal (Bigsby et al. 2011).

MANAGEMENT PRACTICES

PREVENTION STRATEGIES

Preventing movement at all stages of the gypsy moth's life-cycle is key. Currently, outbreaks occur throughout southern Ontario, up to and including Sault Ste. Marie. Quarantines are enforced by the CFIA to help prevent further spread. Before moving to areas outside of the quarantine zone it is important to inspect vehicles and outdoor equipment for egg masses, larvae, cocoons or adult moths (CFIA, 2011a).

EARLY DETECTION TECHNIQUES

Monitoring is the first step to detecting new or re-occurring infestations. Inspect all outdoor equipment for egg masses. Placing a burlap sack around the lower trunk of a preferred host tree such as oak may attract gypsy moth larvae as it provides shelter during the day (Fig. 277). Regularly monitoring the contents of the sack can not only enable early detection but also inform the woodlot owner as to the state and severity of infestation. Any trapped gypsy moth caterpillars should be destroyed to help reduce local populations (McManus et al, 1989).

Figure 277: Using a burlap sack as a method to attract gypsy moth larvae[82].

CONTROL OPTIONS

Eradication programs involving the gypsy moth in North America have not been successful. The goal has changed to suppression and control. The CFIA enforces quarantines in infested areas to prevent further spread. Pheromone traps are used as a monitoring tool outside of the quarantine zones. Outbreaks within the quarantine zone are the responsibility of municipalities and/or private woodlot owners (Régnière et al. 2009).

Woodlot owners are encouraged to actively manage gypsy moth infestations on their property. Performing a regular survey of outdoor equipment for egg masses is an important first step because each can contain up to 1000 eggs. Egg masses should be destroyed by placing them in hot, soapy water or by burning. Attention: the hairs of gypsy moth caterpillars and fibers from egg masses may cause allergic reactions in some people (McManus et al. 1989).

Maintaining the health of the woodlot is another important factor when dealing with re-occurring gypsy moth infestations; healthy trees are less likely to die as a result of defoliation. Good woodlot management practices help to increase habitat for wildlife and promote populations of natural gypsy moth predators such as small mammals and birds (Nealis & Erb, 1993). Pesticides may be used in conjunction with other management techniques. The most commonly used pesticide for gypsy moth control is *Bacillus thuringiensis (Btk)*, which must be applied by a licenced exterminator. This pesticide consists of a bacterium that produces protein crystals that are toxic to gypsy moth larvae (Hajek & Tobin, 2010). Although it should be taken into consideration that Btk is also toxic to native caterpillars, there is evidence that negative impacts are confined to the first year of Btk application (Solter & Hajek, 2009).

5.2.6
Dutch Elm Disease
(*Ophiostoma* spp.)

Other common names:
DED

Priority Rating: HIGH

Figure 278: Elm affected by Dutch Elm Disease[83].

IDENTIFICATION

CAUSAL ORGANISMS

Dutch elm disease is caused by three species of ascomycete fungi that cut off sap movement in elm trees (*Ulmus* spp.). These species are *Ophiostoma ulmi*, *O. novo-ulmi*, and *O. himal-ulmi*. These pathogenic fungi belong to a group called the *Ophiostoma piceae* complex, which is characterized by fungi with fruiting bodies containing two distinct spore-bearing structures (Harrington et al. 2001): black perithecia (i.e., fruiting body containing spores) and orange asexual spores (Chung et al. 2006)(Fig. 279).

Figure 279: Fruiting bodies and asexual spores of *Ophiostoma ulmi*[84].

HOSTS

Dutch elm disease affects all three native species of elm, including white elm (*Ulmus americana*), slippery elm (*U. rubra*), and rock elm (*U. thomasii*) (Fig. 280). The disease also affects two introduced elms: wych elm (*U. glabra*) and English elm (*U. procera*). Conversely, Siberian elm (*U. pumila*) is an introduced ornamental that has shown resistance to Dutch elm disease (Farrar, 1995).

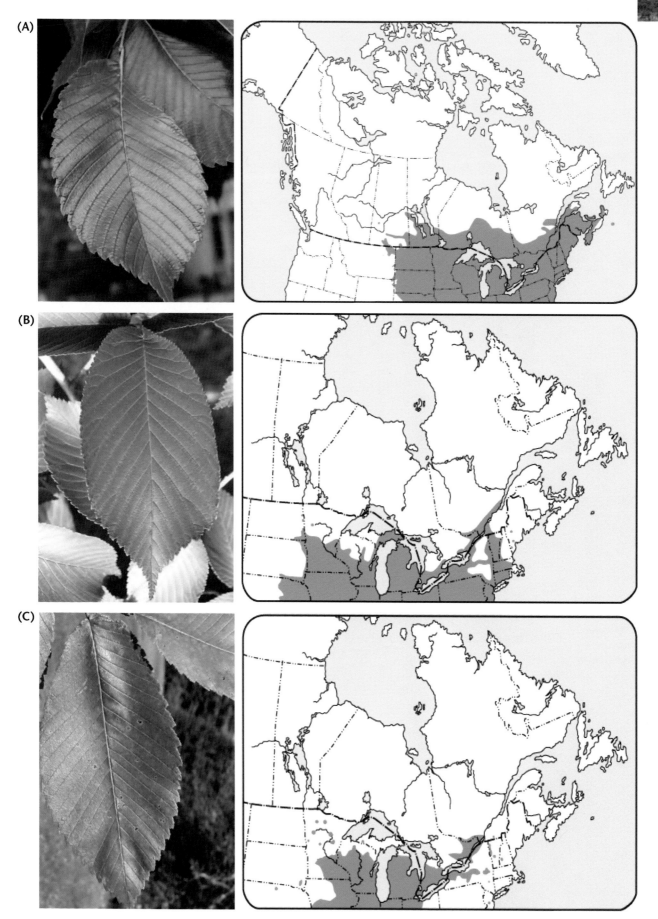

Figure 280: Leaves and native range distribution[64] of white elm[5] (A), slippery elm[5] (B) and rock elm[5] (C).

SIGNS & SYMPTOMS

WILTING LEAVES

The first signs of infection usually appear in early summer. The leaves on isolated branches turn yellow and begin to wilt (Fig. 281). As the infection spreads and more branches wilt, the crown will show bare areas where the leaves have wilted and fallen off the tree. Eventually the entire crown becomes infected and the tree dies. Tree mortality usually occurs between 1 to 3 years after infection (Davis & Meyer, 1997).

Figure 281: Wilted foliage as a result of Dutch elm disease[41].

SAPWOOD DISCOLOURATION

Signs of infection, which usually begins within individual branches, can be seen in the sapwood. As the fungus spreads the sapwood turns dark brown (Fig. 282). Cutting a cross section of the inner wood will reveal a dark brown ring indicating the presence of the fungus. Peeling off the bark will also reveal a dark brown streaking on the outer sapwood (Sinclair & Lyon, 2005).

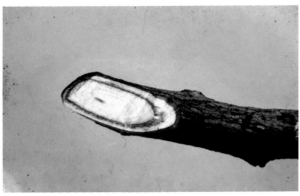 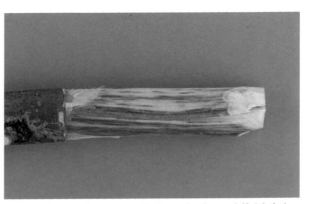

Figure 282: Streaking shown in a cross section[85] (left) and on the outer sapwood of an elm branch[59] (right).

SIMILAR DISEASES, SIGNS & SYMPTOMS

Elm Yellows (*Candidatus Phytoplasma* spp.)

Elm yellows disease is caused by phytoplasmas (i.e., small specialized obligate parasitic bacteria of plant tissue that lack a cell wall) (Lee et al. 2004). As with Dutch elm disease, it also affects the vascular system of elm trees causing the leaves to turn yellow and wilt (Fig. 283). However, the entire crown wilts simultaneously whereas Dutch elm disease starts in individual branches and gradually spreads through the entire crown. Elm yellows will also cause discolouration of the inner sapwood but it produces a distinct wintergreen odour (Sinclair, 2000).

Figure 283: Comparing the symptoms of elm yellows[40] (left) and Dutch elm disease[65] (right).

Verticillium Wilt (*Verticillium* spp.)

Soil-borne fungi that affect the vascular system of trees and shrubs causes Verticillium wilt. This disease can be confused with Dutch elm disease because it causes similar yellowing of leaves and sapwood discolouration (Fig. 284). However, even though Verticillium wilt may cause tree mortality, it is often much less severe than Dutch elm disease. Cankers may also form as a response to Verticillium wilt, which is a symptom associated with Dutch elm disease (Ash, 1994).

Figure 284: Leaf wilting[41] (left) and sapwood discolouration[69] (right) associated with Verticillium wilt.

BIOLOGY

TAXONOMIC HIERARCHY

Kingdom	Fungi
Division	Ascomycota
Class	Sordariomycetes
Order	Ophiostomatales
Family	Ophiostomataceae
Genus	*Ophiostoma*
Species	*Ophiostoma ulmi*
	Ophiostoma novo-ulmi
	Ophiostoma himal-ulmi

ORIGIN & DISTRIBUTION

Dutch elm disease is caused by three species of pathogenic fungi. *Ophiostoma ulmi* was the first of the three species to cause widespread mortality. It was introduced to Europe around 1910 and subsequently to North America in the 1940's (Brasier, 1990; 1991). In Ontario, the first reports of Dutch elm disease date from 1946, two years after having been found in Quebec (Hubbes, 1999). *Ophiostoma ulmi* has been described as a relatively weak pathogen causing 10 to 40% tree mortality. A more aggressive pathogen, causing nearly 100% mortality in affected elms, was discovered in the 1940's in both North America and Europe (Brasier, 1990; 1991). This pathogen, *O. novo-ulmi*, was found to be two distinct subspecies, initially separated geographically (Brasier & Kirk, 2001). *Ophiostoma novo-ulmi* subsp. *americana* spread throughout North America in less than 40 years and was discovered in Europe in the 1960's. *Ophiostoma novo-ulmi* subsp. *novo-ulmi* has seen similar spread in Eurasia (Brasier & Buck, 2001). The origin of Dutch elm disease is unknown. However, surveys in the Himalayas led to the discovery of a third species associated with Dutch elm disease: *Ophiostoma himal-ulmi*. This species, considered endemic to the Himalayas, is an aggressive pathogen of both North American and European elms (Brasier & Mehrotra, 1995).

DISEASE CYCLE

The spread of Dutch elm disease is facilitated by elm bark beetles (*Scolytus* spp.), which preferentially breed in unhealthy trees. The Dutch elm disease fungus produces spores in the dead wood tissue surrounding the larval galleries. As these larvae develop into adults they become covered in spores, which can hitch a ride to other elm trees. As the adult beetles feed on the twigs and branches of healthy elm they create wounds and allow the spores to enter and spread through the vascular system of the tree (Pscheidt, 2011). Figure 285 shows the cycle of Dutch elm disease.

Elm bark beetles transport spores to new hosts[44].

The fungus infects a new host and spreads through the vascular system[88].

Fungal spores are produced, ready to attach to emerging adult beetles[89].

Fungus cuts off sap transport causing wilting[70].

Figure 285: Cycle of Dutch elm disease.

IMPACTS

Elm is a popular ornamental tree commonly used to line urban roadsides. Dutch elm disease devastated the majority of these large picturesque elms (Fig. 286). Most trees die as a direct result of the disease or become weakened and succumb due to other environmental stresses. Elm mortality decreases forest biodiversity and wildlife habitat (NRCan, 2011). Economic impacts result from reductions in the quality and quantity of elm timber products as well as the negative effects associated with quarantine measures (CFIA, 2010).

Figure 286: Comparing a road with healthy elm trees[41] (left) with one with elms affected by Dutch elm disease[90] (right).

VECTORS & PATHWAYS

The fungus that causes Dutch elm disease grows under the bark, along the vascular system of the tree, effectively blocking water transport from the roots to the leaves. The disease spreads via intermingling root systems or elm bark beetles, which can carry the spores. If the roots of neighbouring elm trees are close enough to each other, the fungus will spread from one tree to the other. Once in the roots the fungus can quickly spread as spores are carried through the vascular system (Haugen, 1998).

There is one native and two exotic elm bark beetles that contribute to the long distance dispersal of Dutch elm disease (Fig. 287). See section 5.2.7 for detailed information on the biology and management of exotic elm bark beetles. These beetles complete part of their life cycle in the inner sapwood of elm trees. Beetles emerging from infected trees as adults carry fungal spores on their bodies to new healthy trees. They will often infest the upper branches and burrow into the wood to deposit their eggs and to feed. The spores can enter the tree through these wounds (Haugen, 1998).

Figure 287: Banded elm bark beetle (*Scolytus schevyrewi*)[44].

MANAGEMENT PRACTICES

PREVENTION STRATEGIES

Prevention strategies for Dutch elm disease include destroying the breeding areas of insect vectors and eliminating other ways through which the disease can spread. Elm bark beetles breed in dead or dying elm material. It is best to burn or bury dead or infected branches. Elm firewood should not be left out in the open. If it cannot be burned or utilized right away it is best to completely encase the wood in plastic or tarps with the ends securely fastened or buried. Infected elm wood should be promptly disposed of (Davis & Meyers, 1997). Since Dutch elm disease can spread through root contact it is recommended to dig a trench around infected elm trees that are in close proximity to healthy elms. Ensure that the trench is deep enough to completely sever all connecting roots (Pscheidt, 2011).

EARLY DETECTION TECHNIQUES

Become familiar with the signs and symptoms of Dutch elm disease as well as those associated with elm bark beetles (See section 5.2.7). Look for signs of infected elm trees both in the woodlot and in the region. Contact a professional arborist to confirm the presence of Dutch elm disease and for help with management of infected trees (Davis & Meyers, 1997).

CONTROL OPTIONS

Controlling Dutch elm disease involves removing any dead branches from apparently healthy trees or completely removing infected trees. Pruning dead branches from elm trees effectively removes any potential breeding grounds for elm bark beetles. This will greatly reduce the likelihood of infection. Pruning may also be employed to save infected elms if done early enough. Branches suspected of being infected should be debarked until no sapwood discolouration is observed. This is because discolouration is a result of infection and will aid in detecting how far the disease has spread. It is recommended to remove some of the healthy tissue below the infection. It is also very important to clean cutting tools between each use with rubbing alcohol to prevent spreading spores to other healthy trees or branches (Haugen, 1998).

It is good practice to remove elm trees that have been infected by Dutch elm disease. If sapwood discolouration has spread to the trunk this indicates that the tree can no longer be saved (Haugen, 1998). The presence of infected trees only contributes to the dispersal of Dutch elm disease. The resulting wood should be burned immediately. The stump should also be removed and burned. An alternative involves grinding the stump so that it is 10cm below the soil line and then completely covering it with soil (Davis & Meyer, 1997).

Fungicide injections have been used to control Dutch elm disease but they can be costly and problematic. These injections may wound the tree, causing discolouration and decay around the injection area (Shigo & Campana, 1977). In addition, Dutch elm disease seems to be developing a certain level of resistance to these fungicides, thereby decreasing their effectiveness. Fungicide applications are only feasible for use on high value ornamental trees. Application across an entire woodlot is considered impractical. Management activities that promote diverse and healthy woodlots are the best means of control for Dutch elm disease (Hubbes, 1999).

5.2.7
Elm Bark Beetles
(*Scolytus multistriatus & S. schevyrewi*)

Other common names:
Lesser European elm bark beetle, Smaller European elm bark beetle, Banded elm bark beetle

Priority Rating: **HIGH**

Figure 288: Elm bark beetles[44].

IDENTIFICATION

ORGANISMS

There are two exotic elm bark beetles in Ontario: the banded elm bark beetle (*Scolytus schevyrewi*) and the European elm bark beetle (*S. multistriatus*) (Fig. 289). The banded elm bark beetle is brown with a dark band across its wing covers. It is generally 3 to 4mm long. The European elm bark beetle lacks the band and does not exceed 3mm in length. Only the European elm bark beetle has a spine on the lower abdomen (Lee et al. 2006).

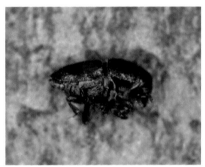

Figure 289: Comparing the banded elm bark beetle[44] (left) and the European elm bark beetle[31] (right).

HOST TREES

The European and the banded elm bark beetle are both host specific, feeding and breeding on elm trees (*Ulmus* sp.). Three native species of elm occur in Ontario: white elm (*U. americana*), slippery elm (*U. rubra*), and rock elm (*U. thomasii*). See figure 280 (section on Dutch elm disease) for a comparison of leaf morphologies and native range maps for these species. Elm is a popular ornamental tree planted along roadsides and parks (Fig. 290). Many are exotic. Exotic elms found in Ontario include wych elm (*U. glabra*), English elm (*U. procera*) and Siberian elm (*U. pumila*); all are susceptible to European or banded elm bark beetles (Sargent et al. 2008; Farrar, 1995).

Figure 290: Elm is a popular ornamental tree[41].

SIGNS & SYMPTOMS

EXIT & ENTRANCE HOLES

Female European and banded elm bark beetles create an entrance hole and lay their eggs in the bark of elm trees. When the eggs hatch, the larvae develop inside the tree and emerge as adults through 2mm circular exit holes in the trunk or branches (Sargent et al. 2008) (Fig. 291).

Figure 291: Exit holes created by the European elm bark beetle[92] (left) and the banded elm bark beetle[44] (right).

LARVAL GALLERIES

Female European and banded elm bark beetles create and lay their eggs in a vertical tunnel under the bark. Larvae make tunnels in an outward fashion, creating a fan-like appearance on both sides of the egg gallery (Fig. 292). Developing and feeding larvae create sawdust that can be seen in the larval tunnels and exit holes (Lee et al. 2006) (Fig. 293).

Figure 292: Larval galleries created by the European elm bark beetle[57].

Figure 293: Sawdust created by banded elm bark beetle larvae[44].

SIMILAR SPECIES, SIGNS & SYMPTOMS

Native Elm Bark Beetle (*Hylurogoplinus rufipes*)

The native elm bark beetle can be distinguished from exotic elm bark beetles by its metallic gold colour (Fig. 294). Adult females create egg galleries by tunneling horizontally across the wood grain, whereas exotic elm bark beetles create vertical tunnels (Fig. 295). Native elm bark beetles leave behind V-shaped markings beside their exit holes, a characteristic not seen for exotic elm bark beetles (CFS, 2011).

Figure 294: Comparing native[92] (left) and European elm bark beetles[92] (right).

Figure 295: Comparing larval galleries of the native elm bark beetle[64] (left) with those of the European elm bark beetle[41] (right).

BIOLOGY

TAXONOMIC HIERARCHY

European Elm Bark Beetle (*S. multistriatus*)		**Banded Elm Bark Beetle (*S. schevrewi*)**	
Kingdom	Animalia	Kingdom	Animalia
Phylum	Arthropoda	Phylum	Arthropoda
Class	Insecta	Class	Insecta
Order	Coleoptera	Order	Coleoptera
Family	Curculionidea	Family	Curculionidea
Genus	*Scolytus*	Genus	*Scolytus*
Species	*Scolytus multistriatus*	Species	*Scolytus schevrewi*

ORIGIN & DISTRIBUTION

As its common name indicates, the European elm bark beetle is native to Europe. First found in Massachusetts in 1909 (Lee et al. 2009), it has since spread throughout Canada (NRCan, 2011). The banded elm bark beetle is native to Asia and is a relatively recent introduction to North America. It was first observed in 2003 in both Colorado and Utah but evidence from past collections indicates that it has been in North America since the 1990's (Negrón et al. 2005). In Canada, it was first detected in Alberta in 2006 with subsequent introductions in Manitoba, Ontario, Saskatchewan (Langor et al. 2009), and, most recently, British Columbia (Humble et al. 2010).

LIFE CYCLE

Elm bark beetles overwinter as adults under the bark of elm trees. They emerge in the spring and begin feeding on the inner tissues of small twigs and branches. It is at this stage that the elm bark beetle can transmit Dutch elm disease to new hosts (Ohmart, 1989). After feeding, the adult beetles seek out weak or dying elm trees to breed, which can become infected with Dutch elm disease (Rudinsky, 1962). Fallen elm logs with intact bark also attract breeding adults. Females create tunnel-like galleries in which they lay their eggs. Eggs hatch in the spring and the larvae feed and pupate for approximately 2 months before emerging as adults (Ascerno & Wawrzynski, 1994) (Fig. 296).

Adult feeding on a healthy elm[44]

Breeding on dead or stressed elm[44]

Adults emerge[44]

Larval development in dead or stressed elm[44].

Figure 296: Life-cycle of elm bark beetles.

IMPACTS

Elm bark beetles alone appear to have minimal ecological impact. Although the larval tunnels under the bark may affect lumber value, considering that elm bark beetles usually breed in dead or dying elm trees, the risk to lumber value is low. Their greatest impact lies in their role as vectors of Dutch elm disease, a deadly condition that affects the tree's vascular system (Seybold et al. 2008). See section 5.2.6 for information on Dutch elm disease.

VECTORS & PATHWAYS

Elm bark beetles were most likely introduced in North America via wood packaging materials. Any materials with intact bark are capable of carrying elm bark beetles. Dispersal is likely facilitated by the transportation of nursery stock and elm wood products such as firewood. Adult beetles are not strong flyers. Instead, wind currents may be more important factors in their natural dispersal (Sargent et al. 2008).

MANAGEMENT PRACTICES

PREVENTION STRATEGIES

Adult elm bark beetles are attracted to wounded elm trees. Destroy all dead or dying elm trees and elm wood by chipping, burning or burying. This will decrease the number of potential breeding sites available for elm bark beetles. Do not use or transport elm firewood. Elm bark beetles are capable of completing their life cycle on elm logs provided there is a small patch of bark left intact (Sargent et al. 2008). If pruning activities are scheduled it is best to wait until the late fall or winter when adult beetles are less active (Byers et al. 1980). The fungal agent of Dutch elm disease has been shown to release chemical signals that attract elm bark beetles (McLeod et al. 2005). Look for signs and symptoms of this disease and consider eliminating infected trees. Refer to section 5.2.6 for management strategies for Dutch elm disease.

Figure 297: Larval galleries of European elm bark beetle[94.]

EARLY DETECTION TECHNIQUES

Regularly look for signs and symptoms of elm bark beetle establishment, including yellowing or wilting foliage, circular exit holes in the bark, and declining elm tree health. When signs or symptoms of the beetle are found peeling the bark away to determine whether the characteristic larval galleries are present can aid in identification (Sargent et al. 2008) (Fig. 297).

CONTROL OPTIONS

Dead elm trees, logs and branches should be destroyed through chipping, burning or burying. This will decrease the number of available breeding sites and prevent populations of elm bark beetles from increasing (Sargent et al. 2008). Keep elm trees healthy and properly pruned. However, only prune during the late fall and winter when adult beetles are less active (Byers et al. 1980).

Woodlot management activities should be geared towards increasing tree health because elm bark beetles are attracted to stressed trees. This can be done by increasing tree species diversity, thinning to reduce competition and removing damaged or diseased trees (Seybold et al. 2008). Elm bark beetles will also invade freshly cut logs, recently fallen trees, and those affected by fire. Thus, it is important to monitor elm trees in the woodlot and eliminate any potential breeding grounds (Rudinsky, 1962).

Since elm bark beetles spend the majority of their life cycle within the tree, insecticides are generally applied to the outer bark only as a preventative measure. This is because these chemicals are only effective if they come into direct contact with the adult beetles. Consequently, insecticide use may be impractical (Seybold et al. 2008).

5.2.8
Butternut Canker
(*Ophiognomonia clavigignenti-juglandacearum*)

Other common names:
Butternut disease

Priority Rating: **HIGH**

Figure 298: Butternut Canker[41].

IDENTIFICATION

CAUSAL ORGANISM

Butternut (*Juglans cinerea*) is native to Ontario and the primary host of the butternut canker fungus (*Ophiognomonia clavigignenti-juglandacearum*). Previously classified as *Sirococcus*, this fungus has recently been reclassified to the genus *Ophiognomonia* (Broders & Boland, 2011). Species in the *Ophiognomonia* genus are characterized by their elongated ascospores that infect a variety of plant families, including Juglanaceae to which butternut belongs (Walker et al. 2012). *Ophiognomonia claviginenti-juglandacearum* reproduces asexually. Fungal spores enter butternut trees through wounds or cracks in the bark. The fungus forms projecting structures under the bark called hyphal pegs (Fig. 299). These hyphal pegs cause the bark to crack and split open. Spores are released into the environment through these openings (Nair et al. 1979).

Figure 299: Hyphal pegs of *Ophiognomonia clavigignenti-juglandacearum*[95].

HOST TREES

Butternut (*Juglans cinerea*) is the main host of *O. clavigignenti-juglandacearum* (Fig. 300). A native to North America, this tree species generally occurs in isolated patches in Ontario, Quebec and New Brunswick (NRCan, 2011). Butternut has been federally and provincially listed as an endangered species due to the devastating impacts of *O. clavigignenti-juglandacearum* (Environment Canada, 2011; OMNR, 2012b). Other members of the walnut family have shown some susceptibility to the disease but, unlike butternut, do not appear to be killed by it (Ostry et al. 1996).

Figure 300: Butternut leaves[5] (left) and fruit[5] (right).

SIGNS & SYMPTOMS

CANKERS

The main symptom of *O. clavigignenti-juglandacearum* infection is the formation of stem and branch cankers. These cankers appear as large black spots on the branches and trunks of butternut trees (Fig. 301). Cankers are black and often release a black sappy substance in the spring. In the summer they dry out, having a sooty black appearance with shades of white along the outer edges (Davis & Meyer, 1997).

Figure 301: Butternut cankers in the spring[41] (left) and summer[41] (right).

SAPWOOD DISCOLOURATION

Removing the bark in areas where a suspected canker is forming will reveal a black, darkened area (Fig. 302). As cankers form and the infection spreads, the sapwood underneath the bark decays and turns black. The fungus will continue to spread and, as the disease intensifies, large areas of dead and blackened cambium tissue appear (Ostry et al. 1994).

MORTALITY

As infection progresses and decay continues within the cambium layer, branches become girdled and die. During heavy rainfall, spores are carried downward and establish new infections in multiple areas of the main trunk. The numerous cankers formed on the main trunk eventually kill the tree (Fig. 303). Epicormic branching is common on stressed trees. However, these branches quickly become infected and die (Davis & Meyer, 1997).

Figure 302: Sapwood discolouration from dead cambium tissue[96].

Figure 303: Butternut killed as a result of *O. clavigignenti-juglandacearum* infection[69].

SIMILAR SPECIES, SIGNS & SYMPTOMS

Butternut trees form similar cankers and experience crown dieback as a result of agents other than *O. clavigignenti-juglandacearum*. A similar fungus, *Melanconis oblongum*, which can co-occur with *O. clavigignenti-juglandacearum* infects dead butternut tissue. However, it is not known to cause butternut mortality (Ostry et al. 1994). Bacterial blight caused by *Xanthomonas arboricola* pv. *juglandis* infection also causes cankers in the form of black lesions but branch and crown dieback does not generally occur as a result. Bunch disease, caused by unknown bacteria, does not produce cankers but has been shown to cause increased lateral growth that may be mistaken for the epicormic shoots produced in response to butternut canker (Pijut, 2006). Cankers can also form from physical injury or frost damage (Harrison & Hurley, 2001). It is recommended to consult a professional to help identify the cause of butternut decline (Fig. 304).

Figure 304: Butternut affected by butternut canker[97].

BIOLOGY

TAXONOMIC HIERARCHY

Kingdom	Fungi
Phylum	Ascomycota
Class	Sordariomycetes
Order	Diaporthales
Family	Gnomoniaceae
Genus	*Ophiognomonia*
Species	*Ophiognomonia clavigignenti-juglandacearum*

ORIGIN & DISTRIBUTION

The origin of *O. clavigignenti-juglandacearum* is unknown. The fungus was first observed in North America in 1967 but it was not until 1979 that it was identified as the causative agent of butternut canker. Today it is found in the eastern United States and southeastern Canada where it has spread throughout the entire range of its host species (Schlarbaum et al. 1997; Harrison & Hurley, 2001) (Fig. 305). It was confirmed in Ontario in 1991 from a sample collected in Ipperwash Provincial Park, south of Lake Huron (Davis et al. 1992).

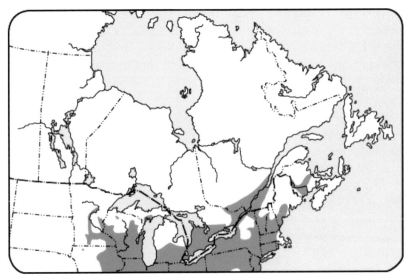

Figure 305: Native range of butternut in Ontario[64].

DISEASE CYCLE

Spores of *O. clavigignenti-juglandacearum* infect butternut trees through buds, leaf scars and other wounds found in the bark. The fungal infection causes cankers under which hyphal pegs exert pressure on the inner bark, causing it to split. Fungal spores can then escape through these cracks and be carried by water, wind or other organisms such as insects, birds and rodents, to new butternut hosts (Nair et al. 1979). Heavy rainstorms can accelerate the infection in individual butternut trees because the water runs down the trunk collecting spores and transporting them downward. As such, multiple cankers can form on the same tree (Tisserat & Kuntz, 1983). The fungus has been reported to survive for up to 2 years on dead trees (Ostry, 1996). Figure 306 shows the cycle of butternut canker.

Hyphal pegs rupture the bark and spores are released.[95]

Spores are transported by wind, rain or biota to new host trees[52]

Establishes itself under the bark and forms fruiting bodies[41]

Spores infect through buds, leaf scars and wounds in the bark[5].

Figure 306: Cycle of butternut canker.

IMPACTS

The introduction of butternut canker has had devastating impacts on butternut populations and forest biodiversity. The fungal infection can kill trees of all ages and sizes (Innes et al. 2001). The majority of infected trees die rapidly after initial infection. Both the above and below-ground portions of the tree die as a result of the disease (Environment Canada, 2010). Butternut produces a seed crop that is a highly valued food source for wildlife such as small mammals and birds (Rink, 1990). Humans can also benefit from the commercial value of the fruits. In addition, the lumber is considered to be of high value when unaffected by the disease for its uses in wood-working (Ostry & Pijut, 2000).

VECTORS & PATHWAYS

The butternut canker fungus can spread within the host tree. Externally, as water runs down from the top branches it collects spores from existing cankers and transports them to lower wounds (Tisserat & Kuntz, 1983). Spores have also been shown to travel up to 45m away from their original host via wind currents. Insects such as beetles can carry the spores on their bodies if they come into physical contact with cankers. It has also been speculated that birds play a role in the spread of butternut canker (Halik & Bergdahl, 2002). Humans also contribute to the spread of butternut canker through the movement of firewood, seeds and nursery stock (Ostry & Woeste, 2004).

MANAGEMENT PRACTICES

PREVENTION STRATEGIES

There is a lack of known preventative measures against butternut canker other than practicing appropriate woodlot management practices and keeping the forest healthy. Butternut canker can easily infect butternut trees through wounds in the bark. Minimizing physical damage during management activities is recommended. Healthy trees are generally less susceptible to insect attack and disease than stressed or weakened trees. Keeping a diverse and healthy woodlot could help to prevent the introduction of pathogens such as the causing agent of butternut canker (Ostry et al, 1996).

EARLY DETECTION TECHNIQUES

Monitor butternut trees in the woodlot and look for signs and symptoms of the disease. It is prohibited to cut down a naturally occurring butternut tree as the species is protected under Ontario's Endangered Species Act. Woodlot owners considering removal of butternut should contact the OMNR, even if the tree(s) is/are infected (OMNR, 2011).

CONTROL OPTIONS

As a woodlot owner, the best management strategy to prevent butternut canker is to promote a healthy woodlot. When performing woodlot management or timber harvest activities it is best to remove groups of trees that may be shading out butternut. Butternut is a shade intolerant species and requires canopy gaps to promote regeneration and healthy growth. Managing both healthy and infected butternut trees is an important goal in the conservation of this species. Infected butternut trees may develop a certain level of resistance, which may be beneficial in future breeding programs (DesRochers, 2009). Butternut trees showing little to no signs of infection may possess a certain level of natural resistance to the disease. Woodlot owners are encouraged to report these trees to the Forest Gene Conservation Association. This organization has been recording the locations of potentially resistant butternut trees for possible use in breeding programs. These programs consist of crossing resistant individuals with the objective of creating a disease-resistant population (FGCA, n.d.).

Federal law currently protects butternut. Given its status, even heavily infected trees should be treated, not cut down. It is an offense to possess or sell naturally occurring butternut wood under the Endangered Species Act, 2007. In fact, a woodlot owner can only remove a butternut tree if considered non-retainable. That is, if infection is so severe that it is no longer possible to save the tree. An expert accredited as a Butternut Health Assessor must identify the tree as non-retainable. Woodlot owners can find a Butternut Health Assessor by contacting the OMNR (OMNR, 2011).

5.2.9
Dogwood Anthracnose
(*Discula destructiva*)

Other common names:
Dogwood disease

Priority Rating: **MODERATE**

IDENTIFICATION

Dogwood anthracnose (*Discula destructiva*) is an airborne fungal disease of flowering dogwood (*Cornus florida*) and Pacific dogwood (*C. nuttallii*) (Hibben, 1990). The origin of D. destructiva is unknown (Zhang & Blackwell, 2001). Black or brown spots bordered in purple on the leaves are indicative of dogwood anthracnose (Fig. 307). These spots eventually turn into holes. These symptoms first appear in the lower crown and progress upwards. Infection on the leaves can spread through the petioles into the twigs. Cankers begin to appear and can eventually girdle and kill the tree (Sinclair & Lyon, 2005).

Figure 307: Leaf lesions[83] (left) and cankers[83] (right) caused by dogwood anthracnose.

IMPACTS

An abundance of white showy flowers and bright red berries contribute to flowering dogwood's popularity as an ornamental tree (Fig. 308). Its fruit and seeds have a high nutritional content that makes them an invaluable food source for wildlife (Rossell et al. 2001).

Dogwood anthracnose has had devastating effects on flowering dogwood in Ontario with an estimated decline of 7-8% per year. This decline has led to the provincial and federal governments listing flowering dogwood as an endangered species (Bickerton & Thompson-Black, 2010).

Figure 308: Showy flowers[15] (top) and bright red berries[66] (bottom) of flowering dogwood.

CONTROL

Flowering dogwood is an endangered species protected by the Endangered Species Act, 2007. In Canada, the native range of flowering dogwood is the Carolinian forest of southern Ontario (Bickerton & Thompson-Black, 2010)(Fig. 309). A healthy flowering dogwood is less susceptible to infection than a weakened or stressed tree. As such, dead or infected branches should be pruned, removed and destroyed. Clean cutting tools with rubbing alcohol between each use to prevent spreading the disease (Pecknold et al. 2001). Report any potentially resistant trees to a species-at-risk biologist at the OMNR. Potentially resistant trees may be useful for research programs investigating ways of saving flowering dogwood populations and controlling dogwood anthracnose (Bickerton & Thompson-Black, 2010).

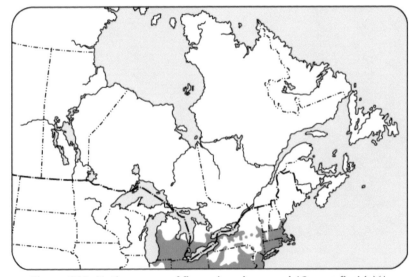

Figure 309: Native range of flowering dogwood (*Cornus florida*)[64].

5.2.10
Thousand Cankers Disease
(*Geosmithia morbida*)

Other common names:
TCD

Priority Rating: **MODERATE**

IDENTIFICATION

Thousand cankers disease is caused by a fungal pathogen (*Geosmithia morbida*) and dispersed by the native walnut twig beetle (*Pityophthorus juglandis*) (Fig. 310). The disease mainly affects black walnut (*Juglans nigra*). Yellowing of the leaves is the first sign of infection followed by dying branches. Cankers form around entry wounds created by the beetle (Fig. 311). Trees usually die within three years as a result of the disruption of nutrient transport (Leslie et al. 2010). The disease received its name for the numerous cankers that form on the trunk and branches of infected trees (Cranshaw & Tisserat, 2008).

Figure 310: Walnut twig beetle (*Pityophthorus juglandis*)[99.]

Figure 311: Cankers caused by thousand cankers disease on a walnut sapling[100] (left) and in the sapwood of a mature walnut tree[101] (right).

IMPACTS

Thousand cankers disease can wipe out entire native populations of black walnut (Fig. 312). Until recently, the disease was confined to western North America where it was causing widespread mortality of ornamental black walnut. It has recently been detected in Tennessee (2010), Virginia (2011) and Pennsylvania (2011), which is a major problem as this comprises the native range of black walnut (Grant et al. 2011). Black walnut is an economically important species that is harvested for both its lumber and fruit (MacDaniels & Lieberman, 1979). They produce a nut crop rich in protein, which is an important energy source for wildlife (Smith & Follmer, 1972).

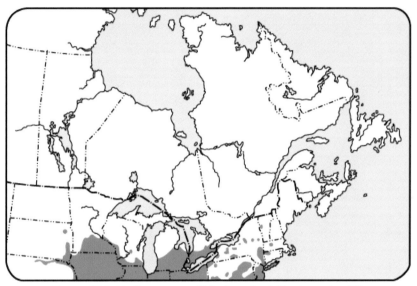

Figure 312: Native range of black walnut (*Juglans nigra*)[64].

CONTROL

Thousand cankers disease is not present in Ontario. However, it is important to be prepared in the event that the disease complex finds its way into Canada. Monitor the health of black walnut trees on the property and look for signs and symptoms of disease. If you suspect that you have a black walnut tree infected with thousand cankers disease contact the CFIA and/or the OMNR. In areas infested by thousand cankers disease, infested walnut trees should be removed to eliminate sources of infection (Fig. 313). Walnut wood should be heat-treated and the bark should be removed. Walnut twig beetles complete their life cycle under the bark. Therefore, logs without bark will not support these insect vectors. Contaminated wood should never be moved outside of infested areas (Cranshaw & Tisserat, 2008).

Figure 313: Controlling thousand cankers disease[100].

5.2.11
Pear Thrips
(Taeniothrips inconsequens)

Other common names:
Fruit tree thrips

Priority Rating: MODERATE

IDENTIFICATION

Pear thrips (*Taeniothrips inconsequens*) are small, black insects that are approximately 1.5mm in length (Fig. 314). They spend part of their life cycle in the soil and part on hardwood trees. In the spring, adults emerge from the soil and enter tree buds. They feed on immature leaves and lay their eggs within leaf tissues. Larvae are clear and very hard to see. They eventually drop to the soil where they pupate and emerge as adults the following year (Hoover, 2002).

Figure 314: Pear thrips in the adult[40] (left) and larva[40] (right) life stages.

IMPACTS

Pear thrips were introduced to North America from Eurasia in the early 1900's (Palm & Gardescu, 2008). Sugar maple seems to be the preferred host for this exotic insect, although damage has been observed on a variety of other hardwoods such as beech, ash, serviceberry and cherry as well as on a variety of herbaceous plants commonly found in forest understories (Palm & Gardescu, 2008). The feeding adults cause leaves to crinkle and wilt (Fig. 315). Crown defoliation and yellowing is often a sign of a high density of pear thrips. Seed production and sap yields may also be adversely affected, which in turn could have negative effects on regeneration and future forest diversity. Hardwoods affected by pear thrips defoliation may be more susceptible to other insect pests and pathogens (Hoover, 2002). Gardescu (2003) found that pear thrips were the primary cause of hardwood seedling mortality in a sugar maple forest in New York.

Figure 315: Damage to maple leaves caused by pear thrips[102].

CONTROL

Pear thrips can be very difficult to control when populations reach high densities. Insecticides are not very effective because the adults spend most of the time within the leaf buds and tissues. Furthermore, insecticides should not be applied to sugar maples in woodlots utilized for maple syrup production. In years of severe defoliation, maple syrup producers may have to avoid tapping infected trees to counteract the effect of the insects and prevent maple mortality (Hoover, 2002).

Several native insects and fungal pathogens affect pear thrips in North America but more research is needed to determine whether they can be augmented to provide any level of biological control. However, heavy infestations seldom last for more than one year (Palm & Gardescu, 2008). More research on the potential long-term consequences of this invasive species is necessary.

6.0
APPENDICES

Appendix 1: Invasive plants considered a high priority for management based on their associated risks.

Species	Risk Category	Risk	References
Norway maple (*Acer platanoides*)	Economic	Cause reduced hardwood growth	Galbraith-Kent & Handel, 2012
		Suppress hardwood regeneration	Fang & Wang, 2011 Galbraith-Kent & Handel, 2008 Martin, 1999 Reinhart et al. 2005; 2006 Wycoff & Webb, 1996
	Environmental	Cause the loss of biodiversity	Bertin et al. 2005 Fang, 2005 Reinhart et al. 2005 Wyckoff & Webb, 1996
		Affect ecosystem function	Gómez-Aparicio & Canham, 2008a
Tree-of-heaven (*Ailanthus altissima*)	Economic	Suppress hardwood regeneration	Heisey, 1990 Lawrence et al. 1991 Mergen, 1959
	Environmental	Cause the loss of biodiversity	Knapp & Canham, 2000 Small et al. 2010
		Affect ecosystem function	Gómez-Aparicio & Canham, 2008b
	Social	Impacts on human health	Ballero et al. 2003 Derrick & Darley, 1994
Garlic mustard (*Alliaria petiolata*)	Economic	Cause reduced hardwood growth	Stinson et al. 2006
		Suppress hardwood regeneration	Meekins & McCarthy, 1999 Stinson et al. 2006
	Environmental	Cause the loss of biodiversity	Stinson et al. 2007
		Affect ecosystem function	Burke, 2008 Cantor et al. 2011 Koch et al. 2011 Rodgers et al. 2008
		Harm species-at-risk	Renwick, 2002 Porter, 1994

Appendix 1: cont'd.

Species	Risk Category	Risk	References
Barberry (*Berberis* spp.)	Economic	Cause reduced hardwood growth	Silander Jr. & Klepeis, 1999
	Environmental	Cause the loss of biodiversity	Kourtev et al. 1998
		Affect ecosystem function	Ehrenfeld et al. 2001 Kourtev et al. 1998; 2002a; 2002b; 2003
	Social	Impacts on human health	Elias et al. 2006 Williams et al. 2009
English Ivy (*Hedera helix*)	Economic	Cause hardwood mortality	Schnitzer & Bongers, 2002 Swearingen & Diedrich, 2006 Thomas, 1980
		Suppress hardwood regeneration	Dlugosch, 2005 Schnitzer & Bongers, 2002
	Environmental	Cause the loss of biodiversity	Dlugosch, 2005 Harmer et al. 2001 Thomas, 1980
	Social	Impacts on human health Affect recreational enjoyment	Swearingen et al. 2010
Himalayan balsam (*Impatiens glandulifera*)	Economic	Suppress hardwood regeneration	Maule et al. 2000 Pyšek & Prach, 1995
	Environmental	Cause the loss of biodiversity	Andrews et al. 2009 Clements et al. 2008 Perrins et al. 1993
Japanese knotweed (*Fallopia japonica*)	Economic	Suppress hardwood regeneration	Beerling et al. 1994 Weber, 2003
	Environmental	Cause the loss of biodiversity	Aguilera et al. 2010 Beerling et al. 1994 Maerz et al. 2005
Common buckthorn (*Rhamnus cathartica*)	Economic	Suppress hardwood regeneration	Delanoy & Archibold, 2007 Mascaro & Schnitzer, 2007
	Environmental	Cause loss of biodiversity	Klionsky et al. 2010 Knight et al. 2007
	Environmental	Affect ecosystem function	Heneghan et al. 2004; 2006; 2007 Knight et al. 2007
Periwinkle (*Vinca minor*)	Economic	Suppress hardwood regeneration	Darcy & Burkart, 2002
	Environmental	Cause loss of biodiversity	Drake et al. 2003
	Environmental	Affect ecosystem function	Bultman & DeWitt, 2008
Dog-strangling vine (*Vincetoxicum* spp.)	Economic	Suppress hardwood regeneration	DiTommaso et al. 2005
	Environmental	Cause loss of biodiversity	Cappuccino, 2004 Kricsfalusy & Miller, 2010
	Environmental	Affect ecosystem function	Smith et al. 2008
	Environmental	Harm a species-at-risk	DiTommaso & Losey, 2003 Ladd & Cappuccino, 2005

Appendix 2: Invasive insects and pathogens considered a high priority for management based on their associated risks.

Species	Risk Category	Risk	References
Emerald ash borer (*Agrilus planipennis*)	Economic	Cause hardwood mortality	Cappaert et al. 2005 MacFarlane & Meyer, 2005 Poland & McCullough, 2006 Raupp et al. 2006
	Environmental	Cause loss of biodiversity	Gandhi & Herms, 2010 Kimoto & Duthie-Holt, 2006 Poland & McCullough, 2006;
	Social	Interfere with a traditional lifestyle	Herms et al. 2004
	Social	Reduce aesthetic values of the forest	Cartwell, 2007
Asian long-horned beetle (*Anoplophora glabripennis*)	Economic	Cause reduced hardwood growth	Dodds & Orwig, 2011
	Economic	Cause hardwood mortality	Cartwell, 2007 Hu et al. 2009 Raupp et al. 2006
	Environmental	Cause loss of biodiversity	Kimoto & Duthie-Holt, 2006
	Social	Interfere with a traditional lifestyle	Cartwell, 2007
	Social	Reduce aesthetic values of the forest	Cartwell, 2007 Nowak et al. 2001
Chestnut Blight (*Cryphonectria parasitica*)	Economic	Cause reduced hardwood growth	McEwan et al. 2006 Paillet, 2002 Tindall et al. 2004
	Economic	Cause hardwood mortality	Griffin, 2000 Sinclair & Lyon, 2005
	Environmental	Cause loss of biodiversity	Sinclair & Lyon, 2005
	Environmental	Harm a species-at-risk	OMNR, 2012b Sinclair & Lyon, 2005
	Social	Interfere with a traditional lifestyle	Youngs, 2000
	Social	Reduce aesthetic values of the forest	Anagnostakis, 1982; 1987
Gypsy moth (*Lymantria dispar*)	Economic	Cause reduced hardwood growth	Baker, 1941 Tobin & Liebold, 2011
	Economic	Cause hardwood mortality	Baker, 1941 Davidson et al. 1999 Fajvan & Wood, 1996 Tobin & Liebold, 2011
	Social	Reduce aesthetic values of the forest	Hollenhorst et al. 1991 Régnière et al. 2009
	Social	Affect recreational enjoyment	Leuschner et al. 1996 Régnière et al. 2009
	Social	Impacts on human health	McManus et al. 1989

Appendix 2: Cont'd.

Species	Risk Category	Risk	References
Beech bark disease (*Neonectria faginata*)	Economic	Cause hardwood mortality	Houston, 1994 McCullough et al. 2005 Shigo, 1972
	Economic	Suppress hardwood regeneration	Hane, 2003 Nyland et al. 2006
	Environmental	Cause loss of biodiversity	McCullough et al. 2005
	Environmental	Affect ecosystem function	McCullough et al. 2005 Storer et al. 2005
	Social	Reduce aesthetic values of the forest	Sinclair & Lyon, 2005
	Social	Affect recreational enjoyment	Heyd, 2005
Dutch elm disease (*Ophiostoma* spp.)	Economic	Cause hardwood mortality	Gibes, 1978
	Environmental	Cause loss of biodiversity	NRCan, 2011
	Social	Reduce aesthetic values of the forest	Davis & Meyer, 1997 Sinclair & Lyon, 2005
Elm bark beetles (*Scolytus* spp.)	Economic	Cause hardwood mortality	Negrón et al. 2005 Seybold et al. 2008
	Environmental	Cause loss of biodiversity	NRCan, 2011
Butternut canker (*Ophiognomonia clavigignenti-juglandacearum*)	Economic	Cause hardwood mortality	Davis & Meyer, 1997
	Environmental	Cause loss of biodiversity	Davis & Meyer, 1997 Schlarbaum et al. 1997
	Environmental	Harm a species-at-risk	OMNR, 2012b
	Social	Reduce aesthetic values of the forest	Davis & Meyer, 1997 Ostry et al. 1994

7.0
REFERENCES

Adams, J., Fang, W., Callaway, R., Cipollini, D., & Newell, E. (2009). A cross-continental test of the enemy release hypothesis: Leaf herbivory on ` (L.) is three times lower in North America than in its native Europe. *Biological Invasions* 11(4): 1005-1016.

Agrios, G.N. (2005). *Plant pathology* (5th ed.). Burlington, MA: Elsevier Academic Press.

Aguilera, A. G., Alpert, P., Dukes, J. S., & Harrington, R. (2010). Impacts of the invasive plant *Fallopia japonica* (Houtt.) on plant communities and ecosystem processes. *Biological Invasions* 12: 1243-1252.

Allen, E. A., & Humble, L. M. (2002). Nonindigenous species introductions: A threat to Canada's forests and forest economy. *Canadian Journal of Plant Pathology* 24: 103-110.

Ammer, C., Schall, P., Wördehoff, R., Lamatsch, K., & Bachmann, M. (2011). Does tree seedling growth and survival require weeding of Himalayan balsam (*Impatiens glandulifera*)? *European Journal of Forest Research* 130: 107-116.

Anagnostakis, S. L. (1982). Biological control of chestnut blight. *Science* 215(4532): 466-471.

Anagnostakis, S. L. (1987). Chestnut blight: The classical problem of an introduced pathogen. *Mycologia* 79(1): 23-37.

Anderson, R. (1999). Disturbance as a factor in the distribution of sugar maple and the invasion of Norway maple into a modified woodland. *Rhodora* 101(907): 264-273.

Anderson, R. C., Dhillion, S. S., & Kelley, T. M. (1996). Aspects of the ecology of an invasive plant, garlic mustard (*Alliaria petiolata*), in central Illinois. *Restoration Ecology* 4(2): 181-191.

Andrews, M., Maule, H.G., Hodge, S., Cherrill, A., & Raven, J.A. (2009). Seed dormancy, nitrogen nutrition and shade acclimation of *Impatiens glandulifera*: Implications for successful invasion of deciduous woodland. *Plant Ecology & Diversity* 2(2): 145-153.

Anulewicz, A. C., McCullough, D. G., & Cappaert, D. L. (2007). Emerald ash borer (*Agrilus planipennis*) density and canopy dieback in three North American ash species. *Arboriculture and Urban Forestry* 33(5): 338-349.

Anulewicz, A.C., McCullough, D.G., Cappaert, D.L., & Poland, T.M. (2008). Host range of the emerald ash borer (*Agrilus planipennis* Fairmaire) (Coleoptera: Buprestidae) in North America: Results of multiple-choice field experiments. *Environmental Entomology* 37(1): 230-241.

Armson, K.A. (2001). *Ontario's forests: An historical perspective*. Toronto, ON: Fitzhenry & Whiteside.

Ascerno, M. E., & Wawrzynski, R. P. (1994). *Native elm bark beetle control*. University of Minnesota Extension. Retrieved November 12, 2011, from http://www.extension.umn.edu/distribution/horticulture/DG1420.html

Ash, C. (1994). *Verticillium wilt of trees and shrubs*. University of Minnesota Extension. Retrieved November 6, 2011, from http://www.extension.umn.edu/distribution/horticulture/DG1164.html

Averill, K. M., DiTommaso, A., & Morris, S. H. (2008). Response of pale swallow-wort (*Vincetoxicum rossicum*) to triclopyr application and clipping. *Invasive Plant Science and Management* 1: 196-206.

Bailey, H. (1969). *Manual of cultivated plants: Most commonly grown in the continental United States and Canada*. Toronto, ON: The MacMillan Company.

Baker, W. L. (1941). Effect of gypsy moth defoliation on certain forest trees. *Journal of Forestry* 39(12): 1017-1022.

Ballero, M., Ariu, A., Falagiani, P., & Piu, G. (2003). Allergy to *Ailanthus altissima* (tree of heaven) pollen. *Allergy* 58: 532-533.

Bancroft, J. S., & Smith, M. T. (2005). Dispersal and influences on movement for *Anoplophora glabripennis* calculated from individual mark-recapture. *Entomologia Experimentalis et Applicata* 116: 83-92.

Barto, E., Powell, J., & Cipollini, D. (2010). How novel are the chemical weapons of garlic mustard in North American forest understories? *Biological Invasions* 12(10): 3465-3471.

Bartomeus, I., Vilà, M., & Steffan-Dewenter, I. (2010). Combined effects of *Impatiens glandulifera* invasion and landscape structure on native plant pollination. *Journal of Ecology* 98: 440-450.

Bean, C., & Russo, M. J. (1988). *Element stewardship abstract for Vinca major (periwinkle)*. Virginia, USA: The Nature Conservancy. Retrieved April 18, 2011, from http://www.imapinvasives.org/GIST/ESA/esapages/documnts/vincmaj.pdf.

Beerling, D. J., Bailey, J. P., & Conolly, A. P. (1994). *Fallopia japonica* (Houtt.) Ronse Decraene. *Journal of Ecology* 82: 959-979.

Beerling, D. J., & Perrins, J. M. (1993). *Impatiens glandulifera* Royle (*Impatiens roylei* Walp.). *Journal of Ecology* 81(2): 367-382.

Bell, F. W., & Newmaster, S. G. (2002). The effects of silvicultural disturbances on the diversity of seed-producing plants in the boreal mixedwood forest. *Canadian Journal of Forest Research* 32: 1180-1191.

Benoit, P., & Lachance, D. (1990). *Gypsy moth in Canada: Behavior and control.* Information Report DPC-X-32. Sainte-Foy, QC: Forestry Canada, Quebec Region.

Bergmann, C., & Swearingen, J. M. (2005). *Fact sheet: Kudzu.* Plant Conservation Alliance's Alien Plant Working Group. Weeds Gone Wild: Alien Plant Invaders of Natural Areas. Retrieved November 2, 2011, from http://www.nps.gov/plants/alien/fact/pdf/pumo1.pdf

Bertin, R. I., Manner, M. E., Larrow, B. F., Cantwell, T. W., & Berstene, E. M. (2005). Norway maple (*Acer platanoides*) and other non-native trees in urban woodlands of central Massachusetts. *Journal of the Torrey Botanical Society* 132(2): 225-235.

Bickerton, H., & Thompson-Black, M. (2010). *Recovery strategy for the eastern flowering dogwood (Cornus florida) in Ontario.* Ontario Recovery Strategy Series. Peterborough, ON: Ontario Ministry of Natural Resources. Retrieved October 6, 2011, from http://www.ontla.on.ca/library/repository/mon/23012/297385.pdf.

Bigsby, K.M., Tobin, P.C., & Sills, E.O. (2011). Anthropogenic drivers of gypsy moth spread. *Biological Invasions* 13: 2077-2090.

BioForest. (2012). *TreeAzin systemic insecticide: Trees saving trees.* BioForest Technologies Inc. Retrieved November 2, 2012, from http://www.bioforest.ca/index.cfm?fuseaction=content&menuid=18&pageid=1026

Bisessar, S., McLaughlin, D.L., & Linzon, S.N. (1985). The first occurrence of the beech scale insect on American beech trees in Ontario. *Journal of Arboriculture* 11(1): 13-14.

Boland, G., Ambrose, J., Elliott, K., Husband, B., Melzer, M., & Waldron, G. (2000). *National recovery plan for American chestnut (Castanea dentata (Marsh.) Borkh.).* World Wildlife Fund and Canadian Wildlife Service.

Bory, G., & Clair-Maczulajtys, D. (1980). (Production, dissemination and polymorphism of seeds in *Ailanthus altissima*.). *Revue Générale de Botanique* 88: 297-311.

Bothwell, R. (1986). *A short history of Ontario.* Edmonton, AB: Hurtig.

Bourchier, R. S., & Van Hezewijk, B. H. (2010). Distribution and potential spread of Japanese knotweed (*Polygonum cuspidatum*) in Canada relative to climatic thresholds. *Invasive Plant Science and Management* 3: 32-39.

Brandt, R. W. (1964). *Nectria canker of hardwoods.* Forest Pest Leaflet 84. U.S. Department of Agriculture, Forest Service. Retrieved November 2, 2012, from http://www.fs.fed.us/outernet/r6/nr/fid/fidls/fidl-84.pdf

Brasier, C.M. (1990). China and the origins of Dutch elm disease: An appraisal. *Plant Pathology* 39: 5-16.

Brasier, C.M. (1991). *Ophiostoma novo-ulmi* sp. nov., causative agent of current Dutch elm disease pandemics. *Mycopathologia* 115: 151-161.

Brasier, C.M., & Buck, K.W. (2001). Rapid evolutionary changes in a globally invading fungal pathogen (Dutch elm disease). *Biological Invasions* 3: 223-233.

Brasier, C.M., & Kirk, S.A. (2001). Designation of the EAN and NAN races of *Ophiostoma novo-ulmi* as subspecies. *Mycological Research* 105: 547-554.

Brasier, C.M., & Mehrotra, M.D. (1995). *Ophiostoma himal-ulmi* sp. nov., a new species of Dutch elm disease fungus endemic to the Himalayas. *Mycological Research* 99(2): 205-215.

Brewer, L.G. (1995). Ecology of survival and recovery from blight in American chestnut trees (*Castanea dentata* (Marsh.) Borkh.) in Michigan. *Bulletin of the Torrey Botanical Club* 122(1): 40-57.

Broders, K.D., & Boland, G.J. (2011). Reclassification of the butternut canker fungus, *Sirococcus clavigignenti-juglandacearum*, into the genus *Ophiognomonia. Fungal Biology* 115: 70-79.

Bultman, T. L., & DeWitt, D. J. (2008). Effect of an invasive ground cover plant on the abundance and diversity of a forest floor spider assemblage. *Biological Invasions* 10: 749-756.

Burch, P. L., & Zedaker, S. M. (2003). Removing the invasive tree *Ailanthus altissima* and restoring natural cover. *Journal of Arboriculture* 29(1): 18-24.

Burke, D. (2008). Effects of *Alliaria petiolata* (garlic mustard: Brassicaceae) on mycorrhizal colonization and community structure in three herbaceous plants in a mixed deciduous forest. *American Journal of Botany* 95(11): 1416-1425.

Burke, D., Elliott, K., Falk, K., & Piraino, T. (2011). *A land manager's guide to conserving habitat for forest birds in southern Ontario.* Ontario Ministry of Natural Resources, Science and Information Resource Division and Trent University. Retrieved November 2, 2011, from http://www.ont-woodlot-assoc.org/pdf/August%202011%20-%20Land_Manager's_Guide_2011.pdf

Byers, J. A., Svihra, P., & Koehler, C. S. (1980). Attraction of elm bark beetles to cut limbs of elm. *Journal of Arboriculture* 6(9): 245-246.

Byford, B. (2009). *A landowner's guide to careful logging.* Ontario Woodlot Association (OWA). Retrieved November 2, 2011, from http://www.ont-woodlot-assoc.org/pdf/Careful-Logging-web.pdf

Canadian Food Inspection Agency (CFIA). (2008). *D-01-04: Plant protection import and domestic movement requirements for barberry (Berberis, Mahoberberis and Mahonia spp.) under the Canadian barberry certification program.* Ottawa, Ontario: Canadian Food Inspection Agency. Government of Canada. Retrieved April 25, 2011, from http://www.inspection.gc.ca/english/plaveg/protect/dir/d-01-04e.shtml

Canadian Food Inspection Agency (CFIA). (2010). *D-97-07: Phytosanitary requirements for the importation from the United States and domestic movement of elm material (Ulmus spp. and Zelkova spp.) to prevent the introduction and spread of Dutch elm disease Ophiostoma ulmi (Buisman) Nannf. and Ophiostoma novo-ulmi (Brasier) within Canada.* Ottawa, Ontario: Canadian Food Inspection Agency. Government of Canada. Retrieved November 17, 2011, from http://www.inspection.gc.ca/english/plaveg/protect/dir/d-97-07e.shtml#e

Canadian Food Inspection Agency (CFIA). (2011a). *D-98-09: Comprehensive policy to control the spread of North American gypsy moth, Lymantria dispar in Canada and the United States.* Ottawa, Ontario: Canadian Food Inspection Agency. Government of Canada. Retrieved November 14, 2011, from http://www.inspection.gc.ca/plants/plant-protection/directives/forestry/d-98-09/eng/1323885774950/1323886065560

Canadian Food Inspection Agency (CFIA). (2011b). *Emerald ash borer infested places order.* Ottawa, Ontario: Canadian Food Inspection Agency.Government of Canada. Retrieved November 11, 2011, from http://www.inspection.gc.ca/english/plaveg/pestrava/agrpla/20110325minoe.shtml

Canadian Food Inspection Agency (CFIA). (2012b). *Anoplophora glabripennis:* Asian long-horned beetle. Ottawa, Ontario: Canadian Food Inspection Agency. Government of Canada. Retrieved November 2, 2012, from http://www.inspection.gc.ca/plants/plant-protection/insects/asian-long-horned-beetle/eng/1337792721926/1337792820836

Canadian Food Inspection Agency (CFIA). (2012a). *Firewood.* Ottawa, Ontario: Canadian Food Inspection Agency. Government of Canada. Retrieved June 18, 2012, from http://www.inspection.gc.ca/plants/forestry/firewood/eng/1330963478693/1330963579986

Canadian Forest Service (CFS). (2011). *Insects and diseases of Canada's forests.* Natural Resources Canada. Retrieved September 23, 2011, from http://imfc.cfl.scf.rncan.gc.ca/accueil-home-eng.html

Cantor, A., Hale, A., Aaron, J., Traw, M. B., & Kalisz, S. (2011). Low allelochemical concentrations detected in garlic mustard – invaded forest soils inhibit fungal growth and AMF spore germination. *Biological Invasions* 13: 3015-3025.

Cappaert, D., McCullough, D. G., Poland, T. M., & Siegert, N. W. (2005). Emerald ash borer in North America: A research and regulatory challenge. *American Entomologist* 51(3): 152-165.

Cappuccino, N. (2004). Allee effect in an invasive alien plant, pale swallow-wort *Vincetoxicum rossicum* (Asclepiadaceae). *Oikos 106*: 3-8.

Cartwell, C. G. (Ed.). (2007). *Invasive forest pests.* New York, NY: Nova Science Publishers Inc.

Cavers, P. B., Heagy, M. I., & Kokron, R. F. (1979). The biology of Canadian weeds. 35. *Alliaria petiolata* (M. Bieb.) Cavara and Grande. *Canadian Journal of Plant Science* 59: 217-229

Chamberlain, A. F. (1891). The maple amongst the Algonkian tribes. *American Anthropologist* 4(1): 39-44.

Chambers, B., Legasy, K., & Bentley, C. V. (1996). *Forest plants of central Ontario.* Edmonton, AB: Lone Pine Publishing.

Chapeskie, D., & Hendersen, J. (2007). *What you should know about maple syrup factsheet.* Ontario Ministry of Agriculture, Food and Rural Affairs (OMAFRA). Retrieved December 6, 2010, from http://www.omafra.gov.on.ca/english/crops/facts/07-069.htm

Chapeskie, D., Richardson, M., Wheeler, A., Sajan, B., & Neave, P. (2006). *A guide to improving and maintaining sugar bush health and productivity.* Kemptville, ON: Eastern Ontario Model Forest.

Cheng-Yuan, X., Griffin, K. L., & Schuster, W. S. F. (2007). Leaf phenology and seasonal variation of photosynthesis of invasive *Berberis thunbergii* (Japanese barberry) and two co-occurring native understory shrubs in a northeastern United States deciduous forest. *Oecologia* 154: 11-21.

Chung, W., Kim, J., Yamaoka, Y., Uzunovic, A., Masuya, H., & Breuil, C. (2006). *Ophiostoma breviusculum* sp. nov. (Ophiostomatales, Ascomycota) is a new species in the *Ophiostoma piceae* complex associated with bark beetles infesting larch in Japan. *Mycologia* 98(5): 801-814.

Cincotta, C. L., Adams, J. M., & Holzapfel, C. (2009). Testing the enemy release hypothesis: A comparison of foliar insect herbivory of the exotic Norway maple (*Acer platanoides* L.) and the native sugar maple (*A. saccharum* L.). *Biological Invasions* 11(2): 379-388.

Clark, J. (2003). *Invasive plant prevention guidelines.* Bozeman, MT: Center for Invasive Plant Management. Retrieved March 21, 2011, from http://www.weedcenter.org/store/docs/CIPM_prevention.pdf

Clark, R. V., Seaman, W. L., & Martens, J. W. (1986). *Puccinia graminis* on barberry and oats in eastern Ontario from 1968 to 1983. *Canadian Journal of Plant Pathology* 8(2): 193-200.

Clauson, K. (2011). *Norway maple (Acer platanoides): A serious threat to Iowa's woodlands.* The Hawkeye Cooperative Management Area (HCWMA). Retrieved July 29, 2011, from http://hawkeyecwma.org/brochures/woodland/Norway%20Maple%20brochure.pdf

Clements, D. R., Feenstra, K. R., Jones, K., & Staniforth, R. (2008). The biology of invasive alien plants in Canada. 9. *Impatiens glandulifera* Royle. *Canadian Journal of Plant Science* 88: 403-417.

Clout, M. N., & Williams, P. A. (2009). Introduction. In M. N. Clout, & P. A. Williams (Eds.), *Invasive species management: A handbook of principles and techniques* (pp. v-ix). Oxford, NY: Oxford University Press.

Coons, C. F. (1992). *Sugar bush management for maple syrup producers.* Toronto, ON: Ontario Ministry of Natural Resources (OMNR).

Cranshaw, W., & Tisserat, N. (2008). *Pest alert: Walnut twig beetle and thousand cankers disease of black walnut.* Colorado State University. Retrieved November 12, 2011, from http://wci.colostate.edu/Assets/pdf/ThousandCankers.pdf

Crook, D.J., Khrimian, A., Francese, J.A., Fraser, I., Poland, T.M., Sawyer, A.J., & Mastro, V.C. (2008). Development of a host-based semiochemical lure for trapping emerald ash borer *Agrilus planipennis* (Coleoptera: Buprestidae). *Environmental Entomology* 37(2): 356-365.

Crooks, J. A. (2005). Lag times and exotic species: The ecology and management of biological invasions in slow-motion. *EcoScience* 12(3): 316-329.

Daily, G. C., Alexander, S., Ehrlich, P. R., Goulder, L., Lubchenco, J., Matson, P. A., Mooney, H. A., Postel, S., Schneider, S. H., Tilman, D., & Woodwell, G. M. (1997). Ecosystem services: Benefits supplied to human societies by natural ecosystems. *Issues in Ecology* 2: 1-16.

Darcy, A. J., & Burkart, M. C. (2002). Allelopathic potential of *Vinca minor*, an invasive exotic plant in west Michigan forests. *Bios* 73(4): 127-132.

Davidson, C. B., Gottschalk, K. W., & Johnson, J. E. (1999). Tree mortality following defoliation by the European gypsy moth (*Lymantria dispar* L.) in the United States: A review. *Forest Science* 45(1): 74-84.

Davis, C., & Meyer, T. (1997). *Field guide to tree diseases of Ontario.* Sault Ste Marie, Ontario: Canadian Forest Service, Great Lakes Forestry Centre, Natural Resources Canada.

Davis, C. N., Myren, D. T., & Czerwinski, E. J. (1992). First report of butternut canker in Ontario. *Plant Disease* 76(9): 972.

de Groot, P., Grant, G.G., Poland, T.M., Scharbach, R., Buchan, L., Nott, R.W., Macdonald, L., & Pitt, D. (2008). Electrophysiological response and attraction of emerald ash borer to green leaf volatiles (GLVs) emitted by host foliage. *Journal of Chemical Ecology* 34: 1170-1179.

Delanoy, L., & Archibold, O. W. (2007). Efficacy of control measures for European buckthorn (*Rhamnus cathartica* L.) in Saskatchewan. *Environmental Management* 40: 709-718.

Department of Canadian Heritage (DCH). (2008). *The maple leaf.* Government of Canada. Retrieved December 7, 2010, from http://www.pch.gc.ca/pgm/ceem-cced/symbl/o3-eng.cfm

Derrick, E. K., & Darley, C. R. (1994). Contact reaction to the tree of heaven. *Contact Dermatitis* 30: 178.

DesRochers, P. (2009). Can we still save the butternut from extinction? *Branching Out* 47: 1-2.

Dickinson, T., Metsger, D., Bull, J., & Dickinson, R. (2004). *The ROM field guide to wildflowers of Ontario.* Toronto, ON: The Royal Ontario Museum.

Diller, J. D. (1965). *Chestnut blight.* Forest Pest Leaflet 94. U.S. Department of Agriculture, Forest Service. Retrieved November 2, 2012, from http://dnrc.mt.gov/Forestry/Assistance/Pests/Documents/FIDLs/ChestnutBlight094.pdf

Diskin, M., Steiner, K.C., & Hebard, F.V. (2006). Recovery of American chestnut characteristics following hybridization and backcross breeding to restore blight-ravaged *Castanea dentata*. *Forest Ecology and Management* 223: 439-447.

DiTommaso, A., Lawlor, F. M., & Darbyshire, S. J. (2005). The biology of invasive alien plants in Canada. 2. *Cynanchum rossicum* (Kleopow) Borhidi [= *Vincetoxicum rossicum* (Kleopow) Barbar.] and *Cynanchum louiseae* (L.) Kartesz & Gandhi [= *Vincetoxicum nigrum* (L.) Moench]. *Canadian Journal of Plant Science* 85(1): 243-263.

DiTommaso, A., & Losey, J. E. (2003). Oviposition preference and larval performance of monarch butterflies (*Danaus plexippus*) on two invasive swallow-wort species. *Entomologia Experimentalis et Applicata* 108: 205-209.

Dlugosch, K. M. (2005). Understory community changes associated with English ivy invasions in Seattle's urban parks. *Northwest Science* 79(1): 52-59.

Dodds, K.J., & Orwig, D.A. (2011). An invasive urban forest pest invades natural environments – Asian longhorned beetle in northeastern US hardwood forests. *Canadian Journal of Forest Research* 41: 1729-1742.

Dodds, K. J., & Seybold, S. J. (1996). *Pest alert: Forest tent caterpillar.* Newton Square, PA: United States Department of Agriculture, Forest Service, Northeastern Area State & Private Forestry. Retrieved November 16, 2011, from http://www.na.fs.fed.us/spfo/pubs/pest_al/ftc/ftc.htm

Douglass, C. H., Weston, L. A., & DiTommaso, A. (2009). Black and pale swallow-wort (*Vincetoxicum nigrum* and *V. rossicum*): The biology and ecology of two perennial,

exotic and invasive vines. In Inderjit (Ed.), *Management of invasive weeds* (pp. 261-277). Springer Netherlands.

Drake, S. J., Weltzin, J. F., & Parr, P. D. (2003). Assessment of non-native invasive plant species on the United States Department of Energy Oak Ridge National Environmental Research Park. *Castanea* 68(1): 15-30.

Drayton, B., & Primack, R. B. (1999). Experimental extinction of garlic mustard (*Alliaria petiolata*) populations: Implications for weed science and conservation biology. *Biological Invasions* 1(2): 159-167.

Drewitz, J. (2000). *Vinca major.* In C. C. Bossard, J. M. Randall & M. C. Hoshovsky (Eds.), *Invasive plants of California`s wildlands.* (pp. 326-328). Berkeley, CA: University of California Press. Retrieved April 29, 2011, from http://www.calipc.org/ip/management/ipcw/online.php

Easterbrook, W. T., & Aitken, H. G. J. (1988). *Canadian Economic History.* Toronto, ON: University of Toronto Press.

Ehrenfeld, J. G. (1997). Invasion of deciduous forest preserves in the New York metropolitan region by Japanese barberry (*Berberis thunbergii* DC.). *Journal of the Torrey Botanical Society* 124(2): 210-215.

Ehrenfeld, J. G. (1999). Structure and dynamics of populations of Japanese barberry (*Berberis thunbergii* DC.) in deciduous forests of New Jersey. *Biological Invasions* 1: 203-213.

Ehrenfeld, J. G., Kourtev, P., & Huang, W. (2001). Changes in soil functions following invasions of exotic understory plants in deciduous forests. *Ecological Applications* 11(5): 1287-1300.

Ehrlich, J. (1934). The beech bark disease: A *Nectria* disease of *Fagus*, following *Cryptococcus fagi* (Baer.). *Canadian Journal of Research* 10(6): 593-692.

Elias, S. P., Lubelczyk, C. B., Rand, P. W., Lacombe, E. H., Holman, M. S., & Smith, R. P. (2006). Deer browse resistant exotic-invasive understory: An indicator of elevated human risk of exposure to *Ixodes scapularis* (Acari: Ixodidae) in southern coastal Maine woodlands. *Journal of Medical Entomology* 43(6): 1142-1152.

Environment Canada (2004). *An invasive alien species strategy for Canada.* Government of Canada. Retrieved March 21, 2011, from http://www.ec.gc.ca/eeeias/default.asp?lang=En&n=1A81B051-1

Environment Canada. (2010). Recovery strategy for the butternut (*Juglans cinerea*) in Canada. *Species at Risk Act Recovery Strategy Series.* Environment Canada, Ottawa vii + 24 pp.

Environment Canada. (2011). *Species at risk public registry.* Retrieved October 23, 2011, from http://www.sararegistry.gc.ca

Fajvan, M. A., & Wood, J. M. (1996). Stand structure and development after gypsy moth defoliation in the Appalachian Plateau. *Forest Ecology and Management* 89: 79-88.

Fang, W., & Wang, X. (2011). Impact of invasion of *Acer platanoides* on canopy structure and understory seedling growth in a hardwood forest in North America. *Trees* 25: 455-464.

Fang, W. (2005). Spatial analysis of an invasion front of *Acer platanoides*: Dynamic inferences from static data. *Ecography* 28: 283-294.

Farrar, J. L. (1995). *Trees in Canada.* Canada: Markham, ON: Fitzhenry & Whiteside Limited and the Canadian Forest Service, Natural Resources Canada.

Fernald, M. L. (1950). *Gray's manual of botany: A handbook of the flowering plants and ferns of the central and northeastern United States and adjacent Canada.* New York, NY: American Book Company.

Forest Gene Conservation Association (FGCA). (n.d.). *Butternut (Juglans cinerea L.)*.Retrieved November 6, 2011, from http://www.fgca.net/conservation/sar/butternut.aspx

Forman, J., & Kesseli, R. V. (2003). Sexual reproduction in the invasive species *Fallopia japonica* (Polygonaceae). *American Journal of Botany* 90(4): 586-592.

Frey, M. N., Herms, C. P., & Cardina, J. (2005). Methods for garlic mustard seed prevention and destruction. In J. Cardina (Ed.), *Ohio invasive plant research conference: Bridging the gap between land management and research* (pp. 123-124). Wooster, Ohio: The Ohio State University & Ohio Agricultural Research and Development Center. Retrieved February 9, 2011, from http://ohioline.osu.edu/sc196/pdf/sc196.pdf.

Galbraith-Kent, S. L., & Handel, S. N. (2008). Invasive *Acer platanoides* inhibits native sapling growth in forest understory communities. *Journal of Ecology* 96: 293-302.

Galbraith-Kent, S. L., & Handel, S. N. (2012). *Acer rubrum* (red maple) growth is negatively affected by soil from forest stands dominated by its invasive cogener (*Acer platanoides*, Norway maple). *Plant Ecology* 213: 77-88.

Gandhi, K. J. K., & Herms, D. A. (2010). North American arthropods at risk due to wide spread *Fraxinus* mortality caused by the alien emerald ash borer. *Biological Invasions* 12: 1839-1846.

Gale, S. W. (2000). Control of the invasive exotic *Rhamnus cathartica* in temperate North American forests. *Restoration and Reclamation Review* 6(5): 1-13.

Gardescu, S. (2003). Herbivory, disease, and mortality of sugar maple seedlings. *Northeastern Naturalist* 10(3): 253-268.

Garske, S., & Schimpf, D. (2005). *Fact sheet: Goutweed.* Plant Conservation Alliance's Alien Plant Working Group. Weeds Gone Wild: Alien Plant Invaders of Natural Areas. Retrieved November 2, 2011, from http://www.nps.gov/plants/alien/fact/pdf/aepo1.pdf

Gibbs, J. N. (1978). Intercontinental epidemiology of Dutch elm disease. *Annual Review of Phytopathology* 16: 287-307.

Gleason, H. A., & Cronquist, A. (1963). *Manual of vascular plants of northeastern United States and adjacent Canada.* New York, NY: D. Van Nostrand Company.

Global Invasive Species Database (GISD). (2006). *Agrilus planipennis (insect)*.The Invasive Species Specialist Group. Retrieved November 11, 2011, from http://www.issg.org/database/species/ecology.asp?si=722&fr=1&sts=&lang=EN

Gómez-Aparicio, L., & Canham, C. D. (2008a). Neighborhood models of the effects of invasive tree species on ecosystem processes. *Ecological Monographs* 78(1): 69-86.

Gómez-Aparicio, L., & Canham, C. D. (2008b). Neighbourhood analyses of the allelopathic effects of the invasive tree *Ailanthus altissima* in temperate forests. *Journal of Ecology* 96(3): 447-458.

Grant, J. F., Windham, M. T., Haun, W. G., Wiggins, G. J., & Lambdin, P. L. (2011). Initial assessment of thousand cankers disease on black walnut, *Juglans nigra*, in eastern Tennessee. *Forests* 2: 741-748.

Greenberg, C. H., Smith, L. M., & Levey, D. J. (2001). Fruit fate, seed germination and growth of an invasive vine - an experimental test of 'sit and wait' strategy. *Biological Invasions* 3: 363-372.

Grice, T. (2009). Principles of containment and control of invasive species. In M. N. Clout, & P. A. Williams (Eds.), *Invasive species management: A handbook of principles and techniques* (pp. 61-76). Oxford, New York: Oxford University Press.

Griffin, G. J. (2000). Blight control and restoration of the American chestnut. *Journal of Forestry* 98(2): 22-27.

Griffin, G.J., Hebard, F.V., Wendt, R.W., & Elkins, J.R. (1983). Survival of American chestnut trees: Evaluation of blight resistance and virulence in *Endothia parasitica*. *Phytopathology* 73(7): 1084-1092.

Griffiths, H.M., Sinclair, W. A., Smart, C. D., & Davis, R. E. (1999). The phytoplasma associated with ash yellows and lilac witches'-broom: "*Candidatus* Phytoplasma fraxini". *International Journal of Systematic Bacteriology* 49: 1605-1614.

Gryzenhout, M., Wingfield, B.D., & Wingfield, M.J. (2006). New taxonomic concepts for the important forest pathogen *Cryphonectria parasitica* and related fungi. *FEMS Microbiology Letters* 258: 161-172.

Gucker, C. L. (2009). *Berberis vulgaris.* In: Fire effects information system (online). U.S. Department of Agriculture, Forest Service, Rocky Mountain Research Station, Fire Sciences Laboratory. Retrieved April 25, 2011, from http://www.fs.fed.us/database/feis/.

Haack, R.A., Jendek, E., Liu, H., Marchant, K.R., Petrice, T.R., Poland, T.M., & Ye, H. (2002). The emerald ash borer: A new exotic pest in North America. *Newsletter of the Michigan Entomological Society* 47(3&4): 1-5.

Hajek, A.E. (2007). Asian longhorned beetle: Ecology and control. In Pimentel, D. (Ed.) *Encyclopedia of pest management* (Vol. II, pp.21-24). Boca Raton, FL: CRC Press.

Hajek, A.E., & Tobin, P.C. (2010). Micro-managing arthropod invasions: Eradication and control of invasive arthropods with microbes. *Biological Invasions* 12: 2895-2912.

Halik, S., & Bergdahl, D. R. (2002). Potential beetle vectors of *Sirococcus clavigiginenti-juglandacearum* on butternut. *Plant Disease* 86: 521-527.

Hane, E. N. (2003). Indirect effects of beech bark disease on sugar maple seedling survival. *Canadian Journal of Forest Research* 33: 807-813.

Harmer, R., Peterken, G., Kerr, G., & Poulton, P. (2001). Vegetation changes during 100 years of development of two secondary woodlands on abandoned arable land. *Biological Conservation* 101: 291-304.

Harrington, T. C., McNew, D., Steimel, J., Hofstra, D., & Farrel, R. (2001). Phylogeny and taxonomy of the *Ophiostoma piceae* complex and the Dutch elm disease fungi. *Mycologia* 93(1): 111-136.

Harrison, K. J., & Hurley, J. E. (2001). *Butternut canker.* Pest Notes No. 2. Fredericton, NB: Natural Resources Canada, Canadian Forest Service, Atlantic Forestry Centre. Retrieved November 2, 2012, from http://cfs.nrcan.gc.ca/pubwarehouse/pdfs/25367.pdf

Haugen, L. (1998). *How to identify and manage Dutch elm disease.* NA-PR-07-98. Radnor, PA: U.S. Department of Agriculture, Forest Service, Northeastern Area, State and Private Forestry. Retrieved November 2, 2012, from http://www.treesearch.fs.fed.us/pubs/10918

Hauser, S. C. (1998). *Sugartime; the hidden pleasures of making maple syrup with a primer for the novice sugarer.* Toronto, Ontario: Key Porter Books Limited.

Havinga, D. (2000). *Sustaining biodiversity: A strategic plan for managing invasive plants in southern Ontario.* Ontario Invasive Plants Working Group. Retrieved March 21, 2011, from http://www.serontario.org/pdfs/sustain.pdf

Heiligmann, R. B., Koelling, M. R., & Perkins, T.D. (2006). *North American maple syrup producers manual.* The Ohio State University Extension & the North American Maple Syrup Council.

Heinrich, B. (1992). Maple sugaring by red squirrels. *Journal of Mammalogy* 73(1): 51-54.

Heisey, R. M. (1990). Allelopathic and herbicidal effects of extracts from tree of heaven (*Ailanthus altissima*). *American Journal of Botany* 77(5): 662-670.

Heneghan, L., Fatemi, F., Umek, L., Grady, K., Fagen, K., & Workman, M. (2006). The invasive shrub European buckthorn (*Rhamnus cathartica*, L.) alters soil properties in Midwestern U.S. woodlands. *Applied Soil Ecology* 32: 142-148.

Heneghan, L., Rauschenberg, C., Fatemi, F., & Workman, M. (2004). European buckthorn (*Rhamnus cathartica*) and its effects on some ecosystem properties in an urban woodland. *Ecological Restoration* 22(4): 275-280.

Heneghan, L., Steffen, J., & Fagen, K. (2007). Interactions of an introduced shrub and introduced earthworms in an Illinois urban woodland: Impact on leaf litter decomposition. *Pedobiologia* 50: 543-551.

Herms, D. A. (2007). *Distinguishing emerald ash borer from native borers (fact sheet).* Ohio State University Emerald Ash Borer Outreach Team. The Ohio State University. Retrieved October 1, 2011, from http://www.oardc.ohiostate.edu/neweab/userfiles/native_borers.pdf

Herms, D. A., Stone, A. K., & Chatfield, J. A. (2004). Emerald ash borer: The beginning of the end of ash in North America? In J. A. Chatfield, E. A. Draper, H. M. Mathers, D. E. Dyke, P. J. Bennett, & J. F. Boggs (Eds.), *Ornamental plants: Annual reports and research reviews* 2003 (pp. 62-71). Wooster, Ohio: The Ohio State University & Ohio Agricultural Research and Development Center.

Henshaw, H. W. (1890). Indian origin of maple sugar. *American Anthropologist* 3(4): 341-352.

Heyd, R. L. (2005). Managing beech bark disease in Michigan. In C. A. Evans, J. A. Lucas & M. J. Twery (Eds.), *Beech bark disease: Proceedings of the beech bark disease symposium. Gen. tech. rep. NE-331.* (pp. 128-132). Newtown Square, PA: U.S. Department of Agriculture Forest Service, Northern Research Station.

Hibben, C.R. (1990). Anthracnose threatens the flowering dogwood: Methods for diagnosing and controlling this new disease. *Arnoldia* 50:16-20.

Hilts, S., & Mitchell, P. (1999). *The woodlot management handbook.* Buffalo, NY: Firefly Books Ltd.

Hinrichs, C. (1995). Off the treadmill? Technology and tourism in the North American maple syrup industry. *Agriculture and Human Values* 12(1): 39-47.

Hinrichs, C. (1998). Sideline and lifeline: The cultural economy of maple syrup production. *Rural Sociology* 63(4): 507-532.

Hirsch, R. (2012). Blight resistance: It's in the DNA. *The Journal of the American Chestnut Foundation* 26(2): 20-22.

Holcombe, T., & Stohlgren, T. J. (2009). Detection and early warning of invasive species. In M. N. Clout, & P. A. Williams (Eds.), *Invasive species management: A handbook of principles and techniques* (pp. 36-45). Oxford, NY: Oxford University Press.

Hollenhorst, S. J., Brock, S. M., Freimund, W. A., & Twery, M. J. (1991). Effects of gypsy moth infestations on near-view aesthetic preferences and recreation behaviour intentions. In L. H. McCormick & K. W. Gottschalk (Eds.), *8th Central Hardwood Forest Conference* (pp. 23-33). Radnor, PA: US Department of Agriculture, Forest Service, Northeastern Experiment Station.

Holt, J. S. (2009). Management of invasive terrestrial plants. In M. N. Clout, & P. A. Williams (Eds.), *Invasive species management: A handbook of principles and techniques* (pp. 126-139). Oxford, NY: Oxford University Press.

Hoover, G. A. (2002). *Entomological notes: Pear thrips.* Penn State, College of Agricultural Sciences, Cooperative Extension. Retrieved November 2, 2011, from http://ento.psu.edu/extension/factsheets/pdf/pearthrips.pdf.

Horst, R.K. (2008). *Westcott's Plant Disease Handbook* (7th ed.). Heidelberg, NY: Springer-Verlag Berlin.

Hortvet, J. (1904). The chemical composition of maple-syrup and maple-sugar, methods of analysis, and detection of adulteration. *Journal of the American Chemical Society* 26(11): 1523-1545.

Hoshovsky, M. C. (1995). *Element stewardship abstract for Ailanthus altissima, tree-of-heaven.* Arlington, Virginia: The Nature Conservancy. Retrieved September 14, 2011, from http://conserveonline.org/library/ailaalt.PDF/view.html

Houston, D. R. (1994). Major new tree disease epidemics: Beech bark disease. *Annual Review of Phytopathology* 32: 75-87.

Houston, D. R., & O'Brien, J. T. (1983). *Beech bark disease.* Forest Insect & Disease Leaflet 75. U.S. Department of Agriculture, Forest Service. Retrieved November 6, 2012, from http://www.na.fs.fed.us/spfo/pubs/fidls/beechbark/fidl-beech.htm

Hu, J., Angeli, S., Schuetz, S., Luo, Y., & Hajek, A.E. (2009). Ecology and management of exotic and endemic Asian longhorned beetle *Anoplophora glabripennis. Agricultural and Forest Entomology* 11: 359-375.

Hu, S. Y. (1979). *Ailanthus. Arnoldia* 39: 29-50.

Hubbes, M. (1999). The American elm and Dutch elm disease. *The Forestry Chronicle* 75(2): 265-273.

Huffman, L. (2005). *Problem weed of the month: Garlic mustard.* Ontario Ministry of Agriculture, Food and Rural Affairs (OMAFRA). Retrieved December 16, 2010, from http://www.omafra.gov.on.ca/english/crops/hort/news/hortmatt/2005/10hrt05a4.htm

Humble, L.M., John, E., Smith, J.J., Zilahi-Balogh, G.M.G., Kimoto, T., & Noseworthy, M.K. (2010). First records of the banded elm bark beetle, *Scolytus scheyrewi* Semenov (Coleoptera: Curculionidae: Scolytinae), in British Columbia. *Journal of the Entomological Society of British Columbia* 107: 21-24.

Innes, L., Harrison, K. J., & Davis, C. N. (2001). Distribution of butternut canker (*Sirococcus clavigignenti-juglandacearum*) in eastern Canada. Frontline Express Bulletin No. 2. Sault Ste Marie, ON: Natural Resources Canada, Canadian Forest Service, Great Lakes Forestry Centre.

Retrieved November 6, 2012, from http://publications. gc.ca/collections/collection_2011/rncan-nrcan/Fo122- 1-2-2001-eng.pdf

Izhaki, I. (2002). Emodin: A secondary metabolite with multiple ecological functions in higher plants. *New Phytologist* 155(2): 205-217.

Jacobi, W.R., Goodrich, B.A., & Cleaver, C.M. (2011). Firewood transport by National and State Park campers: A risk for native or exotic tree pest movement. *Arboriculture and Urban Forestry* 37(3): 126-138.

Jenkins, L., & Jackman, E. R. (1941). *Myrtle*. Extension Bulletin 581. Oregon State College, Corvallis: Oregon State System of Higher Education Federal Cooperative Extension Service. Retrieved April 15, 2011, from http://ir.library.oregonstate.edu/xmlui/bitstream/han- dle/1957/17352/ExtensionBulletin581.pdf?sequence=1

Kashian, D.M., & Witter, J.A. (2011). Assessing the potential for ash canopy tree replacement via current regeneration following emerald ash borer-caused mortality on southeastern Michigan landscapes. *Forest Ecology and Management* 261: 480-488.

Kaufman, S. R., & Kaufman, W. (2007). *Invasive plants: Guide to identification and the impacts and control of common North American species*. Mechanicsburg, PA: Stackpole Books.

Kazmierczak, P., Kim, D. H., Turina, M., & Van Alfen, N. K. (2005). A hyrdrophobin of the chestnut blight fungus, *Cryphonectria parasitica*, is required for stromal pustule eruption. *Eukaryotic Cell* 4(5): 931-936.

Kelly, J., Maguire, C. M., & Cosgrove, P.J. (2008). Best practice management guidelines: Himalayan balsam *Impatiens glandulifera*, Prepared by NIEA and NPWS as part of Invasive Species Ireland. Retrieved February 16, 2012, from http://www.conservationvolunteers.ie/images/ buttons/submenus/news_and_advice/downloads/ naa_bpmg_hb.pdf

Kershaw, L. (2001). *Trees of Ontario*. Edmonton, AB: Lone Pine Publishing.

Kimoto, T., & Duthie-Holt, M. (2006). *Exotic forest insect guidebook*. Canada: Canadian Food Inspection Agency.

Klionsky, S. M., Amatangelo, K. L., & Waller, D. M. (2010). Above- and belowground impacts of European buckthorn (*Rhamnus cathartica*) on four native forbs. *Restoration Ecology* 19(6): 728-737.

Kloeppel, B. D., & Abrams, M. D. (1995). Ecophysiological attributes of the native *Acer saccharum* and the exotic *Acer platanoides* in urban oak forests in Pennsylvania, USA. *Tree Physiology* 15: 739-746.

Knapp, L. B., & Canham, C. D. (2000). Invasion of an old-growth forest in New York by *Ailanthus altissima*: Sapling growth and recruitment in canopy gaps. *Journal of the Torrey Botanical Society* 127(4): 307-315.

Knight, K. S. (2005). Buckthorn biology and invasion history. In L. C. Skinner (Ed.), *Proceedings: Symposium on the biology, ecology, and management of garlic mustard (Alliaria petiolata) and European buckthorn (Rhamnus cathartica)*. (pp. 30-33) USDA Forest Service Publication FHTET-2005-09.

Knight, K. S., Kurylo, J. S., Endress, A. G., Stewart, J. R., & Reich, P. B. (2007). Ecology and ecosystem impacts of common buckthorn (*Rhamnus cathartica*): A review. *Biological Invasions* 9: 925-937.

Koch, A. M., Antunes, P. M., Barto, E. K., Cipollini, D., Mummey, D. L., & Klironomos, J. N. (2011). The effects of arbuscular mycorrhizal (AM) fungal and garlic mustard introductions on native AM fungal diversity. *Biological Invasions* 13: 1627-1639.

Koch, J.L., & Carey, D.W. (2005). The genetics of resistance of American beech to beech bark disease: Knowledge through 2004. In C. A. Evans, J. A. Lucas & M. J. Twery (Eds.), *Beech bark disease: Proceedings of the beech bark disease symposium*. Gen. Tech. Rep. NE-331. (pp. 98-105). Newtown Square, PA: U.S. Department of Agriculture Forest Service, Northern Research Station.

Koch, J.L., Carey, D.W., Mason, M.E., & Nelson, C.D. (2010). Assessment of beech scale resistance in full- and half-sibling American beech families. *Canadian Journal of Forest Research* 40: 265-272.

Kota, N. L., Landenberger, R. E., & McGraw, J. B. (2007). Germination and early growth of *Ailanthus* and tulip poplar in the three levels of forest disturbance. *Biological Invasions* 9: 197-211.

Kourtev, P. S., Ehrenfeld, J. G., & Häggblom, M. (2002b). Exotic plant species alter the microbial community structure and function in the soil. *Ecology* 83(11): 3152-3166.

Kourtev, P. S., Ehrenfeld, J. G., & Häggblom, M. (2003). Experimental analysis of the effect of exotic and native plant species on the structure and function of soil microbial communities. *Soil Biology and Biochemistry* 35: 895-905.

Kourtev, P. S., Ehrenfeld, J. G., & Huang, W. Z. (1998). Effects of exotic plant species on soil properties in hardwood forests of New Jersey. *Water, Air, and Soil Pollution* 105: 493-501.

Kourtev, P. S., Ehrenfeld, J. G., Huang, W. Z. (2002a). Enzyme activities during litter decomposition of two exotic and two native plant species in hardwood forests of New Jersey. *Soil Biology and Biochemistry* 34: 1207-1218.

Kourtev, P. S., Huang, W. Z., & Ehrenfeld, J. G. (1999). Differences in earthworm densities and nitrogen dynamics in soils under exotic and native plant species. *Biological Invasions* 1: 237-245.

Kowarik, I. (1995). Clonal growth in *Ailanthus altissima* on a natural site in West Virginia. *Journal of Vegetation Science* 6(6): 853-856.

Kowarik, I., & Säumel, I. (2007). Biological flora of Central Europe: *Ailanthus altissima* (Mill.) Swingle. *Perspectives in Plant Ecology, Evolution and Systematics* 8: 207-237.

Kowarik, I., & Säumel, I. (2008). Water dispersal as an additional pathway to invasions by the primarily wind-dispersed tree *Ailanthus altissima*. *Plant Ecology* 198: 241-252.

Kricsfalusy, V. V., & Miller, G. C. (2010). Community ecology and invasion of natural vegetation by *Cynanchum rossicum* (Asclepiadaceae) in Toronto region, Canada. *Thaiszia Journal of Botany* 20: 53-70.

Kurylo, J. S., Knight, K. S., Stewart, J. R., & Endress, A. G. (2007). *Rhamnus cathartica*: Native and naturalized distribution and habitat preferences. *The Journal of the Torrey Botanical Society* 134(3): 420-430.

Ladd, D., & Cappuccino, N. (2005). A field study of seed dispersal and seedling performance in the invasive exotic vine *Vincetoxicum rossicum*. *Canadian Journal of Botany* 83: 1181-1188.

Landenberger, R. E., Kota, N. L., & McGraw, J. B. (2007). Seed dispersal of the non-native invasive tree *Ailanthus altissima* into contrasting environments. *Plant Ecology* 192(1): 55-70.

Landis, D., & Evans, J. (2009). *Garlic mustard management: Help for stopping this woodland pest.* Michigan State University Extension. Retrieved on December 16, 2010, from http://www.ipm.msu.edu/garlicMge.htm.

Lane, A. (Ed.). (2007). *Best management practices: Woodlot management.* Agroforestry Series Volume 1. Guelph, ON: Ontario Ministry of Agriculture, Food and Rural Affairs (OMAFRA).

Langor, D.W., DeHaas, L.J., & Foottit, R.G. (2009). Diversity of non-native terrestrial arthropods on woody plants in Canada. *Biological Invasions* 11: 5-19.

Lawlor, F. M., & Raynal, D. J. (2002). Response of swallow-wort to herbicides. *Weed Science* 50: 179-185.

Lawrence, J. G., Colwell, A., & Sexton, O. J. (1991). The ecological impact of allelopathy in *Ailanthus altissima* (Simaroubaceae). *American Journal of Botany* 78(7): 948-958.

Lawrence, M., & Martin, R. (1993). *Sweet maple: life, lore & recipes from the sugarbush.* Shelburne and Montpelier, VT: Chapters and Vermont Life.

Lee, J. C., Aguayo, I., Aslin, R., Durham, G., Hamud, S. M., Moltzan, B. D., Munson, A. S., Negrón, J. F., Peterson, T., Ragenovich, I. R., Witcosky, J. J., & Seybold, S. J. (2009). Co-occurrence of the invasive banded and European elm bark beetles (Coleoptera: Scolytidae) in North America. *Annuals of the Entomological Society of America* 102(3): 426-436.

Lee, I., Martini, M., Marcone, C., & Zhu, S.F. (2004). Classification of phytoplasma strains in the elm yellows group (16SrV) and proposal of 'Candidatus Phytoplasma ulmi' for the phytoplasma associated with elm yellows. *International Journal of Systemic and Evolutionary Microbiology* 54: 337-347.

Lee, J. C., Negron, J. F., McElwey, S. J., Witcosky, J. J., & Seybold, S. J. (2006). *Pest alert: banded elm bark beetle (Scolytus schevyrewi).* U.S. Department of Agriculture, Forest Service, Rocky Mountain Region, Forest Health Protection. Retrieved November 8, 2011, from http://www.na.fs.fed.us/pubs/palerts/banded_elm_beetle/beb.pdf

Leicht-Young, S. A., O'Donnell, H., Latimer, A. M., & Silander Jr., J. A. (2009). Effects of an invasive plant species, *Celastrus orbiculatus*, on soil composition and processes. *American Midland Naturalist* 161(2): 219-231.

Leslie, C. A., Seybold, S. J., Graves, A. D., Cranshaw, W., & Tisserat, N. (2010). Potential impacts of thousand cankers disease on commercial walnut production and walnut germplasm conservation. In D. L. McNeil (Ed.), *Proceedings of the VIth international walnut symposium: Melbourne, Australia, February 25-27, 2009* (Acta Horticulturae: 861, pp. 431-434). International Society for Horticultural Science.

Leuschner, W. A., Young, J. A., & Ravlin, F. W. (1996). Potential benefits of slowing the gypsy moth's spread. *South Journal of Applied Forestry* 20(2): 65-73.

Leuty, T. (2009). *Maple syrup.* Ontario Ministry of Agriculture, Foods and Rural Affairs (OMAFRA). Retrieved December 7, 2010, from http://www.omafra.gov.on.ca/english/crops/facts/info_maple_syrup.htm

Lewis, K., & McCarthy, B. (2008). Nontarget tree mortality after tree-of-heaven (*Ailanthus altissima*) injection with Imazapyr. *Northern Journal of Applied Forestry* 25(2): 66-72.

Liebhold, A.M., & Tobin, P.C. (2008). Population ecology of insect invasions and their management. *Annual Review of Entomology* 53: 387-408.

Locandro, R. R. (1973). Reproduction ecology of *Polygonum cuspidatum*. Ph.D. dissertation, Department of biology, Rutgers University, New Brunswick, New Jersey, USA.

Lower, A. R. M. (1933). The trade in square timber. *Contributions to Canadian Economics* 6: 40-61.

Lumer, C., & Yost, S. E. (1995). The reproductive biology of *Vincetoxicum nigrum* (L.) Moench (Asclepiadaceae), a Mediterranean weed in New York State. *Bulletin of the Torrey Botanical Club* 122(1): 15-23.

Lyons, D. B. (2010). *Emerald ash borer.* Frontline Forestry Research Applications. Technical Note 110. Sault Ste Marie, ON: Natural Resources Canada, Great Lakes Forestry Centre. Retrieved October 31, 2011, from http://cfs.nrcan.gc.ca/publications?id=31501

Lyons, D. B., Caister, C., de Groot, P., Hamilton, B., Marchant, K., Scarr, T., & Turgeon, J. (2007). *Survey guide for detection of emerald ash borer.* Sault Ste Marie and Ottawa, ON: Natural Resources Canada, Canadian Forest Service and the Canadian Food Inspection Agency, Plant Health Division.

MacDaniels, L.H., & Lieberman, A.S. (1979). Tree crops: A neglected source of food and forage from marginal lands. *BioScience* 29(3): 173-175.

MacFarlane, D. W., & Meyer, S. P. (2005). Characteristics and distribution of potential ash tree hosts for emerald ash borer. *Forest Ecology and Management* 213: 15-24.

Maerz, J. C., Blossey, B., & Nuzzo, V. (2005). Green frogs show reduced foraging success in habitats invaded by Japanese knotweed. *Biodiversity and Conservation* 14: 2901-2911.

Magnarelli, L. A., Stafford, K. C., IJdo, J. W., & Fikrig, E. (2006). Antibodies to whole-cell or recominant antigens of *Borrelia burgdorferi*, *Anaplasma phagocytophilum*, and *Babesia microti* in white-footed mice. *Journal of Wildlife Diseases* 42(4): 732-738.

Manion, P.D. (1991). *Tree disease concepts* (2nd ed.). Englewood Cliffs, NJ: Prentice-Hall.

Marinelli, J. (2005). *Plant.* London: DK Publishing.

Martin, P. H. (1999). Norway maple (*Acer platanoides*) invasion of a natural forest stand: Understory consequence and regeneration pattern. *Biological Invasions* 1: 215-222.

Martin, P. H., & Marks, P. L. (2006). Intact forests provide only weak resistance to a shade-tolerant invasive Norway maple (*Acer platanoides* L.). *Journal of Ecology* 94: 1070-1079.

Martin, P. H., Canham, C. D., & Marks, P. L. (2008). Why forests appear resistant to exotic plant invasions: Intentional introductions, stand dynamics, and the role of shade tolerance. *Frontiers in Ecology and the Environment* 7(3): 142-149.

Mascaro, J., & Schnitzer, S. A. (2007). *Rhamnus cathartica* L. (common buckthorn) as an ecosystem dominant in southern Wisconsin forests. *Northeastern Naturalist* 14(3): 387-402.

Maule, H.G., Andrews, M., Watson, C., & Cherrill, A. (2000). Distribution, biomass and effect on native species of *Impatiens glandulifera* in a deciduous woodland in Northeast England. *Aspects of Applied Biology* 58: 31-38.

McCullough, D. G., Heyd, R. L., & O'Brien, J. G. (2005). *Biology and management of beech bark disease: Michigan's newest exotic forest pest.* Extension Bulletin E-2746. Michigan State University. Retrieved September19, 2012, from http://www.baycounty-mi.gov/Docs/Health/GypsyMoth/BeechBark.pdf

McCullough, D. G., Poland, T. M., & Cappaert, D. L. (2006). Attraction of emerald ash borer to trap trees: Effects of stress agents and trap height. In V. Mastro, R. Reardon & G. Parra (Eds.), *Emerald ash borer research and technology development meeting, Pittsburg, PA: 26-27 Sept. 2005.* (pp. 61-62). Morgantown, WV: U.S. Department of Agriculture, Forest Service Publication FHTET-2005-16.

McCullough, D.G., Schneeberger, N.F., & Katovich, S.A. (2008). *Pest alert: Emerald ash borer.* NA-PR-02-04. Newton Square, PA: USDA Foreset Service, Northeastern Area, State and Private Forestry. Retrieved November 6, 2012 from http://www.na.fs.fed.us/spfo/pubs/pest_al/eab/eab.pdf.

McElrone, A. J., Sherald, J. L., & Pooler, M. R. (1999). Identification of alternative hosts of *Xylella fastidiosa* in the Washington, D.C., area using nested polymerase chain reaction (PCR). *Journal of Arboriculture* 25(5): 258-263.

McEwan, R. W., Keiffer, C. H., & McCarthy, B. C. (2006). Dendroecology of American chestnut in a disjunct stand of oak-chestnut forest. *Canadian Journal of Forest Research* 36: 1-11.

McLaughlin, J., & Greifenhagen, S. (2012). Beech bark disease in Ontario: A primer and management recommendations. Forest Research Note No. 71. Sault Ste Marie, ON: Ontario Forest Research Institute, Ontario Ministry of Natural Resources. Retrieved November 5, 2012, from http://www.mnr.gov.on.ca/en/Business/OFRI/Publication/groups/lr/@mnr/@ofri/documents/document/stdprod_096009.pdf

McLeod, G., Gries, R., von Reuß, S.H., Rahe, J.E., McIntosh, R., König, W.A., & Gries, G. (2005). The pathogen causing Dutch elm disease makes host trees attract insect vectors. *Proceedings: Biological Sciences* 272(1580):2 499-2503.

McManus, M., Schneeberger, N., Reardon, R., & Mason, G. (1989). *Gypsy moth.* Forest insect & disease leaflet 162. U.S. Department of Agriculture, Forest Service. Retrieved November 14, 2011, from http://na.fs.fed.us/spfo/pubs/fidls/gypsymoth/gypsy.htm

Meekins, J. F., & McCarthy, B. C. (1999). Competitive ability of *Alliaria petiolata* (garlic mustard, Brassicaceae), an invasive, nonindigenous forest herb. *International Journal of Plant Science* 160(4): 743-752.

Meiners, S. J. (2005). Seed and seedling ecology of *Acer saccharum* and *Acer platanoides:* A contrast between native and exotic congeners. *Northeastern Naturalist* 12(1): 23-32.

Meloche, C., & Murphy, S. D. (2006). Managing tree-of-heaven (*Ailanthus altissima*) in parks and protected areas: A case study of Rondeau Provincial Park (Ontario, Canada). *Environmental Management* 37(6): 764-772.

Melzer, M.S., & Boland, G.J. (1999). CHV3-type dsRNAs and the GH2 genotype in a population of *Cryphonectria parasitica* in Ontario. *Canadian Journal of Plant Pathology* 21: 248-255.

Mergen, F. (1959). A toxic principle in the leaves of *Ailanthus*. *Botanical Gazette* 121(1): 32-36.

Milbrath, L. R. (2010). Phytophagous arthropods of invasive swallow-wort vines (*Vincetoxicum* spp.) in New York. *Environmental Entomology 39*(1): 68-78.

Miller, J. H. (2003). *Nonnative invasive plants of southern forests: A field guide for identification and control.* Gen. Tech. Rep. SRS-62. Asheville, NC: United States Department of Agriculture, Forest Service, Southern Research Station. Retrieved March 21, 2011, from http://www.srs.fs.usda.gov/fia/manual/Nonnative_Invasive_Plants_of_Southern_Forests.pdf

Miller, J. H., Manning, S. T., & Enloe, S. F. (2010). *A management guide for invasive plants in southern forests.* Gen. Tech. Rep. SRS-131. United States Department of Agriculture, Forest Service, Southern Research Station. Retrieved September 7, 2011, from http://www.hort.uconn.edu/cipwg/pdfs/gtr_srs131.pdf

Ministry of Northern Development and Mines (MNDM). (2011). *Ontario's forest industry.* Government of Ontario. Retrieved November 27, 2011, from http://www.mndm.gov.on.ca/forestry/forest_industry_e.asp

Ministry of the Environment (MOE). (2011). *Pesticides.* Government of Ontario. Retrieved March 15, 2011, from http://www.ene.gov.on.ca/environment/en/category/pesticides/index.htm

Mohammed, G. H. (1999). *Non-timber forest products in Ontario: An overview.* Forest Research Information Paper No.145. Sault Ste Marie, ON: Ontario Forest Research Institute, Ontario Ministry of Natural Resources. Retrieved November 27, 2011, from http://www.mnr.gov.on.ca/en/Business/OFRI/Publication/279239.html

Moriarty, J. (2005). Conventional management of buckthorn species. In L. C. Skinner (Ed.), *Proceedings: Symposium on the biology, ecology, and management of garlic mustard (Alliaria petiolata) and European buckthorn (Rhamnus cathartica).* (pp. 53-54). Minnesota: USDA Forest Service Publication FHTET-2005-09.

Murphy, S. D. (2005). Concurrent management of an exotic species and initial restoration efforts in forests. *Restoration Ecology* 13(4): 584-593.

Myers, C. V., Anderson, R. C., & Byers, D. L. (2005). Influence of shading on the growth and leaf photosynthesis of the invasive non-indigenous plant garlic mustard [*Alliaria petiolata* (M. Bieb) Cavara and Grande] grown under simulated late-winter to mid-spring conditions. *The Journal of the Torrey Botanical Society* 132(1): 1-10.

Nair, V. M. G., Kostichka, C. J., & Kuntz, J. E. (1979). *Siroccocus clavigignenti-juglandacearum*: An undescribed species causing canker on butternut. *Mycologia* 71(3): 641-646.

Natural Resources Canada (NRCan). (2011). *Forest Invasive Alien Species (FIAS): Established forest invasive alien species.* Retrieved November 8, 2011, from http://exoticpests.gc.ca/present_eng.asp

Nature Conservancy of Canada (NCC). (2007). *Control methods for the invasive plant garlic mustard (Alliaria petiolata) within Ontario natural areas.* Version 1.0. London, Ontario: NCC - Southwestern Ontario Region. Retrieved on December 14, 2010, from http://www.ontarioweeds.com/media/pdf/garlic_natureconservatory.pdf.

Nealis, V. G. (2002). Gypsy moth in Canada: Case study of an invasive insect. In R. Claudi, P. Nantel & E. Muckle-Jeffs (Eds.), *Alien invaders in Canada's waters, wetlands, and forests.* (pp. 151-159). Ottawa, ON: Canadian Forest Service, Natural Resources Canada.

Nealis, V. G., & Erb, S. (1993). *A sourcebook for management of the gypsy moth.* Sault Ste Marie, ON: Great Lakes Forestry Centre.

Nearing, H., & Nearing, A. (1950). *The maple sugar book.* Social Science Institute, Maine.

Negrón, J.F., Witcosky, J.J., Cain, R.J., LaBonte, J.R., Duerr II, D.A., McElwey, S.J., Lee, J.C., & Seybold, S.J. (2005). The banded elm bark beetle: A new threat to elms in North America. *American Entomologist* 51: 84-94.

Newcomb, L. (1977). *Newcomb's wildflower guide.* New York, NY: Little, Brown and Company.

Nowak, D. J., & Rowntree, R. A. (1990). History and range of Norway maple. *Journal of Arboriculture* 16(11): 291-296.

Nowak, D. J., Pasek, J. E., Sequeira, R. A., Crane, D. E., & Mastro, V. C. (2001). Potential effect of *Anoplophora glabripennis* (Coleoptera: Cerambycidae) on urban trees in the United States. *Journal of Economic Entomology* 94(1): 116-122.

Nuzzo, V. A. (1991). Experimental control of garlic mustard [*Alliaria petiolata* (Bieb.) Cavara and Grande] in northern Illinois using fire, herbicide and cutting. *Natural Areas Journal* 11: 158-167.

Nyland, R.D., Bashant, A.L., Bohn, K.K., & Verostek, J.M. (2006). Interference to hardwood regeneration in northeastern North America: Ecological characteristics of American beech, striped maple, and hobblebush. *Northern Journal of Applied Forestry* 23(1): 53-61.

Ohmart, C.P. (1989). Why are there so few tree-killing bark beetles associated with angiosperms? *Oikos* 54(2): 242-245.

O'Neil, S., Welch, B., Latham, P., & Sarr, D. (2007). Invasive species early detection protocol development in the national parks: Integrating all the pieces. In T. B. Harrington, & S. H. Reichard (Eds.), *Meeting the challenge: Invasive plants in the Pacific Northwest ecosystems* (pp. 13-15). Gen. Tech. Rep. PNW-GTR-694. Portland, Oregon: US Department of Agriculture, Forest Service, Pacific Northwest Research Station. Retrieved January 14, 2011, from http://www.fs.fed.us/pnw/pubs/pnw_gtr694.pdf

Ontario Ministry of Natural Resources (OMNR). (2004). *Ontario tree marking guide.* Version 1.1. Ontario's Forests, Forest Management. Retrieved November 2, 2011, from http://www.mnr.gov.on.ca/en/Business/Forests/Publication/MNR_E000526P.html

Ontario Ministry of Natural Resources (OMNR). (2006). *A guide to stewardship planning for natural areas.* Ontario's Forests, Forest Management. Retrieved November 2, 2011, from http://www.mnr.gov.on.ca/en/Business/Forests/Publication/MNR_E000231P.html

Ontario Ministry of Natural Resources (OMNR). (2010a). *Ontario's cosmetic pesticides ban: What you need to know to protect natural resources.* Retrieved March 15, 2011, from http://www.mnr.gov.on.ca/en/Business/Biodiversity/2ColumnSubPage/270465.html

Ontario Ministry of Natural Resources (OMNR). (2010b). *Emerald ash borer (Agrilus planipennis): Forest health alert.* Ontario's Forests, Forest Health Management (Insects,

Diseases and Invasive Species). Retrieved October 31, 2011, 2011, from http://www.mnr.gov.on.ca/en/Business/Forests/2ColumnSubPage/STEL02_166994.html

Ontario Ministry of Natural Resources (OMNR). (2010c). *Asian long-horned beetle (Anoplophora glabripennis): Forest health alert.* Ontario's Forests, Forest Health Management (Insects, Diseases and Invasive Species). Retrieved October 31, 2011, from http://www.mnr.gov.on.ca/en/Business/Forests/2ColumnSubPage/STEL02_166979.html

Ontario Ministry of Natural Resources (OMNR). (2012b). *Species at risk in Ontario (SARO) list.* Retrieved March 21, 2011, from http://www.mnr.gov.on.ca/en/Business/Species/2ColumnSubPage/276722.html

Ontario Ministry of Natural Resources (OMNR). (2011). *Butternut assessment guidelines: Assessment of butternut tree health for the purposes of the Endangered Species Act 2007. version 1.0.* Retrieved November 8, 2011, from http://www.mnr.gov.on.ca/stdprodconsume/groups/lr/@mnr/@species/documents/document/stdprod_085841.pdf

Ontario Ministry of Natural Resources (OMNR). (2012a). *Ontario's forests: Facts about our forests.* Retrieved November 2, 2012, from http://www.mnr.gov.on.ca/en/Business/Forests/2ColumnSubPage/STEL02_164508.html

Ostry, M. E., Mielke, M. E., & Anderson, R. L. (1996). *How to identify butternut canker and manage butternut trees.* No. HT-70. United States Department of Agriculture, Forest Service, North Central Forest Experiment Station. Retrieved November 28, 2011, from http://na.fs.fed.us/spfo/pubs/howtos/ht_but/ht_but.htm

Ostry, M. E., Mielke, M. E., & Skilling, D. D. (1994). *Butternut - strategies for managing a threatened tree.* Gen. Tech. Rep. NC-165. St. Paul, MN: U.S. Department of Agriculture, Forest Service, North Central Forest Experiment Station.

Ostry, M. E., & Pijut, P. M. (2000). Butternut: An underused resource in North America. *HortTechnology* 10(2): 302-306.

Ostry M.E., & Woeste, K. (2004). Spread of butternut canker in North America, host range, evidence of resistance within butternut populations and conservation genetics. Michler, C.H.; Pijut, P.M.; Van Sambeek, J.W.; Coggeshall, M.V.; Seifert, J.; Woeste, K.; Overton, R.; Ponder, F., Jr., (Eds.). Black walnut in a new century, proceedings of the 6th Walnut Council research symposium; 2004 July 25-28; Lafayette, IN. Gen.Tech. Rep. NC-243. St. Paul, MN: U.S. Department of Agriculture, Forest Service, North Central Research Station.

Paillet, F. L. (2002). Chestnut: History and ecology of a transformed species. *Journal of Biogeography* 29: 1517-1530.

Palm, C. E., & Gardescu, S. (2008). *Sugar maple and the pear thrips.* Ithaca, NY : Insect Diagnostic Laboratory, Cornell University. Retrieved November 25, 2011, from http://entomology.cornell.edu/cals/entomology/extension/idl/upload/Pear-Thrips.pdf

Pannill, P. D. (2000). *Tree-of-heaven control.* United States: Maryland Department of Natural Resources, Forest Service. Retrieved September 14, 2011, from http://www.naturalresources.umd.edu/Publications/PDFs/Other/TreeOfHeaven.pdf

Pecknold, P., Ruhl, G., & Rane, K. (2001). *Ornamental diseases: Dogwood anthracnose*. No. BP-48-W. West Lafayette, IN: Purdue University, Cooperative Extension Service. Retrieved October 6, 2011, from http://www.ces.purdue. edu/extmedia/BP/BP-48.html

Pergams, O. R. W., & Norton, J. E. (2006). Treating a single stem can kill the whole shrub: A scientific assessment of buckthorn control methods. *Natural Areas Journal* 26(3): 300-309.

Perrins, J., Fitter, A., & Williamson, M. (1993). Population biology and rates of invasion of three introduced *Impatiens* species in the British Isles. *Journal of Biogeography* 20(1): 33-44.

Peterson, K. (2007). Garlic mustard control: Is success a possibility? Strategy and potential impact. In T. B. Harrington, & S. H. Reichard (Eds.), *Meeting the challenge: Invasive plants in Pacific Northwest ecosystems* (pp. 59-62). Gen. Tech. Rep. PNW-GTR-694. Portland, Oregon: US Department of Agriculture, Forest Service, Pacific Northwest Research Station. Retrieved January 14, 2011, from http://www.fs.fed.us/pnw/pubs/ pnw_gtr694.pdf

Petrice, T.R., & Haack, R.A. (2007). Can emerald ash borer, *Agrilus planipennis* (Coleoptera: Buprestidae), emerge from logs two summers after infested trees are cut. *The Great Lakes Entomologist* 40: 92-95.

Petrides, G. A. (1972). *A field guide to trees and shrubs: Field marks of all trees, shrubs, and woody vines that grow wild in the northeastern and north-central United States and in southeastern and south-central Canada*. Boston: Houghton Mifflin.

Pijut, P. M. (2006). *Diseases in hardwood tree plantings*. FNR-221. Hardwood Tree Improvement and Regeneration Center, Northern Research Station, UISDA Forest Service, Department of Forestry and Natural Resources, Purdue University.

Poland, T. M., & McCullough, D. G. (2006). Emerald ash borer: Invasion of the urban forest and the threat to North America's ash resource. *Journal of Forestry* 104(3): 118-124.

Poland, T.M., & McCullough, D.G. (2010). SLAM: A multi-agency pilot project to SL.ow A.sh M.ortality caused by emerald ash borer in outlier sites. *Newsletter of the Michigan Entomological Society* 55: 4-8.

Poland, T. M., Rodriguez-Saona, C., Grant, G., Buchan, L., De Groot, P., Miller, J., & McCullough, D. G. (2006). Trapping and detection of emerald ash borer: Identification of stressed-induced volatiles and tests of attraction in the lab and field. In V. Mastro, R. Reardon & G. Parra (Eds.), *Emerald ash borer research and technology development meeting, Pittsburg, PA: 26-27 Sept. 2005*. (pp. 64-65). Morgantown, WV: U.S. Department of Agriculture, Forest Service Publication FHFTET-2005-16.

Porter, A. (1994). Implications of introduced garlic mustard (*Alliaria petiolata*) in the habitat of *Pieris virginiensis* (Peridae). *Journal of the Lepidopterists' Society* 48(2): 171-172.

Pscheidt, J. W. (2011). *An online guide to plant disease control: Elm-Dutch elm disease*. Oregon State University. Retrieved November 10, 2011, from http://plantdisease. ippc.orst.edu/ShowDisease.aspx?RecordID=435

Pyšek, P., & Prach, P. (1995). Invasion dynamics of *Impatiens glandulifera* – A century of spreading reconstructed. *Biological Conservation* 74: 41-48.

Rabaglia, R., & Twardus, D. (1990). *The eastern tent caterpillar*. U.S. Department of Agriculture, Forest Service, Northeastern Area. Retrieved November 16, 2011, from http://na.fs.fed.us/spfo/pubs/pest_al/etc/etc.htm

Raupp, M. J., Cumming, A. B., & Raupp, E. C. (2006). Street tree diversity in eastern North America and its potential for tree loss to exotic borers. *Arboriculture and Urban Forestry* 32(6): 297-304.

Régnière, J., Nealis, V., & Porter, K. (2009). Climate suitability and management of the gypsy moth invasion into Canada. *Biological Invasions* 11: 135-148.

Reichard, S. (2000). *Hedera helix*. In C. C. Bossard, J. M. Randall & M. C. Hoshovsky (Eds.), *Invasive plants of California's wildlands*. (pp. 212-216). Berkeley, CA: University of California Press. Retrieved March 27, 2011, from http://www.calipc.org/ip/management/ipcw/ online.php

Reinhart, K. O., Greene, E., & Callaway, R. M. (2005). Effects of *Acer platanoides* invasion on understory plant communities and tree regeneration in the northern Rocky Mountains. *Ecography* 28: 573-582.

Reinhart, K. O., Gurnee, J., Tirado, R., & Callaway, R. M. (2006). Invasion through quantitative effects: intense shade drives native decline and invasive success. *Ecological Applications* 16(5): 1821-1831.

Remaley, T. (2005). *Fact sheet: Japanese knotweed*. Plant Conservation Alliance's Alien Plant Working Group. Weeds Gone Wild: Alien Plant Invaders of Natural Areas. Retrieved August 23, 2011, from http://www.nps.gov/ plants/alien/fact/faja1.htm

Remaley, T. (2005). *Fact sheet: Japanese knotweed*. Plant Conservation Alliance's Alien Plant Working Group. Weeds Gone Wild: Alien Plant Invaders of Natural Areas. Retrieved August 23, 2011, from http://www.nps.gov/ plants/alien/fact/faja1.htm

Renwick, J. A. A. (2002). The chemical world of crucivores: Lures, treats and traps. *Entomologia Experimentalis et Applicata* 104(1): 35-42.

Ric, J., de Groot, P., Gasman, B., Orr, M., Doyle, J., Smith, M. T., Dumouchel, L., Scarr, T., & Turgeon, J. J. (2007). *Detecting signs and symptoms of Asian longhorned beetle injury- Training guide*. Sault Ste Marie and Ottawa, Ontario: Natural Resources Canada, Canadian Forest Service and the Canadian Food Inspection Agency, Plant Health Division.

Richardson, M. (2003). *Management options for small-scale sugar bush operations. Part I:Planning and management options*. Ontario Woodlot Association (OWA). S&W Report. Retrieved December 9, 2010, from http://www. ont-woodlot-assoc.org/sw_maple1.html

Richardson, M. (2004). *Management options for small-scale sugar bush operations. Part III: Sugar bush safety and liability*. Ontario Woodlot Association (OWA). S&W Report. Retrieved December 9, 2010, from http://www. ont-woodlot-assoc.org/sw_maple3.html

Rink, G. (1990). *Juglans cinerea L.: Butternut. In Silvics of North America.Vol. 2. Hardwoods*. Burns, R.M. & Honkala, B.H. (Eds). Agricultural Handbook No. 654.U.S. Department of Agriculture, Forest Service

Rodgers, V. L., Stinson, K. A., & Finzi, A. C. (2008). Ready or not, garlic mustard is moving in: *Alliaria petiolata* as a member of eastern North American forests. *BioScience* 58(5): 426-436.

Rodriguez-Saona, C., Poland, T.M., Miller, J.R., Stelinski, L.L., Grant, G.G., de Groot, P., Buchan, L., & MacDonald, L. (2006). Behavioural and electrophysiological responses of the emerald ash borer, *Agrilus planipennis*, to induced volatiles of Manchurian ash, *Fraxinus mandshurica*. *Chemoecology* 16: 75-86.

Rossell, I.M., Rossell Jr., C.R., Hining, K.J., & Anderson, R.L. (2001). Impacts of dogwood anthracnose (*Discula destructiva* Redlin) on the fruits of flowering dogwood (*Cornus florida* L.): Implications for wildlife. *American Midland Naturalist* 146(2): 379-387.

Rudinsky, J.A. (1962). Ecology of Scolytidae. *Annual Reviews of Entomology* 7: 327-348.

Sanderson, L. A., & Antunes, P. M. (in press). The exotic invasive plant *Vincetoxicum rossicum* is a strong competitor even outside its current realized climatic temperature range. *NeoBiota*.

Sargent, C., Raupp, M., Sardanelli, S., Shrewsbury, P., Clement, D., & Malinoski, M. K. (2008). *Exotic pest threats: Banded elm bark beetle, Scolytus schevyrewi semenov (Coleoptera: Curculionidae: Scolytinae)*. Maryland Cooperative Extension, University of Maryland. Retrieved November 6, 2011, from http://pestthreats.umd.edu/content/documents/BEBBbulletin.pdf

Schlarbaum, S. E., Hebard, F., Spaine, P. C., & Kamalay, J. C. (1997). Three American tragedies: Chestnut blight, butternut canker, and Dutch elm disease. In K. O. Britton (Ed.), *Proceedings, exotic pests of eastern forests; 1997 April 8-10; Nashville, TN* (pp. 45-54) Tennessee Exotic Pest Plant Council.

Schmidt, K. A., & Whelan, C. J. (1999). Effects of exotic *Lonicera* and *Rhamnus* on songbird nest predation. *Conservation Biology* 13(6): 1502-1506.

Schnitzer, S. A., & Bongers, F. (2002). The ecology of lianas and their role in forests. *Trends in Ecology and Evolution* 17(5): 223-230.

Seybold, S. J., Paine, T. D., & Dreistadt, S. H. (2008). *Bark beetles: Integrated pest management for home gardeners and landscape professionals*. Pest Notes Publication 7421. University of California, Agriculture and Natural Resources. Retrieved November 28, 2011, from http://counties.cce.cornell.edu/wyoming/agriculture/resources/ipd/bark_beetles/bark_beetles.pdf

Shartell, L. M., Nagel, L. M., & Storer, A. J. (2011). Multi-criteria risk model for garlic mustard (*Alliaria petiolata*) in Michigan's upper peninsula. *The American Midland Naturalist* 165(1): 116-127.

Shigo, A.L. (1972). The beech bark disease today in the northeastern U.S. *Journal of Forestry* 70(5): 286-289.

Shigo, A. L., & Campana, R. (1977). Discoloured and decayed wood associated with injection wounds in American elm. *Journal of Arboriculture* 12: 230-238.

Siegel, S., & Donaldson, S. (2003). *Measures to prevent the spread of noxious and invasive weeds during construction activities*. Fact Sheet FS-03-59. University of Nevada Cooperative Extension. Retrieved January 18, 2011, from http://www.unce.unr.edu/publications/files/nr/2003/FS0359.pdf

Siegert, N.W., McCullough, D.G., Liebold, A.M., & Telewski, F.W. (2007). Resurrected from the ashes: a historical reconstruction of emerald ash borer dynamics through dendrochronological analysis. In: Mastro, V., Lance, D., Reardon, R. & Parra, G. comps. Emerald ash borer and Asian longhorned beetle research and development review meeting; Oct. 29- Nov. 2, 2006; Cincinnatti; OH. FHTET 2007-04. Morgantown, WV: U.S. Forest Service, Forest Health Technology Enterprise Team, 18-19.

Silander Jr., A. J., & Klepeis, D. M. (1999). The invasion ecology of Japanese barberry (*Berberis thunbergii*) in the New England landscape. *Biological Invasions* 1: 189-201.

Simberloff, D. (2011). Non-natives: 141 scientists object. *Nature* 475: 36.

Sinclair, W. A. (2000). Elm yellows in North America. In C. P. Dunn (Ed.), *The elms: Breeding, conservation, and disease management*. (pp. 121-136). Massachusetts, USA: Kluwer Academis Publishers.

Sinclair, W. A., & Griffiths, H. M. (1994). Ash yellows and its relationship to dieback and decline of ash. *Annual Review of Phytopathology* 32(1): 49-60.

Sinclair, W. A., & Lyon, H. H. (2005). *Diseases of trees and shrubs* (2nd ed.). Ithaca & London: Cornell University Press.

Sisco, P. (2012). The effects of environment and time on blight resistance. *The Journal of the American Chestnut Foundation* 26(2): 16-17.

Slaughter, B. S., Hochstedler, W. W., Gorchov, D. L., & Carlson, A. M. (2007). Response of *Alliaria petiolata* (garlic mustard) to five years of fall herbicide application in a southern Ohio deciduous forest. *The Journal of the Torrey Botanical Society* 134(1): 18-26.

Small, C. J., White, D. C., & Hargbol, B. (2010). Allelopathic influences of the invasive *Ailanthus altissima* on a native and a non-native herb. *Journal of the Torrey Botanical Society* 137(4): 366-372.

Smallidge, P. J., & Nyland, R. D. (2009). *Woodland guidelines for the control and management of American beech*. Forest Connect Fact Series. Ithaca, NY: Cornell University Cooperative Extension, Department of Natural Resources.

Smith, A.H. (2012). Breeding for resistance: TACF and the Burnham hypothesis. *The Journal of the American Chestnut Foundation* 26 (2): 11-15.

Smith, L. L., DiTommaso, A., Lehmann, J., & Greipsson, S. (2006). Growth and reproductive potential of the invasive exotic vine *Vincetoxicum rossicum* in northern New York State. *Canadian Journal of Botany* 84: 1771-1780.

Smith, L. L., DiTommaso, A., Lehmann, J., & Greipsson, S. (2008). Effects of arbuscular mycorrhizal fungi on the exotic invasive vine pale swallow-wort (*Vincetoxicum rossicum*). *Invasive Plant Science and Management* 1(2): 142-152.

Smith, C.C., & Follmer, D. (1972). Food preferences of squirrels. *Ecology* 53(1): 82-91.

Smith, M. T., Turgeon, J. J., De Groot, P., & Gasman, B. (2009). Asian longhorned beetle *Anoplophora glabripennis* (Motschulsky): Lessons learned and opportunities to improve the process of eradication and management. *American Entomologist* 55(1): 21-25.

Soll, J. (2005). *Controlling English ivy (Hedera helix) in the Pacific Northwest*. The Nature Conservancy. Retrieved May 17, 2011, from http://www.invasive.org/gist/moredocs/hedhel02.pdf

Solter, L.F., & Hajek, A.E. (2009). Control of Gypsy moth, *Lymantria dispar*, in North America. In Hajek, A., Glare, T. & Callaghan, M.O. (Eds.) *Use of microbes for control and eradication of invasive arthropods* (pp.181-212). Dordrecht, Netherlands: Springer Science.

Statistics Canada. (2009). *Production and value of honey and maple products service bulletin.* Catalogue No. 23-2321-X. Government of Canada. Retrieved December 8, 2010, from http://www.statcan.gc.ca/pub/23-221-x2009000-eng.pdf

Steward, A. M., Clemants, S. E., & Moore, G. (2003). The concurrent decline of the native *Celastrus scandens* and the spread of the non-native *Celastrus orbiculatus* in the New York city metropolitan area. *Journal of the Torrey Botanical Society* 130(2): 143-146.

Stinson, K. A., Campbell, S. A., Powell, J. R., Wolfe, B. E., Callaway, R. M., Thelen, G. C., Hallett, S. G., Prati, D., & Klironomos, J. N. (2006). Invasive plant suppresses the growth of native tree seedlings by disrupting below-ground mutualisms. *PLoS Biol* 4(5): 727-731.

Stinson, K., Kaufman, S., Durbin, L., & Lowenstein, F. (2007). Impacts of garlic mustard invasion on a forest understory community. *Northeastern Naturalist* 14(1): 73-88.

Stone, K. R. (2009). *Vinca major, V. minor.* In: Fire effects information system (online). U.S. Department of Agriculture, Forest Service, Rocky Mountain Research Station, Fire Sciences Laboratory. Retrieved March 21, 2011, from http://www.fs.fed.us/database/feis/

Stone, K. R. (2010). *Polygonum sachalinense, P. cuspidatum, P. x bohemicum.* In: Fire effects information system (online).U.S. Department of Agriculture, Forest Service, Rocky Mountain Research Station, Fire Sciences Laboratory. Retrieved March 21, 2011, from http://www.fs.fed.us/database/feis/.

Storer, A.J., Rosemier, J.N., Beachy, B.L., & Flaspohler, D.J. (2005). Potential effects of beech bark disease and decline in beech abundance on birds and small mammals. In C. A. Evans, J. A. Lucas & M. J. Twery (Eds.), *Beech bark disease: Proceedings of the beech bark disease symposium.* Gen. Tech. Rep. NE-331. (pp. 72-78). Newtown Square, PA: U.S. Department of Agriculture Forest Service, Northern Research Station.

Strobl, S., & Bland, D. (2000). *A silvicultural guide to managing southern Ontario forests.* Ontario Ministry of Natural Resources. Retrieved March 21, 2011, from http://www.web2.mnr.gov.on.ca/mnr/forests/public/publications/sil_southern_Ont/toc.pdf

Swearingen, J. M. (2006). *Fact sheet: Oriental bittersweet.* Plant Conservation Alliance's Alien Plant Working Group. Weeds Gone Wild: Alien Plant Invaders of Natural Areas. Retrieved November 2, 2011, from http://www.nps.gov/plants/alien/fact/pdf/ceor1.pdf

Swearingen, J. M., & Pannill, P. D. (2009). *Fact sheet: Tree of heaven.* Plant Conservation Alliance's Alien Plant Working Group. Weeds Gone Wild: Alien Plant Invaders of Natural Areas. Retrieved September 14, 2011, from http://www.nps.gov/plants/alien/

Swearingen, J., & Diedrich, S. (2006). *Fact sheet: English ivy.* Plant Conservation Alliance`s Alien Plant Working Group. Weeds Gone Wild: Alien Plant Invaders of Natural Areas. Retrieved May 17, 2011, from http://www.nps.gov/plants/alien/fact/hehe1.htm

Swearingen, J., Slattery, B., Reshetiloff, K., & Zwicker, S. (2010). *Plant invaders of mid-Atlantic natural areas* (4th ed.). Washington, DC: National Park Service and U.S. Fish and Wildlife Service. Retrieved March 2, 2011, from http://www.nps.gov/plants/alien/pubs/midatlantic/

Swift, C. E., Jacobi, W. R., Schomaker, M., & Leatherman, D. A. (2008). *Diseases: Environmental disorders of woody plants.* No. 2.932. Colorado State University Extension. Retrieved November 10, 2012, from http://www.ext.colostate.edu/pubs/garden/02932.html

Symonds, G. W. (1963). *The shrub identification book: The visual method for the practical identification of shrubs, including woody vines and ground covers.* New York, NY: HarperCollins Publishers Inc.

Tabak, N.M., & von Wettberg, E. (2008). Native and introduced jewelweeds of the Northeast. *Northeastern Naturalist* 15(2): 159-176.

Tattar, T.A. (1978). *Diseases of shade trees.* New York, NY: Academic Press Inc.

Taylor, R.A.J., Bauer, L.S., Poland, T.M., & Windell, K.N. (2010). Flight performance of *Agrilus planipennis* (Coleoptera: Buprestidae) on a flight mill and in free flight. *Journal of Insect Behaviour* 23: 128-148.

Thomas, L. K. (1980). *The impact of three exotic plant species on a Potomac island.* National Park Service Scientific Monograph Series No. 13. Washington DC: Department of the Interior, National Park Service.

Tindall, J. R., Gerrath, J. A., Melzer, M., McKendry, K., Husband, B. C., & Boland, G. J. (2004). Ecological status of American chestnut (*Castanea dentata*) in its native range in Canada. *Canadian Journal of Forest Research* 34: 2254-2563.

Tisserat, N., & Kuntz, J. E. (1983). Dispersal gradients of conidia of the butternut canker fungus in a forest during rain. *Canadian Journal of Forest Research* 13: 1139-1144.

Tobin, P. C., & Liebhold, A. M. (2011). Gypsy moth. In D. Simberloff, & M. Rejmanek (Eds.), *Encyclopedia of biological invasions.* (pp. 298-304). U.S.A.: University of California Press.

Tubbs, C.H., & Houston, D.R. (1990). *Fagus grandifolia*: American beech. In: Silvics of North America, Vol 2: Hardwoods. R.M Burns & B.H. Honkala (Tech. coords.). Agricultural handbook 654 (pp. 653-667). Washington, DC: U.S. Department of Agricultural, Forest Service.

Turchetti, T., & Maresi, G. (2008). Biological control and management of chestnut diseases. In A. Ciancio & K. G. Mukerji (Eds.). *Integrated management of diseases caused by fungi, phytoplasma and bacteria* (pp 85-118). Springer Science and Business Media BV.

Turgeon, J. J., Pedlar, J., de Groot, P., Smith, M. T., Jones, C., Orr, M., & Gasman, B. (2010). Density and location of simulated signs and injury affect efficacy of ground surveys for Asian longhorned beetle. *Canadian Entomologist* 142: 80-96.

United States Department of Agriculture (USDA). (2001). *Guide to noxious weed prevention practices.* United States Department of Agriculture - Forest Service. Retrieved March 21, 2011, from http://www.fs.fed.us/r8/texas/news/pests/guidet_to_nox_weed_prev_practices_07052001.pdf

Vogel, V. J. (1987). The blackout of Native American cultural achievements. *American Indian Quarterly* 11(1): 11-35.

Wainhouse, D. (1980). Dispersal of first instar larvae of the felted beech scale, *Cryptococcus fagisuga*. *Journal of Applied Ecology* 17(3): 523-532.

Wake, W. (1997). *A nature guide to Ontario*. Toronto, ON: Federation of Ontario Naturalists.

Walker, D.M., Castlebury, L.A., Rossman, A.Y., Mejía, L.C., & White, J.F. (2012). Phylogeny and taxonomy of *Ophiognomonia* (Gnomoniaceae, Diaporthales), including twenty-five new species in this highly diverse genus. *Fungal Diversity* 57: 85-147.

Ward, J. S., Williams, S. C., & Worthley, T. E. (2010). Effectiveness of two-stage control strategies for Japanese barberry (*Berberis thunbergii*) varies by initial clump size. *Invasive Plant Science and Management* 3(1): 60-69.

Ward, J. S., Worthley, T. E., & Williams, S. C. (2009). Controlling Japanese barberry (*Berberis thunbergii* DC) in southern New England, USA. *Forest Ecology and Management* 257: 561-566.

Webb, S. L., & Kaunzinger, C. K. (1993). Biological invasion of the Drew University (New Jersey) forest preserve by Norway maple (*Acer platanoides* L.). *Bulletin of the Torrey Botanical Club* 120(3): 343-349.

Webb, S. L., Pendergast IV, T. H., & Dwyer, M. E. (2001). Response of native and exotic maple seedling banks to removal of the exotic, invasive Norway maple (*Acer platanoides*). *Journal of the Torrey Botanical Society* 128(2): 141-149.

Weber, E. (2003). *Invasive plant species of the world: A reference guide to environmental weeds*. Cambridge, Massachusetts: CABI Publishing.

Webster, C. R., Jenkins, M. A., & Jose, S. (2006). Woody invaders and the challenges they pose to forest ecosystems in the eastern United States. *Journal of Forestry* 104(7): 366-374.

Weston, L. A., Barney, J. N., & DiTommaso, A. (2005). A review of the biology and ecology of three invasive perennials in New York State: Japanese knotweed (*Polygonum cuspidatum*), mugwort (*Artemisia vulgaris*) and pale swallow-wort (*Vincetoxicum rossicum*). *Plant and Soil* 277: 53-69.

Whitney, G. G., & Upmeyer, M. M. (2004). Sweet trees, sour circumstances: The long search for sustainability in the North American maple products industry. *Forest Ecology and Management* 200(1-3): 313-333.

Wieseler, S. (2005). *Fact sheet: Common buckthorn*. Plant Conservation Alliance's Alien Plant Working Group.

Weeds Gone Wild: Alien Plant Invaders of Natural Areas. Retrieved on May 12, 2011, from http://www.nps.gov/plants/alien/fact/pdf/rhca1.pdf.

Wilkins, S. (2000). Biology and management of *Alliaria petiolata* (garlic mustard) in woodland communities of North America. *Restoration and Reclamation Review* 6(4): 1-8

Williams, C. E. (2005). *Fact sheet: Exotic bush honeysuckles*. Plant Conservation Alliance's Alien Plant Working Group. Weeds Gone Wild: Alien Plant Invaders of Natural Areas. Retrieved November 2, 2011, from http://www.nps.gov/plants/alien/fact/pdf/loni1.pdf

Williams, S. C., Ward, J. S., Worthley, T. E., & Stafford III, K. C. (2009). Managing Japanese barberry (Ranunculales: Berberidaceae) infestations reduces blacklegged tick (Acari: Ixodidae) abundance and infection prevalence with *Borrelia burgdorferi* (Spirochaetales: Spirochaetaceae). *Environmental Entomology* 38(4): 977-984.

Wilson, L. M. (2007). *Key to identification of invasive knotweeds in British Columbia*. Ministry of Forests and Range, Forest Practices Branch, Invasive Alien Plant Program Retrieved September 2, 2011, from http://www.for.gov.bc.ca/hra/Publications/invasive_plants/Knotweed_key_BC_2007.pdf

Winterrowd, W., & Stagg, P. (1993). In praise of myrtle. *Horticulture* 71(4): 76.

Wittstock, L. W. (1993). *Ininatig's gift of sugar; traditional native sugarmaking*. Minneapolis, MN: Lerner Publications Co.

Wolfe, B. E., Rodgers, V. L., Stinson, K. A., & Pringle, A. (2008). The invasive plant *Alliaria petiolata* (garlic mustard) inhibits ectomycorrhizal fungi in its introduced range. *Journal of Ecology* 96(4): 777-783.

Wyckoff, P. H., & Webb, S. L. (1996). Understory influence of the invasive Norway maple (*Acer platanoides*). *Bulletin of the Torrey Botanical Club* 123(3): 197-205.

Youngs, R. L. (2000). "A right smart little jolt". Loss of the chestnut and a way of life. *Journal of Forestry* 98(2): 17-21.

Zhang, N. & Blackwell, M. (2001). Molecular phylogeny of dogwood anthracnose fungus (*Discula destructiva*) and the Diaporthales. *Mycologia* 93(2): 355-365.

Zouhar, K. (2008). *Berberis thunbergii*. In: Fire effects information system (online). U.S. Department of Agriculture, Forest Service, Rocky Mountain Research Station, Fire Sciences Laboratory. Retrieved April 25, 2011, from http://www.fs.fed.us/database/feis/

8.0
PHOTOGRAPHY CREDITS

1. Lisa Derickx, Invasive Species Research Institute
2. James Smedley, James Smedley Outdoors, www.jamessmedleyoutdoors.com
3. Jeff & JoAnn St. Pierre, North Country Photography, www.jeffnorthcountry.com
4. Jan Samanek, State Phytosanitary Administration, Bugwood.org
5. Paul Wray, Iowa State University, Bugwood.org
6. Leslie J. Mehrhoff, University of Connecticut, Bugwood.org
7. Bill Cook, Michigan State University, Bugwood.org
8. Keith Kanoti, Maine Forest Service, Bugwood.org
9. John Ruter, University of Georgia, Bugwood.org
10. The Dow Gardens Archive, Dow Gardens, Bugwood.org
11. Chuck Bargeron, University of Georgia, Bugwood.org
12. James H. Miller, USDA Forest Service, Bugwood.org
13. Jody Shimp, Illinois Department of Natural Resources, Bugwood.org
14. Walter Muma, Ontario Trees and Shrubs, http://ontariotrees.com
15. Chris Evans, Illinois Wildlife Action Plan, Bugwood.org
16. Karan A. Rawlins, University of Georgia, Bugwood.org
17. Dave Powell, USDA Forest Service, Bugwood.org
18. Gyorgy Csoka, Hungary Forest Research Institute, Bugwood.org
19. John Cardina, Ohio State Weed Lab Archive, The Ohio State University, Bugwood.org
20. Walter Muma, Ontario Wildflowers, http://ontariowildflowers.com
21. Allen Bridgman, South Carolina Department of Natural Resources, Bugwood.org
22. Steve Manning, Invasive Plant Control, Bugwood.org
23. Mary Burrows, Montana State University, Bugwood.org
24. Donna R. Ellis, University of Connecticut, Bugwood.org
25. Forest & Kim Starr, Starr Environmental, Bugwood.org
26. Jil Swearingen, USDI National Park Service, Bugwood.org
27. Charles T. Bryson, USDA Agricultural Research Service, Bugwood.org
28. Deborah L. Miller, USDA Forest Service, Bugwood.org
29. Thaddeus Lewandowski, Algoma University Alumni, Sault Ste. Marie
30. Louisiana State University AgCenter Archive, Louisiana State University AgCenter, Bugwood.org
31. Thérèse Arcand, Natural Resources Canada, Canadian Forest Service, Laurentian Forestry Centre.
32. Robert H. Mohlenbrock @ USDA-NRCS PLANTS/USDA NRCS. 1995. Northeast wetland flora: Field office guide to plant species. Northeast National Technical Center, Chester.
33. Bruce Moltzan, USDA Forest Service, Bugwood.org
34. Vladimir Petko, V.N. Sukachev Institute of Forest SB RAS, Bugwood.org
35. Nancy Loewenstein, Auburn University, Bugwood.org
36. James H. Miller & Ted Bodner, Southern Weed Science Society, Bugwood.org
37. Peggy Greb, USDA Agricultural Research Service, Bugwood.org
38. Erich G. Valley, USDA Forest Service – SRS-4552, Bugwood.org
39. David Cappaert, Michigan State University, Bugwood.org
40. Pennsylvania Department of Conservation and Natural Resources – Forestry Archive, Bugwood.org
41. Joseph O'Brien, USDA Forest Service, Bugwood.org
42. Jared Spokowsky, New York State Department of Agriculture and Markets, Bugwood.org
43. Daniel Herms, The Ohio State University, Bugwood.org
44. Whitney Cranshaw, Colorado State University, Bugwood.org
45. William Jacobi, Colorado State University, Bugwood.org
46. Howard Ensign Evans, Colorado State University, Bugwood.org

47. James A. Copony, Virginia Department of Forestry, Bugwood.org
48. John H. Ghent, USDA Forest Service, Bugwood.org
49. Melody Keena, USDA Forest Service, Bugwood.org
50. Michael Bohne, Bugwood.org
51. Kenneth R. Law, USDA APHIS PPQ, Bugwood.org
52. Steven Katovich, USDA Forest Service, Bugwood.org
53. Dennis Haugen, USDA Forest Service, Bugwood.org
54. Dean Morewood, Health Canada, Bugwood.org
55. Natasha Wright, Florida Department of Agriculture and Consumer Services, Bugwood.org
56. Donald Duerr, USDA Forest Service, Bugwood.org
57. James Solomon, USDA Forest Service, Bugwood.org
58. University of Arkansas Forest Entomology Lab Archive, University of Arkansas, Bugwood.org
59. Claude Moffet, Natural Resources Canada, Canadian Forest Service, Laurentian Forestry Centre
60. Larry R. Barber, USDA Forest Service, Bugwood.org
61. USDA Agricultural Research Service Archive, USDA Agricultural Research Service, Bugwood.org
62. Linda Haugen, USDA Forest Service, Bugwood.org
63. USDA Forest Service – Region 8 – Southern Archive, USDA Forest Service, Bugwood.org
64. Natural Resources Canada, Canadian Forest Service, http://cfs.nrcan.gc.ca/
65. Paul H. Peacher, USDA Forest Service, Bugwood.org
66. David J. Moorhead, University of Georgia, Bugwood.org
67. Andrej Kunca, National Forest Centre – Slovakia, Bugwood.org
68. Louis-Michel Nageleisen, Département de la Santé des forêts, Bugwood.org
69. USDA Forest Service – Northeastern Area Archive, USDA Forest Service, Bugwood.org
70. André Carpentier, Natural Resources Canada, Canadian Forest Service, Laurentian Forestry Centre
71. USDA Forest Service – North Central Research Station Archive, USDA Forest Service, Bugwood.org
72. Tom Coleman, USDA Forest Service, Bugwood.org
73. Manfred Mielke, USDA Forest Service, Bugwood.org
74. Milan Zubrik, Forest Research Institute – Slovakia, Bugwood.org
75. Jeffrey Fengler, Connecticut Agricultural Experiment Station Archive, Connecticut Agricultural Experiment Station, Bugwood.org
76. Ferenc Lakatos, University of West-Hungary, Bugwood.org
77. USDA Forest Service Archive, USDA Forest Service, Bugwood.org
78. Haruta Ovidiu, University of Oradea, Bugwood.org
79. Ronald F. Billings, Texas A&M Forest Service, Bugwood.org
80. Mark Robinson, USDA Forest Service, Bugwood.org
81. Rusty Haskell, University of Florida, Bugwood.org
82. William A. Carothers, USDA Forest Service, Bugwood.org
83. Robert L. Anderson, USDA Forest Service, Bugwood.org
84. Tamla Blunt, Colorado State University, Bugwood.org
85. Petr Kapitola, State Phytosanitary Administration, Bugwood.org
86. Minnesota Department of Natural Resources Archive, Minnesota Department of Natural Resources, Bugwood.org
87. Steven Valley, Oregon Department of Agriculture, Bugwood.org
88. Fabio Stergulc, Università di Udine, Bugwood.org
89. Bruce Watt, University of Maine, Bugwood.org
90. Edward L. Barnard, Florida Department of Agriculture and Consumer Services, Bugwood.org
91. Curtis Utley, CSUE, Bugwood.org
92. J.R. Baker & S.B. Bambara, North Carolina State University, Bugwood.org
93. Ned Tisserat, Colorado State University, Bugwood.org
94. Roland J. Stipes, Virginia Polytechnic Institute and State University, Bugwood.org
95. Shari Halik, University of Vermont
96. Ronald S. Kelley, Vermont Department of Forests, Parks and Recreation, Bugwood.org

9.0
ACRONYMS

9.0

CFIA	Canadian Food Inspection Agency
CFS	Canadian Forest Service
DCH	Department of Canadian Heritage
FGCA	Forest Gene Conservation Association
FIAS	Forest Invasive Alien Species
ISC	Invasive Species Centre
ISRI	Invasive Species Research Institute
NRCan	Natural Resources Canada
GISD	Global Invasive Species Database
MNDM	Ministry of Northern Development and Mines
MOE	Ministry of the Environment
NCC	Nature Conservancy of Canada
OFAH	Ontario Federation of Anglers and Hunters
OMAFRA	Ontario Ministry of Agriculture and Rural Affairs
OMNR	Ontario Ministry of Natural Resources
OWA	Ontario Woodlot Association
PMRA	Pest Management Regulatory Agency
USDA	United States Department of Agriculture